Wales

100 Records

"Huw has really dug in here, cracking open the wide and wonderful world of Welsh popular music. His research and knowledge is impeccable, coming up with a fun and informative read for everyone to enjoy."

— **SIR TOM JONES**

"A superb way of tripping to the heart of Welsh music."

— **CERYS MATTHEWS**

"All too often, Welsh music's power, magic and depth is reduced to a few familiar names. By shining its focus on so many genres, styles and individuals, Huw's book is a blazing, brilliant corrective – a proper lightning bolt, showing everyone what Wales is really made of."

— **JUDE ROGERS**

"Ultimately, this is a book written with passion, skill, dedication and a deep love of Welsh music in all its strange and beautiful variations."

— **NICKY WIRE**

Wales
100 Records

HUW STEPHENS

y Olfa

i Cai a Llew

First impression: 2024

© Huw Stephens & Y Lolfa Cyf., 2024

This book is subject to copyright and may not be reproduced by any means except for review purposes without the prior written consent of the publishers.

© All rights reserved by the copyright holders of all record cover images.

The publishers wish to acknowledge the support of
the Books Council of Wales.

Cover design: Caio Wheelhouse

Design: Richard Huw Pritchard

Author portrait: Two Cats in the Yard Photography

For picture credits, please see section at back of book.

Paperback edition ISBN: 978-1-912631-47-6
Hardback edition ISBN: 978-1-80099-606-9

Published and printed in Wales on paper from well-maintained forests by
Y Lolfa Cyf., Talybont, Ceredigion SY24 5HE

e-mail ylolfa@ylolfa.com
website www.ylolfa.com
tel 01970 832 304

Contents

Introduction	7
The 100 Records	9
Map I: Record stores	197
Map II: 'All Wales is a Land of Song'	198
Appendix I: *Wales: 100 Records* – A–Z by artist	200
Appendix II: *Wales: 100 Records* – by year	203
Further reading	206
Diolch!	207
Picture credits	208
Index	210

Artists with a record featured in the book are marked ●

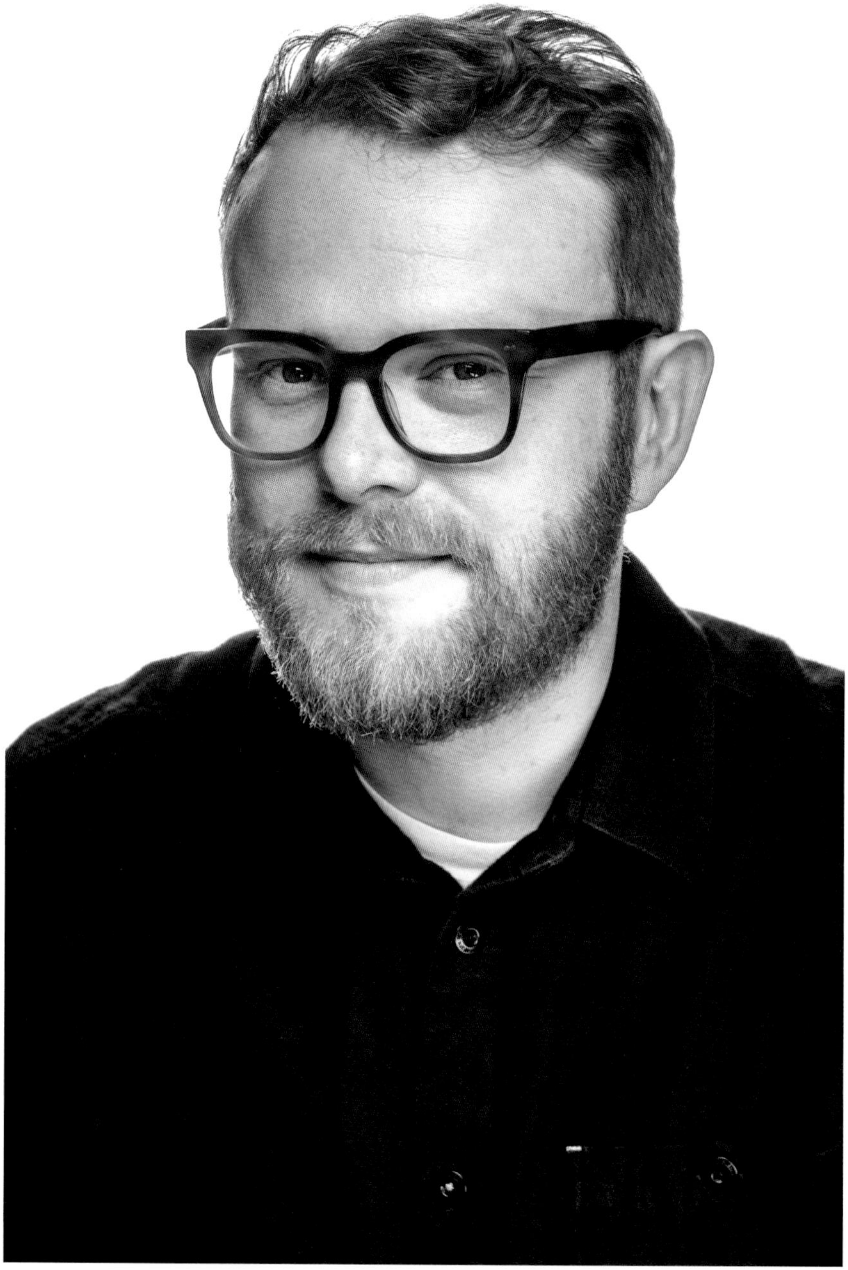

Introduction

In early 1872 it was announced that a singing competition to compete for a Challenge Cup trophy worth a thousand pounds would be held in the Crystal Palace, London. With a choir of 500 voices from across south Wales, Y Côr Mawr/ The Big Choir won this trophy in both 1872 and 1873 – the only times it was contested. In front of the statue of Caradog (their conductor) in Aberdare which commemorates these momentous occasions, are the words:

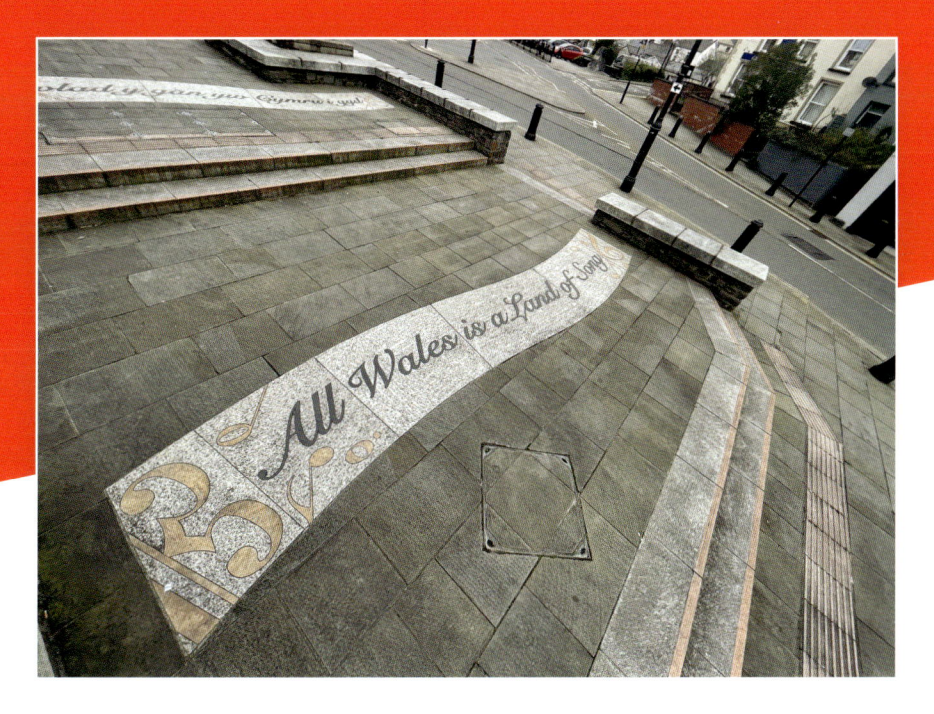

If All Wales is a Land of Song, what is that song and what do all the singers have in common? The sound of Wales has always been hard to pin down, thankfully. It's a choir as much as a house music beat. It's a riff on a guitar as much as a pluck of the harp, a verse of rap as much as a rendition of *cerdd dant*. The music of Wales tells us how we felt at the time and how we found ourselves, or what we loved to lose ourselves to. The music of Wales is a product of its environment, but that differs from village to town to city, from the rural and tranquil to the industrial and noisy. It is from affluence and the middle classes, and from hardship and poverty. Much as there is not one Welsh accent, there is not one Welsh sound. There are many sounds, and many records. In two languages. In every genre. And I, being a jockey of the discs, have selected a hundred of them.

All of these records together, I believe, tell a fascinating and rich story. Some of the albums and artists will be familiar. Others will be new to you. That is, of course, one of the many beautiful things about music: the way that all music is new and fresh and exciting to someone somewhere, no matter when it was originally composed or recorded. There are records from almost every part of Wales here (see the map on page 198!), with quite a few different genres covered.

The USA has been an influence on many of the records. Ffrancon's album *Gwalaxia*, for example, takes inspiration from Machynlleth and its links with Belleville, Detroit – the birthplace of techno. The influence of American rock and pop and soul on the South Wales Valleys is a huge factor in many artists' stories, from Tom Jones' early songbook to Funeral for a Friend's intense emo. Some, like Meredydd Evans and John Cale, made their first recordings in the US. Others, like Paul Robeson and Public Service Broadcasting, came to Wales to sing and compose.

Although a pretty disparate collection of records, there are links between many of them. Harpist Llio Rhydderch played with John Cale in his film *Camgymeriad Gwych/Beautiful Mistake*, Cale was at school with Dafydd Iwan, who founded Sain Records with Huw Jones, whose song 'Dŵr' features Heather Jones, who was in a band with Meic Stevens, who was covered by Super Furry Animals, who were label mates of Rheinallt H. Rowlands, who sang with Gorky's Zygotic Mynci, of whom Sleifar was an early member before going on to form Tystion, whose DJ Jaffa features on the Rounda Records compilation *The Collective* and came up with Me One/MC Eric from Technotronic, who's shared stages with K-klass, who... You get the idea.

There are many records I'd have liked to include here, but it was *Wales: 100 Records*, not *Wales: 1000 Records*. No The Serpents, The Automatic, Iris Williams, The Bug Club, The Darling Buds, Chroma, World Party, Zabrinski, Bryn Terfel, The Crimea, Julian Cope, Malcolm Neon, Topper, Tecwyn Ifan, Charlotte Church, Panic Shack, Dorothy Squires, Steps or Donna Lewis, for now. There are thousands more, of course. There wasn't a lengthy process in finalising the records here – instead I went with my gut instinct of choosing albums that simply had to be in there, and others that I like a lot and hope will be of interest. Each record, naturally, tells a different tale; each one released at a different point in an artist's career. The majority of the records here are albums, some are physical EPs or singles, a few are available solely on streaming services. No cassettes were played in the compiling of this book (maybe that's for next time).

I have, of course, thoroughly enjoyed listening to these records on bits of plastic and various streaming services whilst writing, and hope the overview of the artist's story helps give each record a little context.

Music has been a constant companion in my life. I grew up in a house full of music; my three sisters blasting their favourites, and my parents collecting records from across Europe, including Wales. I also grew up in a house full of books, and I have long hoped a book like this would be published. I feel incredibly lucky to have discovered music in the mid Nineties, a creative and exciting time in Wales. I'd see Catatonia in the pub on New Years Eve (whilst simultaneously playing on Jools Holland's *Hootenanny* on the pub's TV!), Gorky's on a lunch break from their rehearsals and the Manics throwing us a party in the Stadium to welcome a new millennium. I saw pop sensation Robbie Williams walking straight out of Spillers Records and into an awaiting car once, a little red bag in his hand. What had the number one pop star on the planet just bought? The latest Stereophonics and Super Furry Animals CDs, of course! If pop music shaped my life, it has certainly shaped this book, for which I make no apologies.

Whilst filming the BBC documentary *Wales Music Nation* a few years ago, I had the pleasure of listening to the Treorchy Male Voice Choir rehearsing. I was struck by the close-knit community surrounding the choir. One singer drove a three-hour round trip every week from Tenby, just for choir practice. Another member told me at the end of the night, almost in tears, 'You can't buy what this choir gives you.' Music does that to a person: it reminds us we belong.

Huw Stephens

The 100 Records

WORD GETS AROUND
Stereophonics
(V2, 1997)

Having recorded previously as Tragic Love Company, it was the name Stereophonics that accompanied the then Cwmaman-based trio to worldwide fame. Formed by frontman Kelly Jones along with Stuart Cable on drums and Richard Jones on bass, the 'Phonics were a tight-knit group: friends and musical comrades, raised in local pubs and with a deep love of classic rock.

Early observation of everyday life took place when Kelly worked on the fruit 'n' veg stall in the local market. Later, his fascination with film led to him talking to the BBC about a chance to develop his writing for the screen. Filmmaking's loss was music's gain. His honed storytelling abilities were ripe for creating memorable tales in songs that often felt like short films, like 'Local Boy in the Photograph' and 'A Thousand Trees', two successful singles from this album. Although rooted in Kelly's local Cwmaman community, the songs had global appeal and the band soon became a hit on the touring circuit, steadily growing their fanbase and graduating to venues that reflected their mass appeal.

Word Gets Around was released at the height of the Cool Cymru explosion, which saw young, musically ambitious bands from Wales capture music fans' ears worldwide. **Super Furry Animals**, **Catatonia**, **Gorky's Zygotic Mynci**, **60ft Dolls** and **Manic Street Preachers** were all bursting out of Wales and ready to take their music to the masses. They had more in common geographically than musically, and even then some presumed that Wales was a village, unaware of the differences between Cardiff and Carmarthen, Bangor and Blackwood.

It could be argued that Stereophonics were the band most steeped in reality of all these. Their no-nonsense approach to songwriting turned heads, and they were the first signings to Richard Branson's brand-new V2 label, benefitting from a big budget and a big energy for the label's first release. Soon they were headlining Cardiff Castle and gigging relentlessly, though drummer Stuart Cable, a larger-than-life character, much loved and very popular in the Welsh media, left the band in 2003 and sadly died in 2010.

As Kelly's world has got bigger, so have his songs. 30 years on, the band continues to enjoy huge success, with eight number one albums under their belts. Apart from the Manics, they are the only band from the Cool Cymru era still together, and are able to sell out arenas globally, as well as the odd stadium show – including two nights in Cardiff in 2022 with **Tom Jones** as a special guest. Kelly has released two solo studio albums, and a film based on his live album, *Don't Let the Devil Take Another Day*, documenting a harrowing period in his life when he almost lost his voice permanently. Far From Saints, a band he started with Patty Lynn and Dwight Baker from Austin, Texas, surpassed expectations, this side project going on to release a critically acclaimed album and selling out shows across Europe.

The constant throughout all of Stereophonics' back catalogue is Kelly Jones' vocals. They tell tales as he sees them, his filmic instincts creating memorable scenes from everyday life – a talent which makes *Word Gets Around* a spectacularly appreciated record.

Stereophonics

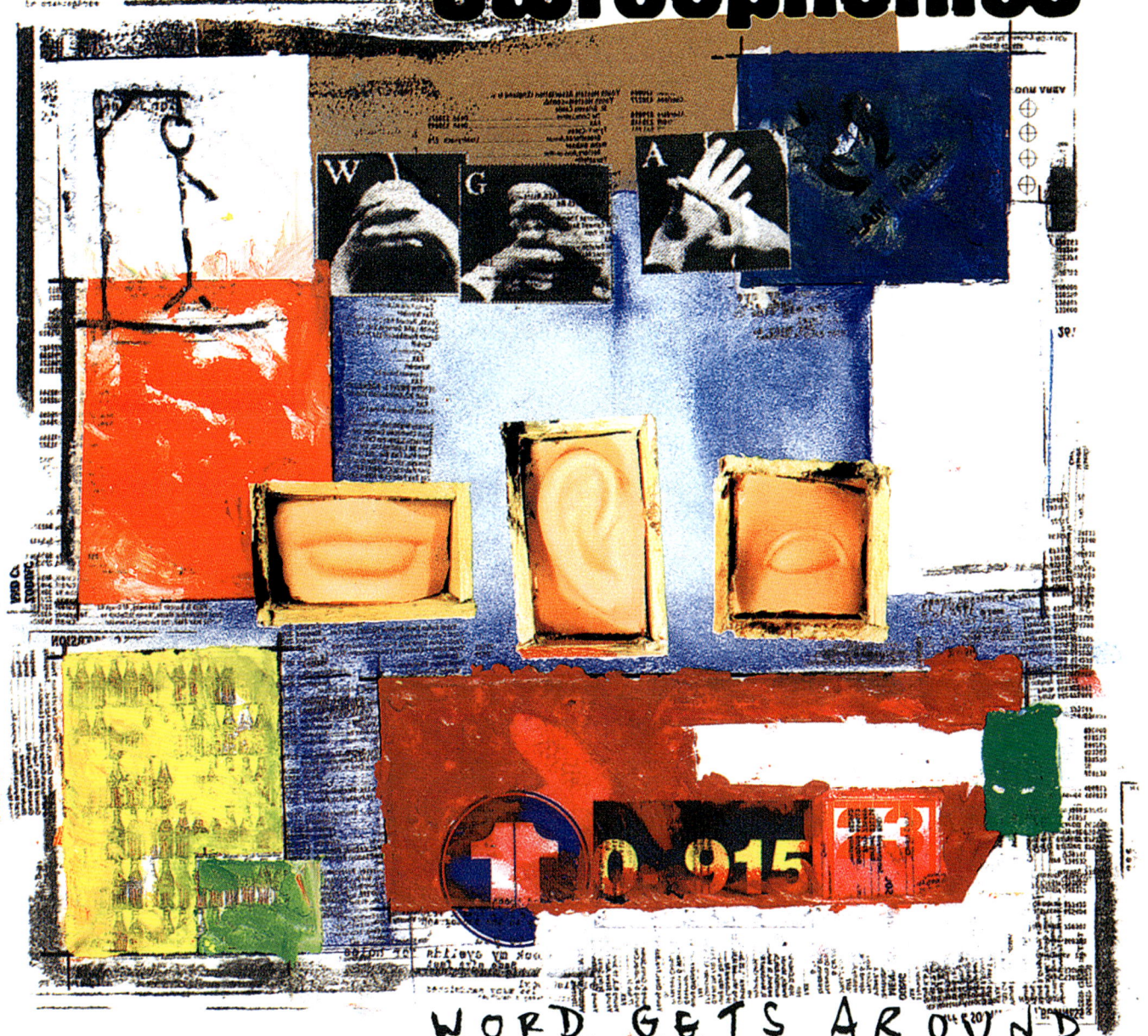

Word Gets Around

WELSH FOLK-SONGS
Meredydd Evans
(FOLKWAYS RECORDS, 1954)

If you happened to be reading *The New York Times* in 1954, you'd have read about Meredydd Evans' *Welsh Folk Songs*, ranked in their Top 10 folk albums that year. Bringing traditional Welsh songs to life, introducing them to a new audience and promoting the heritage of Wales was Evans' life work. He recorded the album for the revered Folkways label, with a curator who engineered a relaxed, informal recording session that made the final cut, although Merêd (as he was affectionately known) himself was then ready to do another 'proper' take for the actual record. Because of the relaxed nature of the session, captured here is a warm, tender collection of songs sung entirely a cappella, and straight from the heart.

Merêd held these songs dear: they'd been with him since his mother sang to him as a baby in Llanegryn in north-west Wales. They had been passed down the generations and somehow avoided being erased by the Methodist revival of the eighteenth century. With recording technology advancements in the mid 1950s, here was a chance to get them on tape for posterity. No one did more to make sure these songs endured than Meredydd Evans.

Married to American singer Phyllis Kinney, he was studying for a PhD at Princeton University when he made this record. After teaching at Boston University for a few years (and being voted Tutor of the Year by students), he then returned to Wales and dedicated his life to his country, language and heritage.

His and Phyllis' personal collection of Welsh folk and traditional songs was unparalleled, and he proudly passed them on to a new generation of musicians who were eager to learn from him. Young musicians would visit their home in Cwmystwyth, near Aberystwyth, where they would receive a warm welcome and a wealth of information.

A broadcaster and media producer, Merêd created several light entertainment programmes in Welsh – often singing himself, sometimes also with Phyllis – entertaining thrilled audiences who hadn't seen this kind of entertainment in their first language before. He sang in Triawd y Coleg (The College Trio), who dominated the Welsh-language popular music scene in the 1940s and 1950s and whose song '*Triawd y Buarth*' (The Farmyard Trio) and its chorus '*Mŵ Mŵ, Me Me, Cwac Cwac*' had audiences howling with laughter.

He brought new talent to the screen – including the hugely popular comedy and singing duo ⊙ **Ryan** & Ronnie and folk troubadour ⊙ **Meic Stevens**, who he introduced to a new audience – and remained an inspirational leading light until his death at the age of 95 in 2015. He campaigned passionately for Cymdeithas yr Iaith (the Welsh Language Society), and in 2015 posthumously won the BBC Radio 2 Folk Awards Good Tradition Award, presented by Cerys Matthews, for his huge contribution to Welsh music culture.

He and Phyllis Kinney were also awarded the Welsh Music Prize's Inspiration Award in 2019. During a lifetime of music, Meredydd and Phyllis contributed enormously to Wales' music history, helping preserve traditions that will live on for generations to come.

WELSH FOLK-SONGS

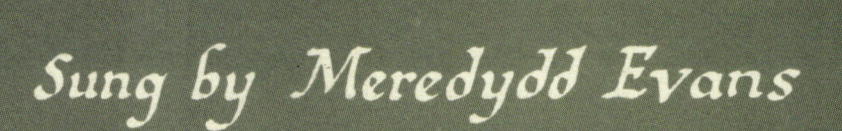

Sung by Meredydd Evans

FP 835 Folkways Records: New York

INNER SONG
Kelly Lee Owens
(SMALLTOWN SUPERSOUND, 2020)

Bagillt in Flintshire, north-east Wales, population around 4,000, might not seem like the natural home of one of the most exciting names in electronic music. But, as we know, Wales is full of surprises.

Kelly Lee Owens has quickly risen as a shining star on the dance music scene, an air of mystery and fantastic beats captivating fans of the genre the world over. Released on Norway's Smalltown Supersound label, this is a striking collection, and was critically acclaimed when it emerged as KLO's second album, the follow-up to her eponymous 2017 debut.

It was in London at a long-gone record shop named Pure Groove that Kelly found her tribe, including producer Daniel Avery, immersing herself in the world of electronica. A series of twelve-inches led to *Inner Song*, with meditative melodies and warm synths twisting and turning throughout.

On 'Jeanette', which is named in tribute to KLO's late grandmother, the pulsating beat seems to come alive, evoking a memory close to the musician's heart. It's playful, evocative and deeply sensual music, crystal clear in its execution and hugely engaging as the album plays on.

'Melt!' is definitely made for the dancefloor, techno rhythms throbbing throughout. Album-opener '*Arpeggi*' is a deconstruction of Radiohead's 'Weird Fishes/*Arpeggi*' – a haunting, minimalistic take that sets the tone for *Inner Song*.

On 'Corner of My Sky', the vocals are provided by one ◉ **John Cale**. This is the sound of old Wales joining young Wales on record, both artists keen to push boundaries, to vanquish stereotypes, to wear their Welsh identity with an international outlook. Both are proud of their Welsh roots, although both felt they had to leave Wales to find their musical selves: John to London then New York (the rest is, of course, history), and Kelly to London to work in record shops and meet like-minded souls. In the video made to accompany the song, Michael Sheen stars as a toast-maker, perplexed by an ever-popping toaster. It is as surreal and as pleasing as the song itself, in which Cale is at first seemingly tired of the rain, turning his anguish to relief as he sings, 'The rain, the rain, thank God, the rain'. He then sings in Welsh for the first time on tape since his version of 'Myfanwy' on S4C's *Heno* magazine programme in 1992. What a great surprise!

Kelly Lee Owens' love of electronic instrumentation is clear, but her voice, calm and warm, is a constant ray of sunshine throughout the album. The final track, 'Wake-Up', is a beautiful closer, with Kelly singing 'Wake up, repeat, again, again, again'. The repetitive nature of our lives, soundtracked by these beautiful repetitive beats.

Inner Song won the Welsh Music Prize in 2021.

Kelly Lee Owens followed this breakthrough album with *LP.8*, which follows in the musical footsteps of its predecessor. It's centred around the track '*Anadlu*' (Breathe), in which KLO instructs us to breathe over some stunningly mellow electronics. She has focused her attention on touring and playing her music live, as support for revered synth masters Depeche Mode, playing enormous venues and engaging audiences around the world.

KELLY LEE OWENS
INNER SONG

LIFE'S NOT OUT TO GET YOU
Neck Deep
(HOPELESS RECORDS, 2015)

Bursting onto the scene in 2012 with an affectionate take on US pop punk, Wrexham five-piece Neck Deep quickly made a name for themselves as one of the most energetic live bands around. They were embraced by the US too, where so many of their musical influences hail from.

Starting as a band making demos in Wrexham bedrooms, their dedication and relentless touring has taken them to countless venues across the UK, building on their live reputation and seeing their gig capacity grow and grow. They soon found a hardcore fanbase enamoured with their chugging guitars, heart-on-their-sleeve lyrics and huge, all-encompassing sound. *Kerrang!* magazine and BBC Radio 1's *Rock Show* declared themselves fans, as Neck Deep took their music to stages around the world.

Led by vocalist Ben Barlow, later joined by his brother Seb, their breakthrough album was 2014's *Wishful Thinking*, released through Hopeless Records from California. Inspired by US skate-punk giants Green Day and Blink 182, their sound made sense to a US audience, who fell in love with their infectious songs and passion for pop-punk culture.

This second album is a step up from their debut. The striking artwork is by Barcelona-based artist Ricardo Cavolo, who has since worked with electronic producer Kaytranada. An anthemic collection of songs, full of tight instrumentation and lyrics drenched in desperation, it's an unrelenting listen in its forward-driving riffs and sharp execution. The song 'December', which their musical hero Mark Hoppus from Blink 182 would later re-record with them, is an album highlight, showing a gentler side to their songwriting craft. A single released from the album, 'Can't Kick Up the Roots', has become a fan favourite, and namechecks Wrexham venue Central Station, now The Rockin' Chair, in this song that's a love letter to life in a small town.

Wrexham's music scene has benefitted greatly from the Focus Wales festival, which began in 2011. It brings musicians in many different genres from around Wales as well as inviting international artists to play across the city, with music fans and industry types descending on the many venues involved to enjoy music and to network. Local bands such as Gallops, The Royston Club, Kidsmoke and Camera have released albums and toured with their music. Football fans have seen their beloved Wrexham FC go global since US actors Ryan Reynolds and Rob McElhenney became the owners, and The Declan Swans provided a soundtrack to the accompanying Disney+ documentary series.

The Peace and the Panic followed this album in 2017, Neck Deep working on songs for it at Monnow Valley Studio, not far from Rockfield, although they eventually recorded in LA. The album *All Distortions are Intentional*, based around the fictional character of Jett, came in 2020, this time recorded at home in Wales at Monnow Valley. A self-titled album was released in 2024, this time recorded at the band's own studio in Wrexham.

For Neck Deep fans, whether it's pogoing down the front at a gig or devouring the artwork and lyrics at home, they're a band with a positive energy and zest for life that is infectious in its message and music, and have found themselves taken to the hearts of their fans worldwide.

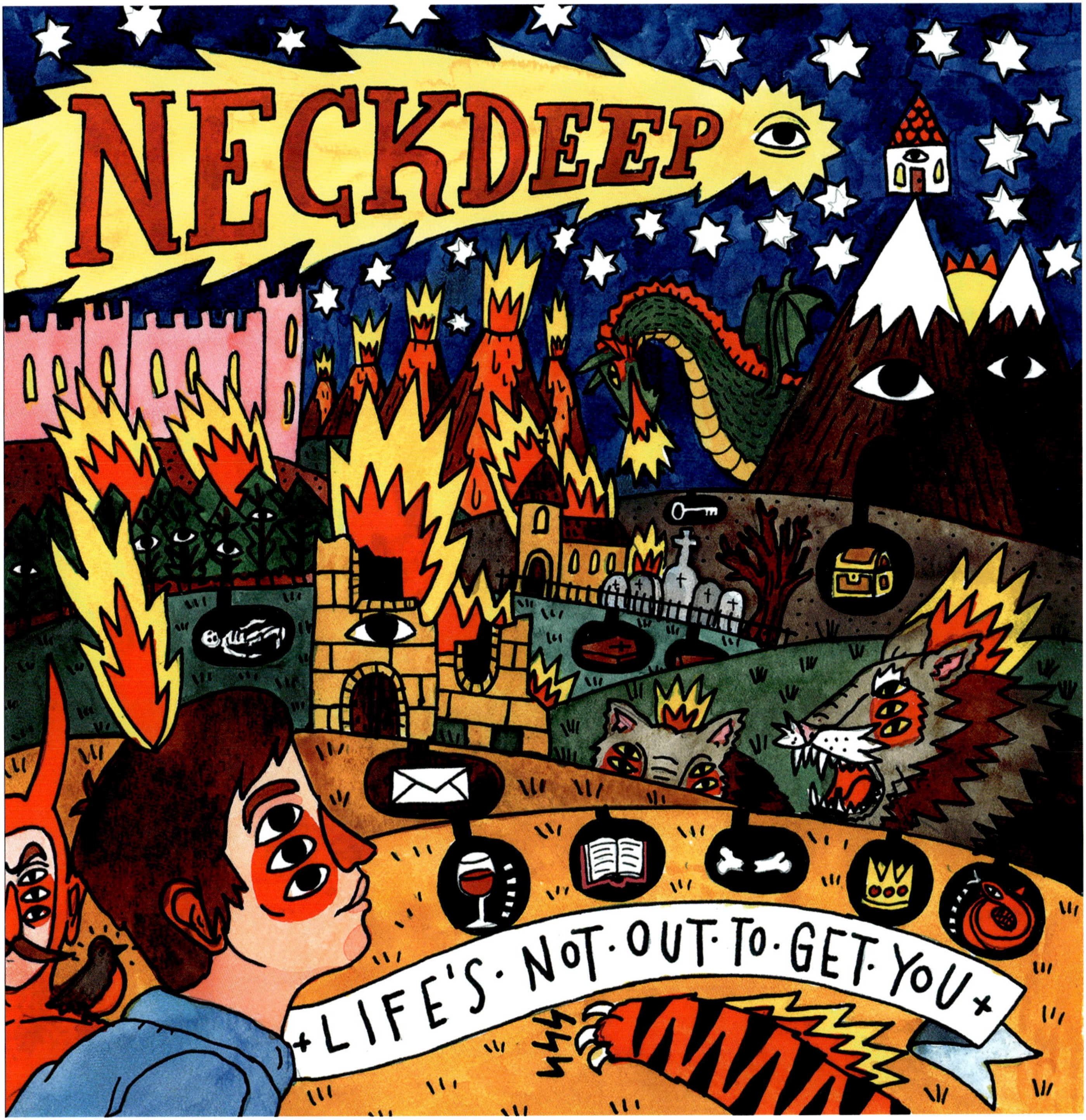
NECKDEEP
LIFE'S · NOT · OUT · TO · GET · YOU

CUPID & PSYCHE 85
Scritti Politti
(VIRGIN, 1985)

Scritti Politti remain a pleasing peculiarity in the world of Welsh – and international – pop.

Born in Cardiff, Green Gartside's family moved around south Wales for much of his early life. Newport remained close to his heart, as he told music journalist and author Robin Turner in a 2011 interview for *The Quietus*: 'I remember growing up with an interest in music, but the very fact that no one from that bit of Wales had ever done it before meant that it couldn't be done. It was without precedent. The whole area was peculiarly bereft of pop.'

After his father had passed away, his mother remarried and the young Paul Strohmeyer used her new husband's surname, and added the Green to stand out in school. Green Gartside was born. His first band was the brilliantly named Heads of the Valleys, but it was in Leeds, where Gartside studied Fine Art, that Scritti Politti was born.

Moving to London and signing to the hugely hip and truly independent Rough Trade record label, the big breakthrough came with 'The Sweetest Girl', a beautifully dreamy single reliant on a drum machine, piano played by Robert Wyatt and Green's distinctive vocals. It remains a truly luxurious-sounding lo-fi song. Green would later reveal it was written with the intention of being a duet between Kraftwerk and Gregory Isaacs; a great idea that never happened, though it was later covered by Madness.

Gartside suffered from illness, including panic attacks, which delayed the release of their debut album, *Songs to Remember*, by a year. When it came out, it was the most commercially successful album Rough Trade had had, getting to number 12 in the album charts.

For the second album, the Scritti Politti line-up had changed, with Green now the only original member remaining. He was obsessed with hip-hop, after trips to Bristol and London from Wales to buy all the rap music twelve-inches he could find in the early Eighties – a musical obsession which continues to this day. Newly signed to Virgin Records, he moved to the birthplace of hip-hop, New York City. The band's second album, *Cupid & Psyche 85*, is a triumph, Green's spectacular and unusually high vocals thrilling at every turn.

'Wood Beez (Pray Like Aretha Franklin)' proved to be a refreshing, remarkable and exciting-sounding single, which made it into the Top Ten. Other sparkling hit singles pepper the record: 'Perfect Way', 'The Word Girl', 'Absolute'. This was slightly skew-whiff modern-day soul pop, intelligent and classy but accessible and memorable, all from the brain of a Welsh visionary who went to Croesyceiliog School in Cwmbran.

Further success, and complications, would follow. Green retreated to Usk after the follow-up to *Cupid & Psyche 85*, *Provision*, was released in 1988. It would then be over a decade until new music appeared, on the excellent *Anomie & Bonhomie* and *White Bread Black Beer* albums. Ill health and the need to rest and recuperate leave seemingly dormant years in the story of Scritti Politti, but when there is action, it is always hugely thrilling. Most recently, live shows and anniversary gigs for these special albums have been joyous occasions, a reminder of their singularity and special place in the story of UK pop music.

SCRITTI POLITTI
Cupid & Psyche 85

MELYN
Adwaith
(LIBERTINO RECORDS, 2018)

This is the debut album from acclaimed indie band Adwaith. Vocalist/guitarist Hollie Singer, bassist Gwenllian Anthony and drummer Heledd Owen arrived as a breath of fresh air on the male-dominated guitar scene in Wales.

The Tangled Parrot record shop in Carmarthen was instrumental in Adwaith's formation. It was a venue, and it's where the members would see gigs, where they would meet up and, once Adwaith were ready, where they would play their own first gigs. The venue has now been renamed Cwrw (Beer) but the record shop is still upstairs, as well as having branches in Hay on Wye and Swansea. A portrait of David R Edwards of ● **Datblygu**, who would call in most days when he lived in Carmarthen, sits behind the counter.

Edwards was a huge presence in the town and the Welsh music scene as a whole, with popular arts app Am, distribution arm Pyst and Libertino Records all named after Datblygu songs or albums. It was to Libertino Records that Adwaith would sign. Their support for Adwaith and many other bands is invaluable. Breichiau Hir, Ynys, ● **Minas**, SYBS, Rogue Jones, Los Blancos, Papur Wal and N'Famady Kouyaté have all released records through the label – with Gruff Owen, who runs the label, also promoting gigs and managing some of the artists. It shows how much good can be done through one person's devotion and energy; the repercussions are hugely positive for a scene.

Melyn (Yellow) is a loose listen, with melodies and an otherworldliness interweaving. '*Fel i Fod*' (How to Be) is a coming-of-age song, with Hollie opening her heart, sounding overwhelmed by modern-day life, taking solace in the bedsheets.

She sings, '*Falle fi moen mynd yn wyllt, falle fi moen mynd i gysgu*' (Maybe I want to go wild, maybe I want to go to sleep). Adwaith share a young, personal perspective. At times there is a charming naivety to these first songs: they are singing about life at home in a relatively small town. Touring and seeing the world would follow.

'*Gartref*' (Home) tells how they occasionally feel far from home, and how it's OK to be lost sometimes. It was later remixed by James Dean Bradfield of ● **Manic Street Preachers**, who added his trademark guitars to the single. The Manics, ever the supportive band, invited Adwaith to support them at a few gigs, as did punk heroes Idles.

Melyn won the Welsh Music Prize in 2019, and Adwaith repeated the feat in 2022 with their second album, *Bato Mato*. Named after a tour guide who accompanied them when they played a gig in Siberia in early 2021, it is tighter and sounds more accomplished.

They became the first all-female headliners at Maes B, the night-time gig element of the National Eisteddfod, and the first Welsh-language band to sell out a gig at Le Pub in Newport in the venue's 30 years of gig-promoting. They've been supported by BBC Radio 6 Music, appearing on their mainstream playlist during the day, and played a standout set on the Introducing stage at Glastonbury. They did all of this while singing in Welsh, which came naturally to them. They are the embodiment of how far the Welsh-language scene has come – or maybe more correctly, how the world now views bands singing in Welsh: a minority language, maybe, but one that connects with people and is used creatively and confidently to create wonderful music.

ADWAITH

AS FAR AS I'M CONCERNED
Me One
(ISLAND RECORDS, 2000)

Eric Martin started his musical journey on Queen St in Cardiff city centre in the mid 1980s. With hip-hop culture everywhere, he and his friends were breakdancing, graffitiing and rapping. While his lifelong friend DJ Jaffa scratched and beat-matched records, starting his lifelong journey in hip-hop, Eric discovered his talent for rapping, recording himself on a cassette deck. He started promoting hip-hop shows when he was just 16, and found a taste for entrepreneurship as well as making music.

Eric met producer Jo Bogaert and Manuela Kamosi (also known as Ya Kid K) in a London studio and ideas began to flow. Technotronic became their pseudonym, and they soon became serious chart contenders. Their single 'Pump up the Jam' was released in 1989, becoming a worldwide smash. Eric was the main vocalist on another hit single, 'This Beat Is Technotronic', and the production-crew-turned-pop stars toured North America as support to Madonna and DJ Jazzy Jeff. They sold millions of albums in the US, the young Eric taking it all in and realising what the music industry looked like when you were as successful an artist as Madonna.

By the end of the Nineties, Eric was ready to show a mellower side to his music as Me One. He'd wanted to record a project using the name since his early days in Riverside, Cardiff. He cut some tracks in London and Jamaica, then in New York at D&D Studios – where Biggie Smalls, Gang Starr and a young Jill Scott recorded – Eric putting the pieces together for what would become his next musical chapter, *As Far as I'm Concerned*. The Roots produced his single 'Frenemy', and when acclaimed guitarist Jeff Beck reached out to him after hearing early Me One tracks, they collaborated on a funky number called 'Pay Me No Mind'. One album highlight is 'In My Room', his take on the Beach Boys classic, with his seamless blending of hip-hop, jazz and electronica making him an exciting name in music at the dawn of a new millennium.

Today Eric works in production and DJs live, mixing tracks from his past and his new compositions, with MCs and singers joining him onstage. He continues to promote live shows and club nights, and composes like he always has done, with the dancefloor and the music connoisseur firmly in his mind as he mixes. He's worked with Anthem, the charity that aims to improve young people's lives through music in Wales, and has been on the board of the Welsh Music Foundation, bringing his expertise, knowledge and many experiences in the industry to the next generation of creatives.

me'

AS FAR AS I'M CONCERNED

AR LAN Y MÔR
Yr Hennessys
(CAMBRIAN, 1970)

Thanks to Cardiff's world-famous docks, thousands of Irish families came to live in the city in the mid 1800s, with the Newtown area becoming known as Little Ireland. It's from this stock that Frank Hennessy can trace his heritage, with his dad's parents originally from County Waterford.

With his Irish blood and a guitar given to him on his thirteenth birthday, Frank learnt his craft and became a hit in the pubs of Cardiff. Frank's lifelong friend Dave Burns, who also played in Ar Log and passed away in 2023, plays mandolin on this four-track EP, with Paul Powell from Adamsdown in the city on guitar. Drawing on traditional Irish songs, their music took them to Ireland, where they were welcomed on the trad scene, the far-reaching Irish diaspora intrigued by these fine musicians from just across the water. Frank Hennessy's song 'The Old Carmarthen Oak' was a particular favourite with the Irish, with even Daniel O'Donnell recording his own version, swapping 'Carmarthen' for 'Dungarvan'.

As Welsh-language TV programming boomed on the BBC and the new third channel for Wales, HTV, a decade before S4C became a reality, English-language songs would be translated into Welsh. Hywel Gwynfryn's talent for turning the English words into Welsh lyrics would be utilised by TV programmes such as *Hob y Deri Dando* and *Disc a Dawn*, often performed by singer-songwriter ● **Meic Stevens** or Yr Hennessys. The latter's song 'The Gipsy' would become '*Y Sipsi*' for this, their first record in the Welsh language. One of Frank's most evergreen songs, 'Goodbye to the Rhondda', translated by dramatist Rhydderch Jones, is heard here as '*Ffarwel i'r Rhondda*': a pessimistic, heartfelt ode to the loss of work in the Rhondda Valleys' mines. It's a melancholic dose of reality about the realities of industry, a close cousin to ● **Max Boyce**'s more innocent 'Rhondda Grey'.

Frank ran popular folk clubs in Cardiff, and the songs he wrote based on the city are the stuff of legend. His song 'Cardiff Born' was a hit on the terraces of Ninian Park at Cardiff City games. It features on the *Cardiff After Dark* album from 1984, along with 'Billy the Seal' and 'Grangetown Whale'.

Frank can still be heard on BBC Radio Wales, where he's been fronting shows since 1984. He can currently be heard presenting the popular *Celtic Heartbeat* programme – a weekly journey through his folk and traditional favourites, old and new, all beautifully linked with Frank's enthusiasm, understanding and indisputable charm.

CAMBRIAN CEP 455

YR HENNESSYS
AR LAN Y MÔR

CHATTY PATTY
Minas
(SILENT KID RECORDS, 2023)

Producer and emcee Minas' rap music crossed with punk has surprised many with his erratic and openly vulnerable sound. Glimmers of electronica combine to create a raw, pulsating sound that is both menacing and mesmerising, something of a trademark for this fascinating artist.

Minas is musician of Welsh and Greek descent, his parents instrumental in the founding of Wales' NoFitState Circus. A stream of consciousness trip through Minas' mind, the lyrics of 'Chatty Patty' are honest, brutal and full of contradictions. He raps about not having much to say, and yet his lyrics tell us more about the state of mind of being young and Welsh than many other artists'. The boredom, the monotony, the relentless feeling of being skint are portrayed in an uncompromising manner, as if Minas is leaving us a personal voice note. We are listening in on a man's innermost thoughts, his words spoken as if he's coming to terms with himself, grappling with everyday anxieties as he comes face to face with the realities of life.

At two and a half minutes, this is a double A-side single with 'The Public Ain't Spoken', and a follow-up to a Welsh-language track called '*Ddoe*' (Yesterday). Minas is a creative force with a special energy, eager to explore his own musical mind and push barriers as far as he can, keen to share his honesty with raw, gripping lyrics. On stage he has made a name for himself as one of the most exciting live performers around, an uncompromising and enthralling artist who, together with his live band including producer Don the Prod, gives it his all.

Minas' impressive debut album *All My Love Has Failed Me* came out to rave reviews in 2022 on Libertino Records. His production work for countless other artists served him in good stead as he turned his attentions to his own music, culminating in this brightly executed collection of tracks.

COLLI IAITH
Heather Jones
(SAIN, 1971)

Heather Jones has been a constant favourite on the Welsh-language scene since she began singing in her home in Cardiff, where she was born in 1949.

Her debut solo release appeared in 1968 on the Welsh Teldisc label, an introduction to her particularly beautiful voice. Her restrained, chiming singing has never been showy or garish; instead she exudes a melodic, controlled delivery on her varied back catalogue of folk, country and rock songs. A pupil in school with ◉ **Geraint Jarman**, they would become romantically linked, and spoke Welsh (which she'd learnt as a second language) to each other as they began courting. Together with ◉ **Meic Stevens** (a few years their senior), they formed Bara Menyn, originally a parody band aimed at mocking and mimicking the light entertainment groups popular in Wales on the *Noson Lawen* (a kind of talent show) scene.

'*Colli Iaith*' translates loosely as 'To Lose a Language'. Arranged by ◉ **Meredydd Evans**, the words are by Harri Webb, the Swansea poet whose extensive work lit up the Welsh literature firmament. Among his many collections of poems is *Looking Up England's Arsehole*, the title of which gives us a glimpse into his thinking. But '*Colli Iaith*' isn't one of Harri's comical poems. In fact it is quite the opposite: a stark, sudden bolt of a poem which mourns the loss of a language, but also of many other things that Webb saw disappearing in Wales. Community and dignity, religion and old melodies are all mourned. The valleys of Elan and Tryweryn are mentioned in the song's most poignant moment, as Webb sees all of Wales under water. Heather's vocal delivery is nothing short of stunning, sung entirely a capella. Glimmers of hope burst through the clouds, as 'Wales begins on its journey' – '*A Chymru'n cychwyn ar eu hymdaith*'. The repetition of the word *colli* throughout the song is unforgiving: a reminder that once it's gone, it's gone.

Heather's vocals are a true treasure of Welsh music, her impressive collection of songs having enriched all those who have heard them over the years.

CHATTY PATTY

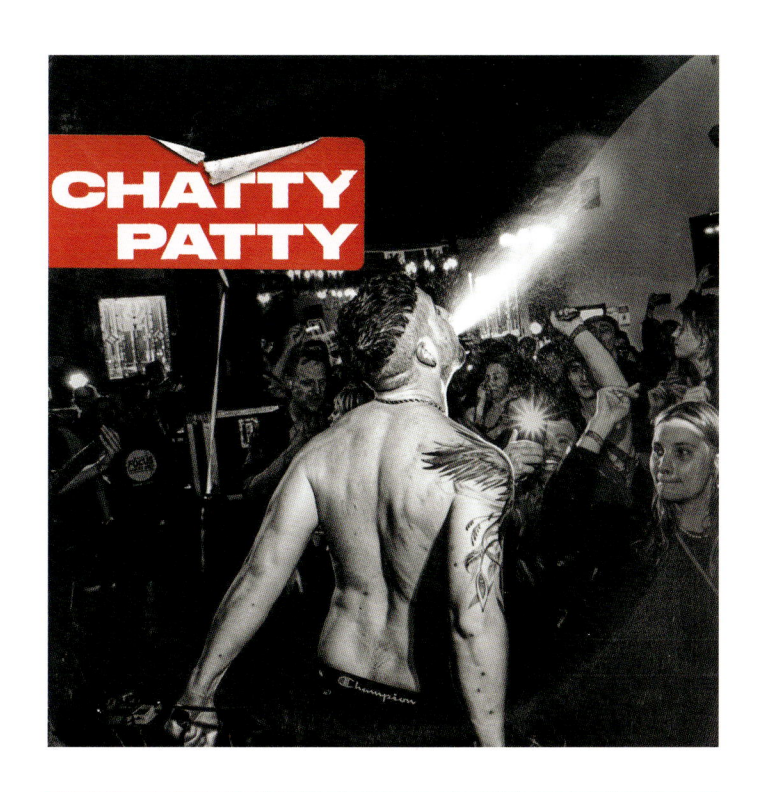

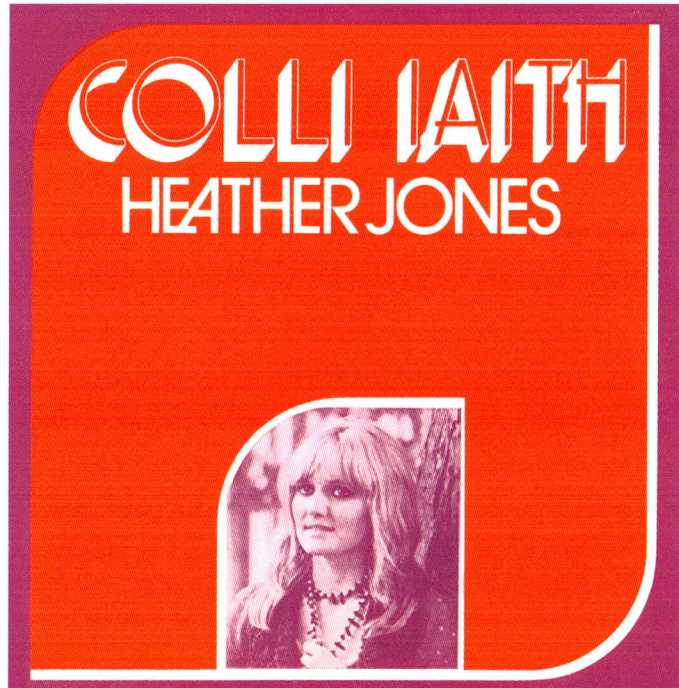

COLLI IAITH
HEATHER JONES

PARIS 1919
John Cale
(REPRISE RECORDS, 1973)

'Our language, our literature and our music gave us a cherished sense of nationhood.' So says John Cale in his 1999 autobiography *What's Welsh for Zen*, writing about growing up in Garnant, 'in the foothills of the Brecon Beacons'.

At a young age he showed great musical promise, joining the National Youth Orchestra of Wales as a violist before he left school in Ammanford. A school where ○ **Dafydd Iwan** was also a pupil at the same time as Cale, although neither remembers the other, life taking them on very different journeys. His Aunt Mai worked on *Welsh Rarebit*, a programme on BBC Wales that showcased new talent, something she nurtured in young John.

Soon, new lands and adventures were calling. After studying music at Goldsmiths in London, Cale arrived in New York in 1963, where he formed a new musical project with Lou Reed. Their work in The Velvet Underground remains untouchable, their music undisputedly iconic. Their 1967 self-titled debut, with Warhol's famous banana as its artwork, is the blueprint for avant-garde rock, widely regarded as a masterpiece. But Cale soon tired of looking back at his musical legacy, preferring instead to immerse himself in new musical projects as a keen creator who wanted to do something new. He would answer questions about his formative years, but there was always a creative itch to be scratched and he became weary of journalists wanting to know only about the past when he felt all he wanted to say had been said. His eyes were fixed firmly on the future.

His friendship with Lou Reed was rekindled after reconnecting at Andy Warhol's funeral in 1987, which led them to work together again on the striking *Songs for Drella* album, a record in tribute to the influential artist. Cale became a respected producer, working with an eclectic list of artists including Patti Smith and The Stooges, Squeeze and Happy Mondays.

An ambitious and surprising record, *Paris 1919* features the UCLA Symphony Orchestra, who lift the record. It's an album that is both melancholy and uplifting, which twists and turns with mini symphonies, and which gives a glimpse of Cale's creative vision in the early 1970s. A lush-sounding record, the lingering 'Half Past France' gives a glimpse of the young poet at work, and album opener 'A Child's Christmas' in Wales is a nod to another great Welsh visionary, Dylan Thomas.

He played *Paris 1919* at the Coal Exchange in Cardiff in 2009 to a delighted audience, the first time he'd ever played the album in full. Next to the historic venue, now a hotel, was former church turned live music locale The Point, where a decade earlier they had set up a studio for Cale to collaborate with young Welsh bands, captured on film by director Marc Evans. The result was the film *Camgymeriad Gwych/Beautiful Mistake* (2000), featuring James Dean Bradfield of ○ **Manic Street Preachers**, poet Patrick Jones, ○ **Gorky's Zygotic Mynci**, harpist ○ **Llio Rhydderch**, Derrero, Julie Murphy, ○ **Big Leaves** and even rap crew ○ **Tystion** performing, their musical hero adding instrumentation to their songs.

Cale's 17th solo album, *Mercy*, was released in his 80th year, featuring collaborations with other forward-looking musicians such as producer Actress, Weyes Blood, Sylvan Esso and Dev Hynes – a fascinating and masterful album that Cale was rightly proud of.

Released a year after *Mercy*, Cale's latest work, *POPtical Illusion*, sees him continue to reinvent and reassess, and includes the song 'Davies and Wales'. A remarkable creator with an audacious appetite to evolve and to create, his music is unmistakably his and his alone.

John Cale Paris 1919.

TRUE COLOURS
High Contrast
(HOSPITAL RECORDS, 2002)

High Contrast is regarded as one of the leading lights in the drum 'n' bass world. D'n'B – or jungle, as some call it – is a fast and furious style of music that emerged during the 1990s rave scene. Like many underground movements, it has since crossed over to infiltrate the mainstream, with producers matching it with rap, rock, house and other styles to create genre-defying worldwide hits.

Music was in Lincoln Barrett's family, his father managing a young ● **Shakin' Stevens** and other rock 'n' roll bands in the 1970s. Growing up in Penarth in the Vale of Glamorgan meant that Cardiff was in easy reach for a young Lincoln to discover the club scene for himself. He'd regularly be found in Catapult in the city centre, an influential dance music shop where drum 'n' bass legends like LTJ Bukem and Grooverider would play instore sets. He worked there for a while and became a regular at Clwb Ifor Bach's Silent Running and Aperture nights, where he was a favourite, keeping the dancefloor bouncing.

After playing some minidisc demos to DJ and producer London Elektricity in Catapult Records, High Contrast was soon signed to his Hospital Records. Known for their epic late-night raves, Hospital ran the label whilst simultaneously promoting their DJs in the live arena. Hospital became a favourite with the D'n'B audience whilst also attracting attention from the mainstream, all tied together under their striking Hospital logo and merchandise.

D'n'B had been a genre where remixes and one-off tracks were usually more common than full albums. Lincoln's appreciation of the album as an art form made sure he'd be constantly releasing full-length albums for the next 20 years. As a former film student in Newport, film samples would weave their way into his music, his understanding of the dancefloor and a sense of adventure in the studio creating memorable, captivating records.

True Colours was his debut album, and whilst bolder collaborations and bigger success would follow, this is where it all started. Recorded quite simply on the equipment he had to hand in a terraced house in Penarth, there's a hard-edged darkness to this record. Like a lot of the best drum 'n' bass music, it hits you over the head whilst you dance, but there are glimmers of Lincoln's future records here too, particularly in 'Global Love' and 'Music is Everything', which have him bending samples and guest vocals to fit around his particular beats.

He worked with fellow Welshman Rick Smith, of electronic music pioneers ● **Underworld**, and Dutch superstar DJ Tiësto on a single called 'The First Note Is Silent' – a huge single in sound and reach. That relationship with Smith continued when Lincoln worked with him and Karl Hyde on the music heard throughout Danny Boyle's spectacular opening ceremony for the 2012 London Olympics.

High Contrast remains one of the most respected and enigmatic D'n'B producers in the world, his eagerness to collaborate and create keeping his fans interested and very much lost in the music.

TRUECOLOURS
HIGHCONTRAST

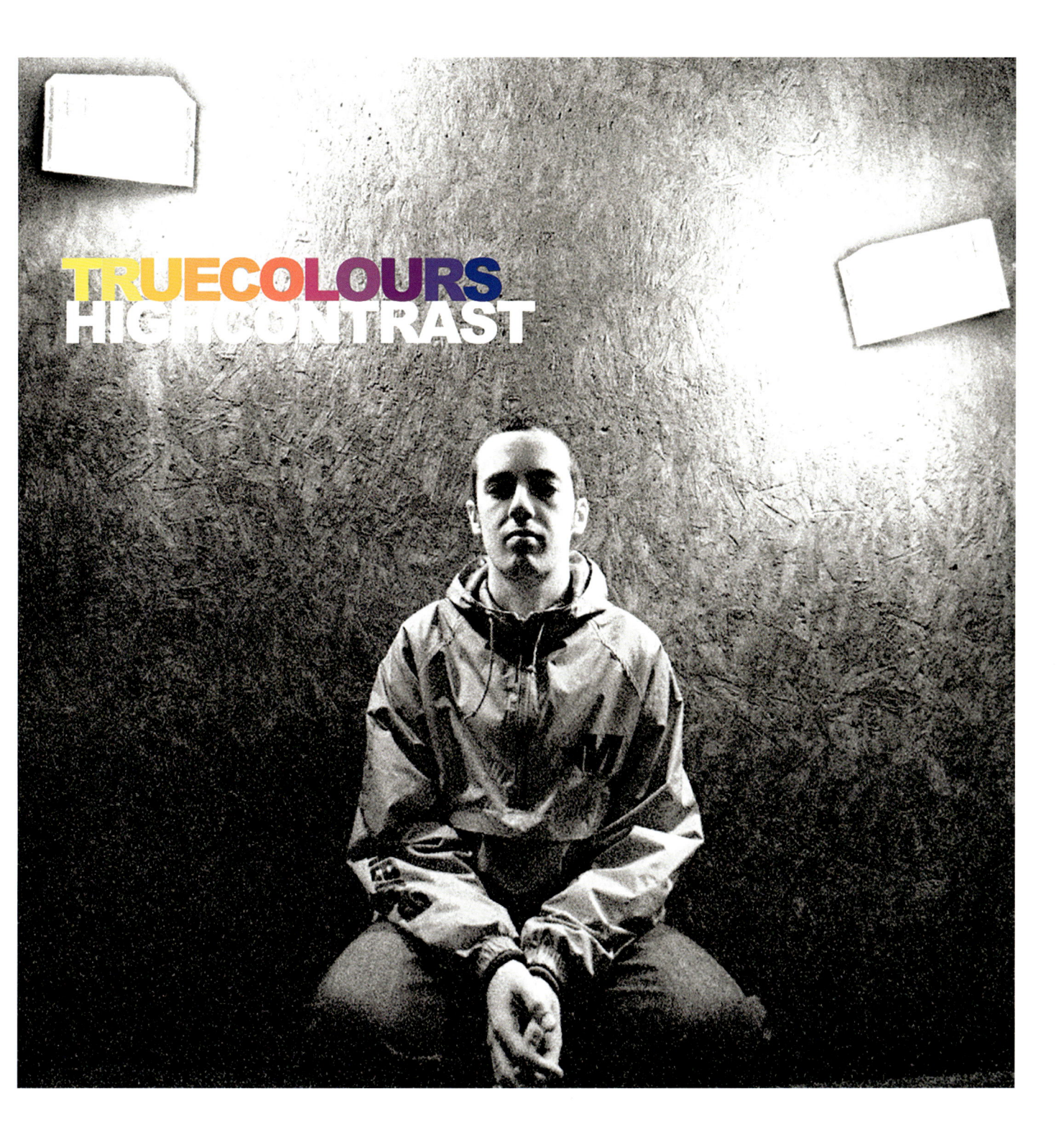

YN ÔL I GWM RHYD Y RHOSYN
Dafydd Iwan ac Edward
(SAIN, 1977)

"Have you heard of Cwm Rhyd y Rhosyn?" asks ⊙ **Dafydd Iwan**, the narrator on this record who guides us from song to song, as well as singing. "It's a wonderful place, halfway between Pen Llŷn and Cardiff, not too far from Avalon. Let's go there together, but remember one thing: you have to sing all the time." Dafydd's narration helps create a fantasy world, describing an idyllic valley where the songs and characters – mostly animals – on this record live, and reminds us that this is a record not just to listen to, but for the kids to join in on (with a little help from the adults, maybe). This they have done, around record players at home, and more recently in cars on long journeys, since the record's release in 1977.

When his father became a preacher in Llanuwchlyn, near Bala, Dafydd moved there from Brynaman with his family. Impressed by Edward Morus Jones' meccano skills and their shared love of Sassie Rees' records for children, Dafydd and Edward started singing together at the local *Noson Lawen* (a night showcasing local talents) and school dances. They went into the studio to record a Welsh-language version of Woody Guthrie's 'This Land is My Land' in 1966, released on the Welsh Teldisc label. But the second track on that EP was their laid-back version of popular children's song '*Gee Ceffyl Bach*' (Gee Up, Little Horse), about a little horse crossing the river to collect some nuts. This laid the foundation for a future record of songs especially for children.

Before long, Dafydd and Edward went on to record what would become their first album together, *Fuoch Chi Rioed yn Morio* (Have You Ever Been Sailing?), in 1973. The title track itself asks, 'Have you ever been sailing? Well yes, in a frying pan.' Edward was a teacher by now and understood the importance of songs for young people. The humour made the language fun, but there were also more serious songs teaching them about Wales and the wider world.

In stark contrast to their later albums, the simple black and white portrait on the cover of *Fuoch Chi Rioed yn Morio* suggested a record that was meant entirely for children to enjoy. And that they did. With televisions unaffordable, music for children was only available through random radio programmes and records, and the album proved a hit, selling thousands of copies across Wales.

In 1968, Edward teamed up with ⊙ **Mary Hopkin** as Mary ac Edward and released an EP on the Cambrian label, mostly of covers. His son is the Plaid Cymru politician Rhun ap Iorwerth, himself once in a band called 69.

Dafydd Iwan was a household name in Welsh-speaking Wales by the time this colourful album was released in 1977. He'd been an activist and a prisoner for his role in Cymdeithas yr Iaith (the Welsh Language Society), a Plaid Cymru politician, and a protest singer of note. But family and Welsh education remained close to his heart, as they still are. There are beautiful, moving, funny and entertaining songs here, many ingrained in the memories of Welsh people thanks to this album.

The beautiful artwork is by Cen Williams, an illustrator who passed away in 2020, with the gatefold vinyl edition of the album showing his work in full effect, complementing this iconic children's album.

YN ÔL I GWM RHYD Y RHOSYN

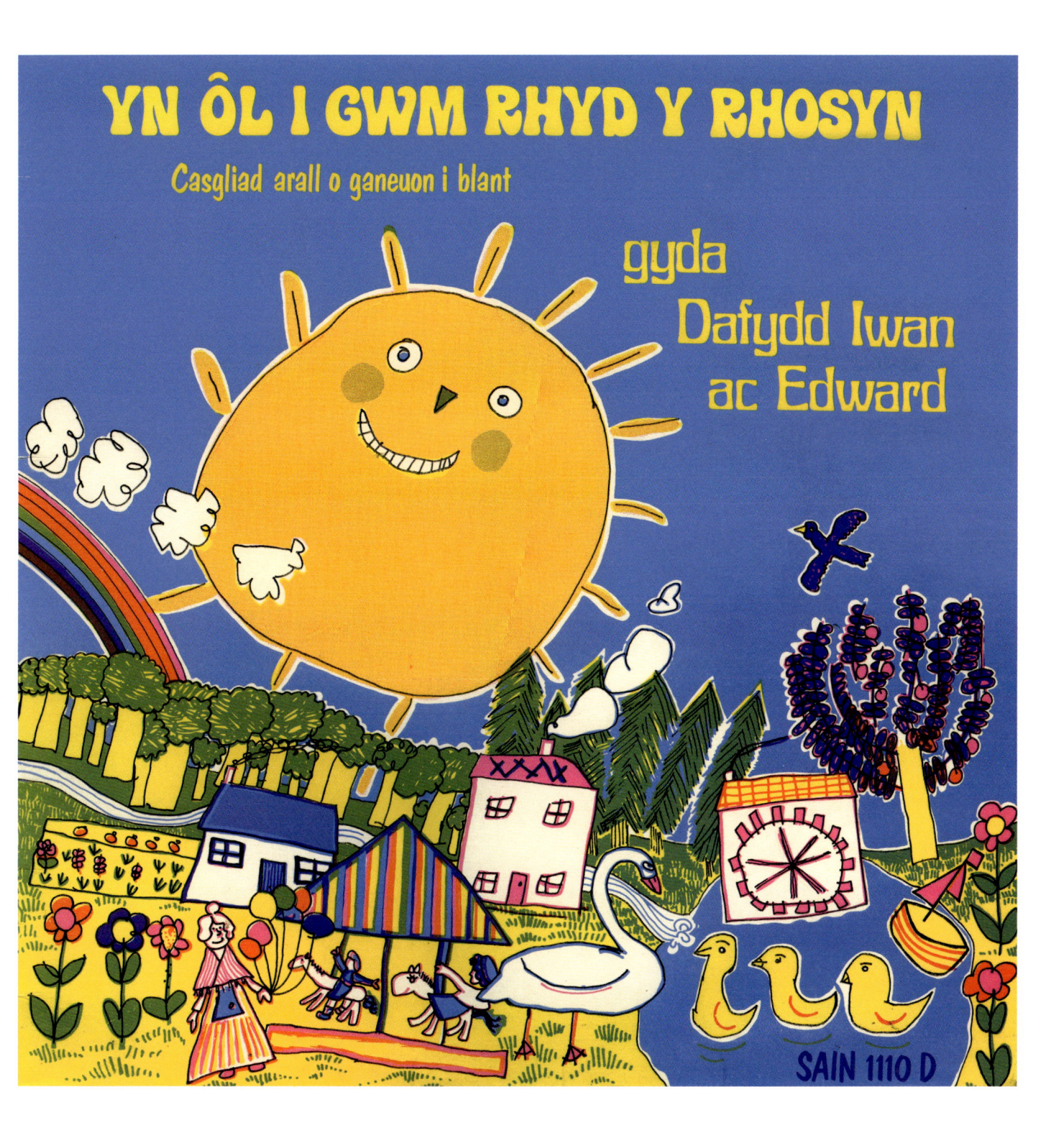

Casgliad arall o ganeuon i blant

gyda
Dafydd Iwan
ac Edward

SAIN 1110 D

ROCKFERRY
Duffy
(A&M RECORDS/ROUGH TRADE, 2008)

In 2008 the debut album from Duffy, *Rockferry*, brought her fame and success that she could only have imagined a few years earlier.

Born on the Llŷn Peninsula and raised there in Nefyn before moving to Fishguard when she was 10, Aimée Duffy was no stranger to isolation and seaside towns. With a love of singing, she became a contestant on S4C music talent show *WawFfactor*, coming second on it in 2003. One of the judges was Owen Powell, guitarist and songwriter in ○ Catatonia and previously member of indie band Crumblowers, from the Whitchurch area of Cardiff. He recognised her talent and was a fan of her voice, and introduced her to his friend Richard Parfitt, lead singer of the now-defunct Newport band ○ **60ft Dolls**. Soon Aimée Duffy would meet Jeanette Lee, a former member of Public Image Ltd and co-owner of the legendary Rough Trade label, where The Smiths, The Strokes and ○ **Scritti Politti** had made their names. Jeanette was also a manager, could hear Duffy had something special, and took her under her wing.

Working with Bernard Butler, a superb guitarist, songwriter and former member of Suede, Duffy's *Rockferry* album started to take shape over the next four years. She studied the greats, listening to The Supremes, Candi Staton and Millie Jackson, falling in love with this sensational old soul music. She worked with Eg White, a songwriter who had formed Brother Beyond and gone on to write for several big names. These sessions brought out the best in Duffy, and they wrote striking, memorable songs.

Wearing her heart on her sleeve, this is an album drenched in love and in heartbreak, with lush orchestration elevating the music throughout. 'Warwick Avenue' – the title coming from a wrong turn Duffy took on the Underground, ending up at this tube stop in London – upbeat stomper 'Mercy' and the forlorn 'Stepping Stone' were big hits, opening the doors to mainstream success for Duffy. Rock Ferry itself is in Birkenhead, and used on the record by Duffy as a metaphor for when one is lost or alone. The album cover photograph, however, was taken in the Ffestiniog Railway station in Porthmadog – opposite Cob Records, a wonderful second-hand record shop.

Rockferry went straight to number 1, and won the Brit Award for British Album of the Year the following year. Its success would be hard to replicate with the follow-up album *Endlessly*, released in 2010. For it she worked with Albert Hammond Senior, and highly regarded US band The Roots, featuring Questlove, provided the instrumentation. It was, however, the last official release we have heard from Duffy. Her stunning rendition of the traditional Welsh folk song '*Ar Lan y Môr*' (By the Sea Shore) on the soundtrack to *Patagonia*, the Marc Evans-directed film based in Wales and Argentina, in which Duffy played the role of a lost young woman from a seaside town, stands as one of her finest and most heartfelt recordings to date.

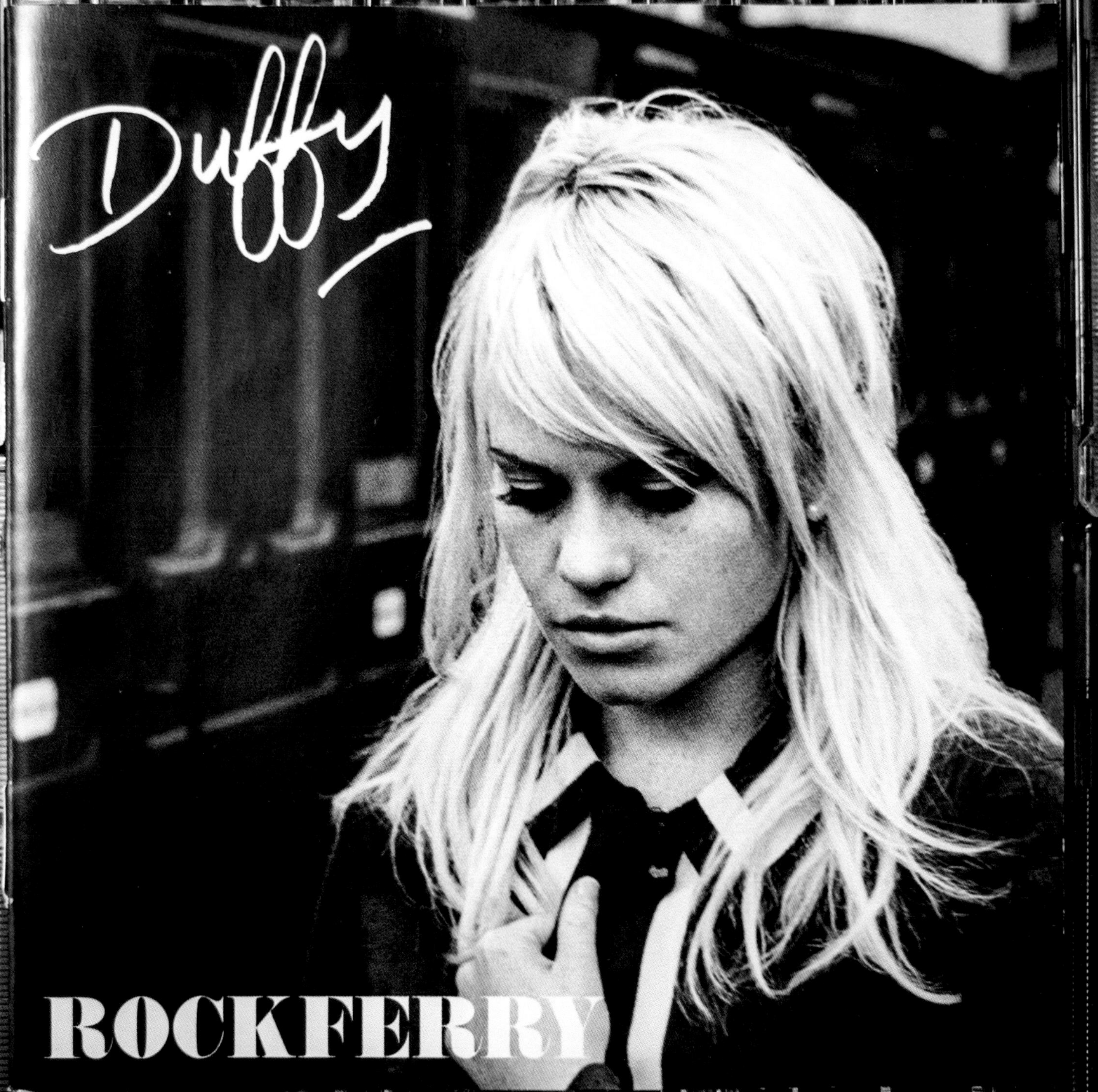
Duffy
ROCKFERRY

GWALAXIA: BELLEVILLE 1315 / MACHYNLLETH 1404
Ffrancon

(ANKSTMUSIK, 2021)

After a few decades releasing home-recorded CDRs, downloads and the occasional extended mix, Ffrancon's *Gwalaxia* album emerged in 2021 on the legendary Ankstmusik label. Geraint Ffrancon, a Rachub, Bethesda-born musician, had been living in Bristol for most of his adult life, immersed in the city's vibrant electronic music scene, but he remained closely involved in Wales' cultural landscape, making music as Stabmaster Vinyl and Blodyn Tatws.

In the early 2000s he, along with electronic music-obsessive friends Pappy and Plyci, brought a much-needed dose of dance music to the Welsh-language scene, which was then saturated with guitars. Ffrancon has also brought a playfulness with his music, encapsulated in this album's artwork: the Welsh flag reimagined with all-too-familiar Welsh sheep rather than the famous mythical Welsh dragon.

This instrumental techno album came about when Ffrancon realised that Machynlleth, the small rural market town in Mid Wales, was twinned with Belleville, Michigan – which boasts a population only slightly bigger than Machynlleth itself, at some 4,000 people. What excited Ffrancon was that Belleville is regarded as the birthplace of techno. It is home to Derrick May, Juan Atkins and Kevin Saunderson, known as The Belleville Three – hugely influential pioneers in the genre.

Machynlleth, meanwhile, was the location of the first Welsh parliament, held in 1404 under Owain Glyndŵr, the last true Prince of Wales. The building said to be his Parliament House is open to visitors to the town today, and his flag is seen the length and breadth of Wales, on bucket hats and car stickers.

If the spirit of Glyndŵr lives on in Wales today, the spirit of Detroit techno caught on worldwide. Known for its hypnotic, repetitive nature and its dark and edgy twists and turns, it goes in hard and heavy at around 150 beats per minute, meaning the relentlessness of the music creates epic odysseys on the dancefloor. I'm sure Glyndŵr would have approved.

Inspired by the last Welshman to hold the title of Prince of Wales, by rebellious politics and by the challenging, untamed nature of techno music, this is a lively, fascinating concept album bringing two of the most unlikely bedfellows together to create a great techno journey.

It was recorded as a post-Brexit statement that underlined Geraint's love of music and Wales' continued interest in independence. *Gwalaxia* is an album that is both international in its appeal, yet rooted in location and specific history. An unusual, surprising record that takes two hugely influential moments in two very different countries' stories to create a memorable album.

FFRANCON

GWALAXIA : BELLEVILLE 1315 / MACHYNLLETH 1404

THE HOLY BIBLE
Manic Street Preachers
(EPIC, 1994)

With artwork by Jenny Saville, it has to be one of the most striking, iconic album covers of all time.

Released in 1994, this is the third album from Manic Street Preachers. Widely regarded by die-hard Manics fans as their best, it is an honest, abrasive work of art that is uncompromising and instantly thrilling. If their ambitious first two albums, *Gold Against the Soul* and *Generation Terrorists*, got the Manics noticed, this was the band scaling everything back and making sure they were being taken seriously – or, as Richey Edwards would infamously have it, *4 Real*. After *The Holy Bible* was heard, there was no doubt that this was a band who were here to stay, and who had a lot to say.

It was recorded in Cardiff's Sound Space Studios, the band purposely choosing this small, low-key studio in the centre of the city to make sure there were no frills, no decadence, and no unnecessary comforts to take away from these songs, which are muscular, taut and straight to the point. The majority of the songs' lyrics are written by Richey, his beautifully poetic writing on full display here. His ability to dwell on the desperate, to highlight the pain and bring his tales of suffering and vulnerability alive, matched with the extraordinarily spiky guitar of James Dean Bradfield, Sean Moore's post punk jazz drumming and the low-slung bass of Nicky Wire, makes for a heady concoction.

'Faster' leaps out at you with its staccato guitars, intellectual heaviness, and bold claims of being stronger than Mensa, Miller and Mailer, spitting out Plath and Pinter, leaving the listener reeling. This is a band whose ambition has been honed, their ideas more audacious and braver than ever. Refusing to participate in anyone's games, they are a working-class band who have seen too much; they will not play by the rules and sit quietly. That is apparent throughout this masterful, beautiful record. Snippets of film and dialogue are sampled throughout the album, adding to the urgency and mystery of the songs.

In the sleeve notes to the remastered 20th anniversary edition of *The Holy Bible*, journalist Keith Cameron notes that '*The Holy Bible* is an ongoing revelation' and 'Many of its riddles remain unresolved.' He also writes, 'Thirteen songs – and every one a toe-tapper, as I once declared to an incredulous band', and that is possibly the greatest achievement of the Manics: the marrying of some devastating lyrics with enormous melodies and chord structures that take those ideas to hearts around the world.

Six months after *The Holy Bible*'s release, Richey would disappear and things would never be the same for Manic Street Preachers. *Everything Must Go* was released in 1996, bringing the band's music to a whole new audience. Huge success followed, and the Manics remain a creative force to be reckoned with. They still play songs from *The Holy Bible* at their gigs, often prompting mass singalongs from long-term fans and new converts to this heavyweight, spectacular album.

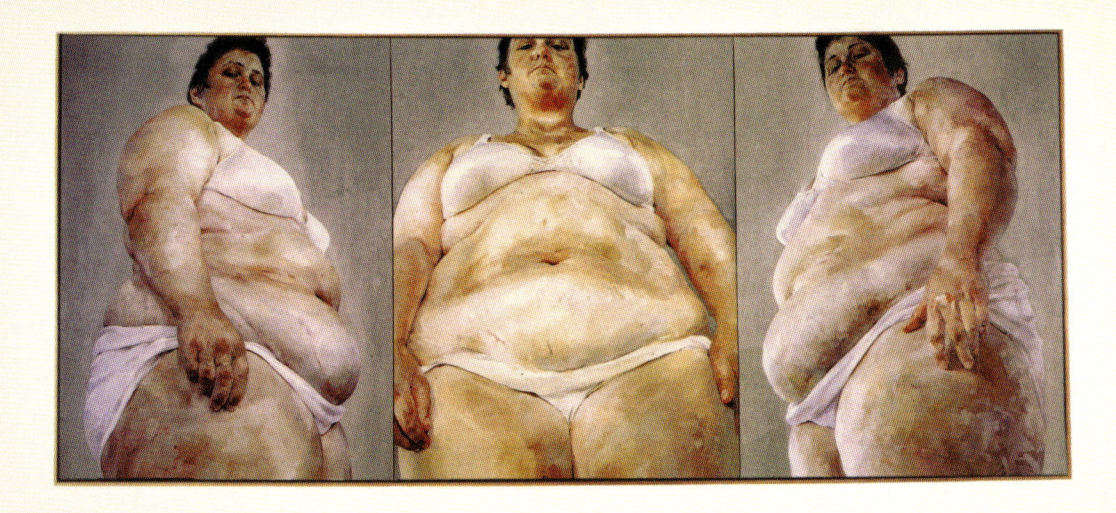

THE HOLY BIBLE
MANIC STREET PREACHERS

1. YES
2. IFWHITEAMERICATOLDTHETRUTHFORONEDAYIT'SWORLDWOULDFALLAPART
3. OF WALKING ABORTION   4. SHE IS SUFFERING   5. ARCHIVES OF PAIN
6. REVOL   7. 4st 7lb   8. MAUSOLEUM   9. FASTER   10. THIS IS YESTERDAY
11. DIE IN THE SUMMERTIME   12. THE INTENSE HUMMING OF EVIL   13. P.C.P.

COLOSSAL YOUTH
Young Marble Giants
(ROUGH TRADE, 1980)

Young Marble Giants are one of the most enigmatic and mysterious Welsh bands of modern times.

Signed to the Rough Trade label, the band's album *Colossal Youth* is regarded as a classic of its kind and Alison Statton's singular voice is immediately striking. The sparse instrumentation and purposefully minimalist production made *Colossal Youth* a cult concern at first, before it was later recognised as a hugely influential album.

When Young Marble Giants formed, enthralled by Kraftwerk and Devo, Cardiff was a relatively young capital, having only gained the title in 1955. Devolution had been voted against in 1979, and the city suffered huge job losses as steelworks closed. Orange buses hurtled round the city, the centre yet to be pedestrianised, and the docks area was seen by developers as ripe for regeneration. This was a Cardiff the band were eager to escape, hoping the music would set them free.

Released in 1980, *Colossal Youth* would be the band's only album, though two EPs followed. Instrumentalist brothers Philip and Stuart Moxham had been in bands before, but started afresh with a group that would do things differently: there would be no drummer in Young Marble Giants, the heavier in-sound of the day ignored in favour of trying something new. Similarly to ○ Datblygu, their keen adoption of drum machines and clever use of home recording gave their sound and their few records a demo feel, with nothing polished or at all grandiose about their music. Again similarly to Datblygu, John Peel was a fan and gave them a session, while the Welsh media didn't really know what to make of them.

Kurt Cobain raved about the band in a *Melody Maker* interview in 1992, naming the album as one of his all-time favourite records, and Courtney Love's band Hole recorded their own thrilling version of the song 'Credit in the Straight World'. Young Marble Giants re-formed for the Hay-on-Wye literature festival in 2007, to support Domino Records' re-release of the album. This reissuing of their one album sparked a renewed interest in the band, with high-profile gigs at Primavera in Barcelona, All Tomorrow's Parties, Sŵn Festival in Cardiff and the 2015 edition of Meltdown, curated by Talking Heads founder David Byrne, all huge successes. But it wasn't to last, and much the same as they had a few years after forming, the band again called it a day in 2016.

Stuart Moxham has recorded several solo albums, and Alison Statton made two albums with Ian Devine as Devine & Statton, including *Cardiffians*, which featured postcard images of the city on its cover.

More recently, US producer and beat-maker Madlib used an alluring sample of 'Searching for Mr Right' on his *Sound Ancestors* album, proving that Young Marble Giants' music continues to enthrall young musicians and those looking for something a little different to this day. They were a band who only made music for a few years, and released so little, yet their cultural influence has been far-reaching and nothing short of astonishing.

YOUNG MARBLE GIANTS

COLOSSAL YOUTH

WELSH RARE BEAT
Various Artists
(FINDERS KEEPERS RECORDS, 2005)

Crate-digging record fanatic Andy Votel is a big collector of psych and strange sounds from around the world. Turkish, Greek, Catalan and French oddities and rarities he was familiar with, but when he heard one rare record, he couldn't place its origin. With no English writing on the sleeve, he thought it might be from a European country he hadn't become familiar with. Then it struck him: it was from Wales, some 60 miles from where he stood in Manchester.

Votel and his friend Dom Thomas knew their musical onions better than most. Gruff Rhys joined them on their trip around Wales, uncovering lost gems in attics and raiding collectors' shelves for grooves and melodies that made them smile. Gruff had grown up with these songs, so could tell Votel and crew about them and put them in context. The result is this remarkable compilation that sounded, looked and felt like a triumph. For those that were familiar with this music, it was presented as something new and exotic; something that wasn't boring and traditional in its style, but special and rare.

It opens with a short spoken-word piece from 1974 rock opera *Nia Ben Aur* (Golden-Haired Nia), before seamlessly mixing into ◯ **Brân** track '*Y Gwylwyr*' (The Watchers). When it comes to rare Welsh records, Brân's are up there with the rarest, next to ◯ **Meic Stevens**' *Gwymon* (Seaweed) and *Outlander* albums.

There are big hitters here, like ◯ **Huw Jones**' '*Mathonwy*' and '*Dŵr*' (Water) ◯ **Heather Jones**' '*Nos Ddu*' (Black Night) and '*Penrhyn Gwyn*' (White Headland), and a few Meic Stevens numbers, including the super-catchy '*Y Brawd Houdini*' (Brother Houdini, or 'Great Houdini', as Meic sang on the 2003 reissue of *Outlander*). The surreal and often hilarious nature of Welsh-language rock is represented perfectly by Y Tebot Piws (The Purple Teapot) with their hit '*Mae Rhywun Wedi Dwyn fy Nhrwyn*' (Someone's Stolen my Nose) and Y Dyniadon Ynfyd Hirfelyn Tesog (The Sultry Long Blond Foolish Subtractions) with '*Cwmwl Gwyn*' (White Cloud). It closes with the great guitarist Tich Gwilym, and his epic version of the Welsh national anthem, '*Hen Wlad fy Nhadau*' (Land of My Fathers) on electric guitar.

Welsh Rare Beat aimed to give the casual listener a snapshot of the remarkably varied scene in Wales from the 1960s to the 1970s, and it did so with a kind of childlike energy, the sweet-shop nature of the tracklisting making it a colourful and brilliant audio journey.

If Votel was incredulous that this music was made not too far from his home city of Manchester, many in Wales saw the irony that a label based outside the country had taken it upon themselves to re-release and re-evaluate all these amazing recordings. Perhaps it had to be this way. By releasing it next to compilations of newly rediscovered gems from around the world, the Finders Keepers label brought a new audience to this music of Wales, giving it a new context and appreciating the incredible sounds featured on this mind-blowing compilation.

Volume 2 soon followed, this time with laverbread on toast on the cover, ensuring the Welsh Rare Beat goes on.

WELSH RARE BEAT

25 LESSER SPOTTED WELSH OBSCURITIES FROM THE ORIGINAL SAIN BACK CATALOGUE

COMPILED BY
ANDY VOTEL
DOM THOMAS
GRUFF RHYS
(SUPER FURRY ANIMALS)

SAFWN YN Y BWLCH
Hogia'r Wyddfa
(WREN RECORDS, 1969)

Wales has seen plenty of close-harmony singing groups named 'Hogia something' over the years, *hogia* being a term in north Wales for a group of boys or men. Hogia Llandegai, Hogia Bryngwran, Hogia'r Ddwylan – these were popular, charismatic and vocally focused groups of men who'd combine romantic, patriotic and occasionally humorous songs, designed to make audiences across Wales cry, sway and laugh in equal measure. Before the advent of television, the *Noson Lawen* would be where audiences would get to see these groups performing. Meaning a 'Night of Fun' or a 'Merry Evening', these *Nosweithiau Llawen* would be a variety show of local talents. The communities would sit on bales of hay, the nights often taking place in cow-sheds, upgrading to a village hall if the amenities were available.

This single was released in 1969 on Wren Records (also known as Recordiau'r Dryw), a label founded by Dennis Rees of Llandybie, and it is a wren that sits in the middle of this beautiful sleeve. A patriotic, bold statement of a song, 'Safwn yn y Bwlch' translates as 'We'll Stand in the Gap'. It dreams of Wales standing on its own two feet – '*Safwn yn y bwlch gyda'n gilydd, mae Cymru ein hangen ni*' (Together we'll stand in the gap, Wales needs us) – and is a rousing, nationalist song that portrays the people standing up for '*ein iaith, ein gwlad, dros ein pobl, dros ein plant*' (for our language, for our country, for our people, for our children). The song builds into an almighty crescendo, an optimistic crowd-pleaser in perfect tune with the audience.

If ◉ **Dafydd Iwan** was the hip young folk kid in the 1960s, a romantic troubadour who'd also get on with your mother, then Hogia'r Wyddfa might have been your mother's best friends' sons. Formed in 1963 in and around Llanberis, Hogia'r Wyddfa were charismatic and welcoming – often pictured in Aran jumpers or comfortable shirts, there was nothing edgy about these singing friends. Along with Dafydd Iwan and Eleri Llwyd, these Hogia were mainstays of the *Noson Lawen*. Arwel Jones, Myrddin Owen, Vivian Williams and Elwyn Jones went on to release several EPs and albums through Sain and Wren Records, and they were among the first artists on the label to receive a gold disc for their sales. They retired in front of a packed-out pavilion at the National Eisteddfod in Denbigh in 2003, after 50 years of singing.

HOGIA'R WYDDFA

W.S.P. 2001
Ochr 1:

"SAFWN YN Y BWLCH"

W.S.P. 2001
Ochr 2:

"BYSUS BACH Y WLAD"

RECORDIAU'R DRYW
Llandybie

MCLUSKY DO DALLAS
mclusky
(TOO PURE, 2002)

In the early 2000s a handful of noisy, carefree bands formed on the DIY Cardiff scene. Mo-Ho-Bish-O-Pi, The Martini Henry Rifles, Cubare and Sammo Hung were proud of their art school sounds, lo-fi guitars and an articulate sense of the absurd. Mclusky however, were made of different stuff.

Led by vocalist and songwriter Andy Falkous from Newcastle, mclusky made a name for themselves with short, sharp, thrilling nuggets of angry punk music. Their debut album *My Pain and Sadness Is More Sad and Painful than Yours* was released through Fuzzbox records, who also had a rehearsal space where the band would hone their sound.

The one-minute-and-fifty-one-second opener of this second album – 'Lightsabre Cocksucking Blues', a song that remains a live favourite today – is the perfect example of their style. Released on the renowned Too Pure label, the album propelled mclusky to a new audience far beyond Cardiff, the city and scene which brought the band together, also thanks in no small part to their relentless touring.

Angry and articulate, mclusky's carefree yet concise spirit is captured perfectly in 'To Hell with Good Intentions', a bass-heavy, direct hit of a song. Opening with 'My love is bigger than your love', switching to 'My band is better than your band' and then 'My dad is bigger than your dad, he's got eight cars and a house in Ireland', it's become a live favourite, the guitars erupting and falling in on themselves throughout, the lyrics vitriol coupled with a sense of the absurd throughout. 'Alan Is a Cowboy Killer' stands out as maybe the most accessible song on the album, swapping the spikiness for an albeit very brief mellower moment, before erupting into an almighty, frazzled chorus.

Riotous album closer 'Whoyouknow' was originally released on the Boobytrap Singles Club, a monthly CD single label that promoted Welsh bands. Texas Radio Band, Zabrinski, El Goodo, MC Mabon (of **Tystion**) and JT Mouse were among those on the label, with mclusky's double A-side single sandwiched between bravecaptain and **Big Leaves**. If mclusky didn't fit in on the roster, neither did any of the others, each release a stand-alone snapshot of an artistic accomplishment.

After Jon Chapple left the band in 2005 and moved to Australia, they called it a day for while, before re-forming in 2014. Falkous had been busy with other musical adventures: Future of the Left and Christian Fitness saw the intensity of his original band, but gave him the chance to delve deeper into sonic experimentation. Mclusky fans were thrilled when the band re-formed, with Jack Egglestone on drums and Rhyl-born musician Damian Sayell on bass. A live concert recording from Clwb Ifor Bach in Cardiff and London's Dingwalls was released in 2021, capturing the intense euphoria of a mclusky gig – the crowd hanging on to Falkous' every word, his on-stage ad libs and his way of dealing with hecklers something he had become famous for.

Too gnarly for mainstream success, and maybe just too clever to play the game, mclusky have remained true to their vision, and their audience true to them.

mclusky

mclusky do dallas

UNIVERSAL
K-klass
(DECONSTRUCTION/PARLOPHONE, 1993)

According to German electro duo Snap, 'Rhythm Is a Dancer'. Gloria Estefan was convinced that 'Rhythm Is Gonna Get You'. But for K-klass, their theory that 'Rhythm Is a Mystery' was a sensible conclusion, as their 1991 single brought them enormous commercial success and became their most well-known single – one that still gets played regularly today.

Their debut album for Deconstruction Records, also home to Black Box and M People, *Universal* is a house music odyssey with the dancefloor firmly in mind throughout.

Having met at the legendary Haçienda nightclub in Manchester – the physical manifestation of music visionary Tony Wilson's ideas – K-klass found themselves booked to perform at the club they frequented, playing their brand of energetic house music to their own people. Wrexham's Andy Williams, along with Russ Morgan, Carl Thomas and Paul Roberts were the founding members, with Andy and Carl previously members of Wrexham band Interstate. K-klass signed to respected independent Deconstruction, who saw the potential of this single, putting it out again soon after it had failed to chart on its original Creed Records release.

With Bobbi Depasois' effortless vocals giving the song crossover appeal in 1991, 'Rhythm Is a Mystery' became a hit across Europe and brought K-klass to the attention of hugely popular artists including Whitney Houston and Janet Jackson, who were keen for them to remix their own singles. This took these well-established artists to the dancefloors, meaning DJs could spin them in club environments – giving them even more exposure, and credibility.

Universal features a remix by Sabres of Paradise, the trio made up of Jagz Kooner, Gary Burns and the late, great Andrew Weatherall, the DJ and producer who reimagined Primal Scream's *Screamadelica* in 1991 to great acclaim. Their darker productions bring an edge to this mostly uplifting album, the synth sounds throughout evoking the dancefloor and the sun rising, possibly simultaneously, with soulful vocals, all sung live as opposed to sampled as was the norm for many producers of the era. Legendary Smiths guitarist Johnny Marr plays on '*La Cassa*', a playful number that closes the album.

K-klass' trademark sound was euphoric, slick and straight to the point: this is music made for the dancefloor, with soul and sweat. It's interesting to note that much of their output, which soundtracked many happy moments around the world, was recorded in an old nuclear bunker in the Borras area of Wrexham, where K-klass set up studio and named it first The Pharmacy and then The Bunker. Llandudno band Catfish and the Bottlemen and Wrexham's ⦿ Neck Deep have since rehearsed there, the studio now known as ROC2 and run by Steve Hywyn Jones, previously a member of Eighties guitar band Brodyr y Ffin.

Russ Morgan and Carl Roberts continue to tour and produce as K-klass, bringing house music to the masses. The highlight of their sets is 'Rhythm Is a Mystery', regarded as one of the greatest dance singles of all time.

K-klass

universal

KEEP THE HOME-FIRES BURNING
Ivor Novello

(ASCHERBERG, HOPWOOD AND CREW LTD., 1915)

There aren't many blue plaques on buildings in Wales for musicians, but on Cowbridge Road East in Cardiff, one commemorates the place where David Ivor Davies – later Ivor Novello – was born in January 1893. In Cardiff Bay there is a statue of him, with some of his lyrics decorating his plinth. These are two great honours for one of the most notable Welsh composers of all time.

'Keep The Home Fires Burning', written in response to the First World War, is a song aimed at rallying the troops and keeping all of those affected by the war positive. Novello was the composer, with lyrics by his American friend Lena Ford. Numerous versions have appeared on war-song compilations over the years.

It was his first hit and has remained something of a British staple, appearing in the 1969 musical *Oh! What a Lovely War* and the 1981 film *Chariots of Fire*. It's been covered by several artists, each interpretation bringing something new to this beautiful song tinged with sadness. Amongst them was a stunning rendition by Cerys Matthews of ○ **Catatonia**, appearing on a ○ **Max Boyce** TV special in 2002, accompanied by harpist Elinor Bennett and Les Morrison on the banjo.

The song has become synonymous with Novello, a proud member of the British songbook canon, perhaps overshadowing his other accomplishments in the worlds of composing, writing and acting, though his musicals and plays were huge hits in the West End.

He died in London, where he had lived for most of his life, in 1951, aged 58. Soon after his death, the Ivor Novello Awards were established and named after him, recognising songwriters and composers since their inception in 1956. They are seen as the pinnacle of the music industry awards, with some of the world's finest songwriters proudly displaying their Ivor Novello on shelves around the world. A prestigious award, named in honour of an extraordinary talent.

I KNOW SOMEONE WHO KNOWS SOMEONE WHO KNOWS ALAN McGEE QUITE WELL
The Pooh Sticks

(FIERCE RECORDINGS, 1988)

Huw (aka Hue) Williams, and Steve Gregory formed The Pooh Sticks in their Swansea bedrooms in the late Eighties, bringing indie pop and quirky lyrics to an underground audience bored with mainstream music. This was one of many singles that found favour on late-night radio and in the indie music press, back when 'indie' meant jangly pop on independent labels, probably destined to sell modestly.

But The Pooh Sticks were loved and, like fellow Swansea indie heroes ○ **Helen Love** and Newport-based The Darling Buds, the UK-wide network of fanzine writers, DIY-gig promoters and those yearning for something real, funny, romantic and innocent found a place for them in their record collections.

Proving their indie credentials, albeit with tongue firmly in cheek, their brag about sort of knowing Alan McGee would raise a smile with those familiar with the Scottish Creation Records head honcho. When this was written in 1987, Creation was a small label, with future fortune and fame the stuff of dreams; the hedonism and crossover of indie in the 1990s a distant prospect. McGee would go on to play an important part in Nineties music, with Oasis, Primal Scream and ○ **Super Furry Animals** becoming key Creation bands.

The Pooh Sticks went on to release four albums, with *The Great White Wonder* and *Million Seller* released on major labels in the US and doing well there, taking them to bigger venues and more mainstream radio. Huw Williams went on to co-found the Townhill Music record label, a management company, and the Welsh Music Foundation. More recently, he and Amelia Fletcher from Talulah Gosh, who sang occasionally with The Pooh Sticks, regrouped to make music as Swansea Sound, an indie-pop band named after the now-closed radio station. Their debut album *Live at the Rum Puncheon* wasn't recorded live at that long-closed venue, either, just to add to the confusion. And that's the way they like it.

THE POOH STICKS

DŴR
Huw Jones
(SAIN, 1969)

'Dŵr' was the debut single on Sain Records, the hugely influential Welsh-language record label founded by 🔘 Dafydd Iwan and the musician responsible for this single, Huw Jones. It came out in 1969, four years after the village of Capel Celyn in the Tryweryn Valley, near Bala, was flooded to create a reservoir to provide water for Liverpool. An incredibly significant moment in the history of modern Wales, the drowning of the valley continues to spark debate on the political landscape of Wales. It continues also to inspire creative statements, with 🔘 Manic Street Preachers frontman James Dean Bradfield using the word *Cofiwch* from the famous *Cofiwch Dryweryn* (Remember Tryweryn) graffiti on his 2020 solo album *Even in Exile*, based on the life of Chilean activist Victor Jara. The Manics also wrote the song 'Ready for Drowning', inspired by Tryweryn.

'Dŵr' remains an impactful, singular track that still haunts. The first voice heard is that of 🔘 Heather Jones, her backing vocal soaring above Huw Jones throughout this stunning single. Heather was already an established voice in Wales, and sang with 🔘 Meic Stevens and 🔘 Geraint Jarman in a pastiche band called Bara Menyn.

Huw Jones' strained, desperate vocals tell the tale as if he was one of those who lived in Capel Celyn:

Dŵr, sy'n llifo dros y wlad
Le bu fy mam a nhad
A'm brodyr a chwiorydd a minnau'n byw

(Water, pouring over the land
Where my mother and father
Brothers and sisters and I lived)

The song is a heartfelt howl that reminds you of the beauty, the innocence and the everyday life that existed in the valley, before the enormity of what happened – the water pouring and crashing in, just as the chorus in this song crashes in and pours throughout the song. There is an urgency: the song never lets up; it is a constant railing against a cruel and unstoppable act.

The story of Welsh pop would be a lot quieter without Rockfield Studios, located just outside the small village of Rockfield, Monmouthshire, where this single was recorded. Now immortalised in books and documentaries as well as in endless record sleeve credits, the studios have been in high demand ever since brothers Charles and Kingsley Ward opened them in 1963, repurposing barns on the family farm. Over the decades, the studios have played host to countless bands, from Queen and Coldplay to Idles and Annie Lennox. Known for its secluded location, homely atmosphere and excellent recording facilities, Rockfield has become an institution, bringing out the best in thousands of recordings. It was also the inspiration for Sain to build their own studios in Gwernafalau, and then in Llandwrog.

The early days of Sain Records caught something very special in Wales, and they have continued to do so since 1969. On 'Dŵr', a young Meic Stevens – then using his original given name, Mike – plays guitar and is credited with the arrangement.

Huw Jones would go on to become an important figure in Wales, running several large television companies, and he had a successful stint as Chairman of S4C. His other singles for Sain included the sardonic '*Dwi Isio Bod yn Sais*' (I Want to Be an Englishman), one of many tongue-in-cheek, slightly surreal singles of the time, along with Y Tebot Piws (The Purple Teapot)'s '*Mae Rhywun Wedi Dwyn fy Nhrwyn*' (Someone Has Stolen My Nose) and Edward H. Dafis' sarcastic '*Tŷ Haf*' (Holiday Home).

DWR

huw jones

Y DYDD OLAF
Gwenno
(PESKI, 2014)

If Gwenno had quit music before releasing her debut solo album in 2014, she would still have achieved more than most. Having danced from a young age, she became a member of Michael Flatley's renowned *Lord of the Dance* when she was 17, before joining the polka-dotted girl group The Pipettes in 2005. A solo EP had been released through Crai Records, featuring electronic pop songs that aimed to bring some populist contemporary styles to the Welsh-language scene, but the story of Gwenno as we know her today was yet to begin.

Gwenno had left Wales at a young age, not fully appreciating the Welsh-language culture that surrounded her. She'd grown up in Cardiff immersed in both the Welsh and Cornish languages, her mother a member of Côr Cochion Caerdydd (Cardiff Reds Choir) – often heard singing in the Hayes, raising money for good causes – and her father a respected poet in Cornish. But the bright lights of Las Vegas and Brighton were calling.

Returning to Wales, she came with a new appreciation of the culture she'd been brought up with, and she was eager to record and contribute. Teaming up with Rhys Edwards, who'd recorded as Jakokoyak and ran the Peski Records label, she released the *Ymbelydredd* (Radioactivity) cassette before working on *Y Dydd Olaf* (The Last Day), which would become her debut solo album.

The record is a concept album inspired by the sci-fi novel *Y Dydd Olaf* by Owain Owain – a story of robots taking over, though one man is able to pass on information to future generations by writing it in Welsh, which the robot overlords don't understand. Originally released in a limited run on Peski Records which quickly sold out, the album was picked up by Heavenly Recordings, the respected and influential indie label. Heavenly's history with Welsh artists begins with ⭕ **Manic Street Preachers'** *Motown Junk* EP in 1991, and continues with Boy Azooga, and producer David Wrench's band, Audiobooks. Gwenno sang with the Manics on a bilingual version of their song 'Spectators of Suicide'. Her music has been remixed by Andrew Weatherall and R. Seiliog, taking her psychedelic, krautrock grooves and giving them a dancefloor focus.

Y Dydd Olaf won the Welsh Music Prize in 2015, and a mural of Gwenno was painted on the outside wall of Clwb Ifor Bach, the iconic live music venue on Womanby St in Cardiff. Her sister Ani Glass has played the venue many times, as well as releasing her own take on synth-driven electropop.

Gwenno followed *Y Dydd Olaf* with *Le Kov* (The Place of Memory), an album in the Cornish language, and *Tresor* (Treasure), also sung mostly in Cornish apart from one song in Welsh: '*Nid Yw Cymru ar Werth*' (Wales Is Not for Sale). This is also a slogan for Cymdeithas yr Iaith (the Welsh Language Society), protesting about the lack of affordable housing for young people – a problem Gwenno could identify with and recognise in both Wales and Cornwall.

Her singing in Cornish, and taking it to a global audience, is widely recognised as a big reason why there's a renewed interest in the language. Her work with film director Mark Jenkin on music for his critically acclaimed films *Bait* and *Enys Men* captured a creative energy in Cornwall, one that is entrenched in a political and linguistic fight. *Tresor* was nominated for the prestigious Mercury Prize, and became the first nominee in the prize's history not sung in English.

Y Dydd Olaf

GWENNO

FUN CITY
Bright Light Bright Light
(YSKWN!, 2020)

In 2009, after several years of recording using his real name, singer-songwriter Rod Thomas released his first music under the name Bright Light Bright Light. Things would never be the same for him again.

Born in Crynant near Neath – a small village that also claims ○ **Amen Corner**'s Mike Smith as one of its own – Thomas found his musical feet whilst busking. Blending traditional songwriting with pop production, he toured with Scissor Sisters and Ellie Goulding, and found a style and an audience that was receptive to his emotional and honest lyrics that wore their heart on their sleeve. His outlook and infectious inquisitiveness have brought him collaborations and friendships with heroes of his, including Elton John, and Thomas has for over a decade lived in New York, the city which has welcomed him with open arms. Bright Light Bright Light's music is high-energy, perfectly moulded modern disco, with Thomas' sweet vocals taking us into his deepest feelings and sharing his most private thoughts in a safe space that he has created for himself and his fans.

His fourth studio album, *Fun City*, is a star-studded disco extravaganza with the occasional quieter moment, and at times feels as though you've gatecrashed a party full of the most surprisingly fabulous names. Big on collaborations, each guest vocal sounds right at home with Thomas holding the fort, on this album which is a celebration of Queer spaces and people.

His old friend Jake Shears duets on 'Sensation', bringing to the album the unmistakable vocals that made Scissor Sisters such a global success. LGBTQ+ icon Andy Bell joins him on 'Good at Goodbyes', a super-catchy number that sounds like an end-of-the-night dancefloor filler. Ironically, it was on an empty dancefloor of the nightclub Bedlam in New York – where Bell's Erasure, Scissor Sisters and gay icon Sylvester thrilled fans over the years – where the vocals for *Fun City* were recorded. Steeped in LGBTQ+ history, it really is a love letter to the community which Thomas has found so welcoming and life-affirming.

Perhaps the most surprising guest on *Fun City* is Mark Gatiss, with a spoken word contribution on 'Next to You'. The respected actor made his name in *The League of Gentlemen*, a TV series Rod Thomas is a huge fan of – and even appeared in, as an extra in 2017's *Return to Royston Vasey*.

Cabaret legend Justin Vivian Bond closes the record, joining Thomas on 'Saying Goodbye Is Exhausting'. Which it might well be, but Thomas does it with such style and seems to be having a truly wonderful time in the process.

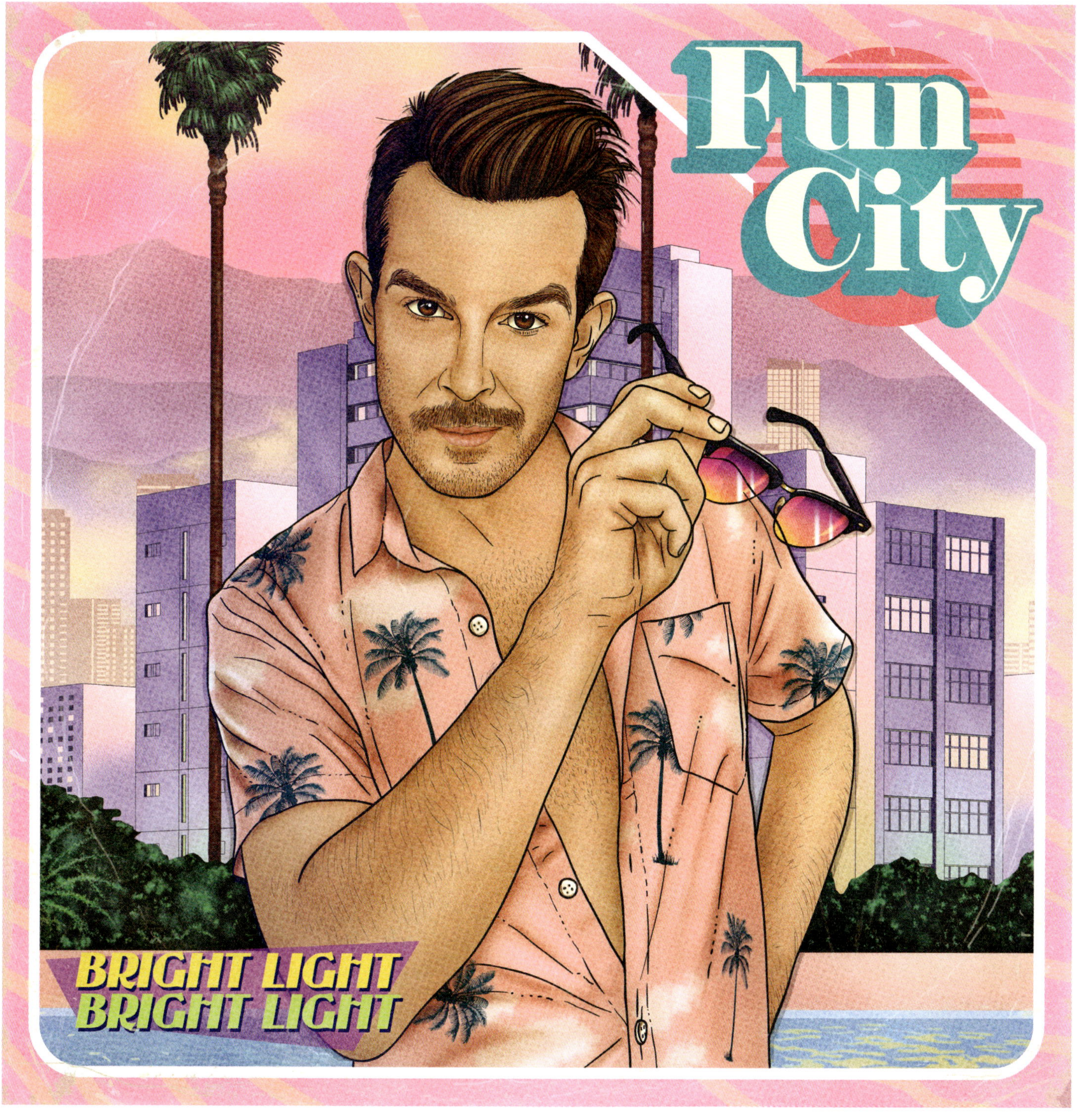
Fun City
BRIGHT LIGHT
BRIGHT LIGHT

GWYMON
Meic Stevens
(WREN RECORDS, 1972)

Meic Stevens has been something of an enigma in Welsh-language music since he first picked up a guitar in the mid 1950s, inspired by the skiffle scene.

His stunning debut album, 1970's mostly English-language *Outlander* on Warner Bros. Records, has become a hugely collectable record, selling for hundreds of pounds. Having cut discs in professional studios in London and keen to record more in Welsh, which he spoke in his hometown of Solva in Pembrokeshire, his second long-player *Gwymon* (Seaweed) would be the beginning of that Welsh-language musical journey, which would continue into his later years. This is one of the rarest records in Welsh.

Meic had a long relationship with Sain Records and its sub-labels, and would also release one album through Fflach. *Gwymon*, however, was originally released on Wren Records – or Recordiau'r Dryw – based in Llandybie, and produced by Meic himself in London. It would later be re-released by Sunbeam Records, who would reissue several of Meic's most sought-after early recordings.

Meic's music is the sound of a Welsh-speaking Pembrokeshire, a sad, longing sound that captures the beauty and magic of this part of Wales before the roads were improved, before the theme parks and the holiday homes. You can almost taste Solva harbour when you listen to Meic's voice, and the village and area are described beautifully in his autobiographies.

Opening with the jubilant stomp of '*Shwd Mae? Shwd Mae?*' (Hello? Hello?), it's clear that this is an album which has a lighter side to it. '*Mynd i Weld y Byd*' (Off to See the World) and '*Carangarw*' (Kangaroo) pick up on the guitar-laden fun and frolics of the opener, but the real album highlights are the deeper, balladesque songs. One in particular, '*Merch o'r Ffatri Wlan*' (The Girl from the Wool Factory) is a beautiful, sad track about his mother, and remains one of his most popular songs.

This is a young Meic Stevens making his name in the Welsh-language world, and letting us know that he's here to stay, with buckets of talent, a carefree attitude and a way around a tune or too. He made his name on Welsh television too, with BBC Wales and HTV showcasing his music on programmes like *Disc a Dawn*.

He would go on releasing well-received and much-cherished albums over the next four decades, and continued to play live – once with the BBC National Orchestra of Wales, often with a full band, and even more regularly on his own. His acoustic guitar would accompany him as he travelled around Wales by public transport, often with a bottle of wine for company.

He returned to his love of painting in his later years, and gigged less frequently. His reputation now precedes him, his tales over the years becoming the stuff of legend – not least his claim that he was there on the night Jimi Hendrix drank too much red wine and died in his sleep. Upsetting some along the way with his views on Wales and the world, Meic's onstage talk would often leave audience members entertained, shocked or perplexed, waiting with bated breath for the next song to start as he tuned his guitar mid anecdote.

The leading expert on Meic Stevens, author Hefin Wyn, has published several excellent books on the singer and his life in music. One is titled *Y Swynwr o Solfach*: a nickname for Stevens that has stuck, meaning 'the Solva Sorcerer'. His musical magic and influence on the Welsh music scene is undeniable – a maverick who made his mark with talent, charisma and songs that have worked their way into the nation's psyche.

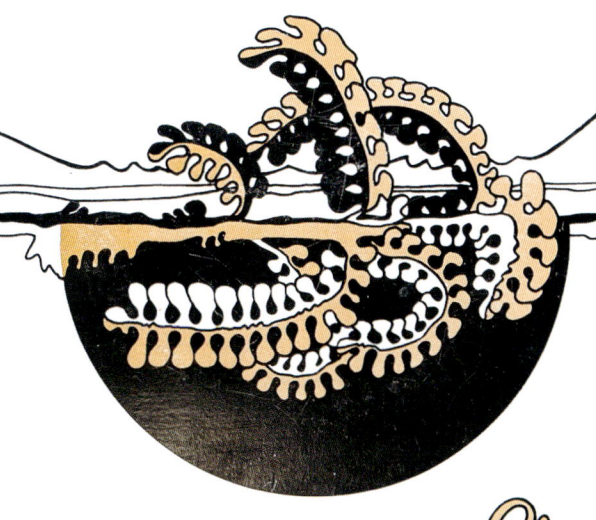

Meic Stevens.

Gwymon

SEFYLL AR Y SGWÂR
Ail Symudiad
(SAIN, 1982)

Richard and Wyn Jones were brothers and the founding members of Ail Symudiad, who formed in Cardigan in 1978, after hearing records by The Undertones, Buzzcocks and the Sex Pistols. Y Trwynau Coch, a punky power-pop band who formed in Ystalyfera high school in Neath Port Talbot, were a big influence as well, as young Welsh speakers who loved popular culture realised that it was possible to enjoy music in their own language too.

Rehearsing in their local Tabernacl Chapel in downtown Aberteifi, they would later set up a recording studio there, the whole town keen to support the enigmatic and often hilarious Jones brothers. Malcolm Gwyon was a friend from the outset, helping the young Ail Symudiad record their first singles and get to grips with performing live. Gwyon himself found fame as Malcolm Neon later, with his experimental pop records steeped in the new electronic movement of the 1980s.

But it was punk and new wave that made Ail Symudiad happy, and soon the word spread about this melodic group from west Wales. *Sgrech* (Scream) magazine was the Welsh-language music publication championing new Welsh sounds at the time, and the group found fans through its readership.

In their formative days, S4C hadn't started, so Welsh-language programming was on the BBC and the new third channel, ITV, with the BBC's *Sosban* programme hosted by lifelong fan Richard Rees and the *Sêr* television show on HTV showcasing the band. Matched with an incredibly busy gigging schedule in every corner of Wales, Ail Symudiad saw their hard work and perseverance pay off, and they won *Sgrech* magazine's Band of the Year award, voted for by the readers, in 1982.

This inspired a young David R Edwards to form his own band, ◉ **Datblygu**. He later acknowledged their importance in making him realise that young people from his part of Wales could make music and find an audience – it wasn't the preserve only of people from north Wales or university students.

Releasing their first single on the omnipresent Sain, through their pioneering Sain Singles Club, in which a different band released a seven-inch every so often, '*Whisgi a Soda*' was a hit and remained a favourite with the band at gigs over the subsequent decades. *Sefyll ar y Sgwâr*, their debut album, was also recorded at and released by Sain, and is a perfect document of their spiky, humorous sound.

With members coming and going in the band, Rich and Wyn set up their own Fflach label in 1981. It was a part of their lives that would remain a constant and would have a hugely positive impact on the scene, nurturing bands and releasing children's music, hugely popular singers and choirs. In 1997 a subsidiary label, fflach:tradd, was set up to focus on the traditional scene the brothers admired so much. Harpist ◉ **Llio Rhydderch**, singer Julie Murphy and *crwth* player Cass Meurig were among those welcomed to the roster, and fflach:tradd was welcomed as a label that could focus on and champion the reburgeoning trad scene in Wales.

Ail Symudiad continued to record and play until 2019. The brothers' eccentricities and often hilarious rapport grew over the years, with Richard often speaking on the phone in character as 'Lord Mwldan'. Both were known for putting everyone at ease with their jokes and flowing conversation.

Wales lost two incredibly important individuals when both Richard and Wyn died within a month of each other in 2021. They left an incredible legacy, which richly served Wales and its music world.

SEFYLL

AR Y SGWÂR

AIL SYMUDIAD

OF SNOWDONIA
Daedelus
(PLUG RESEARCH, 2004)

When a 13-year-old classically trained Alfred Darlington visited Wales with their family on holiday in the early 1990s, it was a dream come true. Their hard-to-explain infatuation with Wales had seemingly come from nowhere, and yet here they were, as they took in the scenery, met The People and fell in love with a new kind of music. Staying at a YMCA in London en route to Wales, a pirate radio station was playing rave music. Young Alfred was hooked. The music they heard in the UK stayed with them and formed the foundation of a renowned musical career. When I first heard *Of Snowdonia*, I presumed the artist responsible for this incredible music was Welsh. Daedelus, it turns out, is a Los Angeles native.

With producer Flying Lotus and others, they were a pivotal member of the Low End Theory club night in LA. They've released records on Brainfeeder, Ninja Tune, Alpha Pup Records and Plug Research, amongst others, and have worked closely with dublab, an experimental music hub based in LA and broadcasting around the world. Daedelus' beats are uncompromising, surprising, and quite unlike any other producer's. With 19 albums to their name, they have made their mark, their relentless work ethic taking them around the world as an in-demand live performer and a unique producer.

On stage, Daedelus often wears Victorian-era outfits, their love of Dandyism informing their fashion sense, whilst the music is at the very cutting edge of electronics. It's a wonderful contrast.

Beautiful, sun-drenched rhythms merge with propelling beats to create pieces of music that can seem dislocated, as Daedelus mashes up samples, twisting and turning them into something altogether otherworldly and beautiful. This album was made using mostly acoustic instruments, and on 'Something Bells' features vocals by emcees Busdriver and Pigeon John. Alfred has called *Of Snowdonia* their 'intimate love letter to Wales' – the culmination of an obsession with a country.

Hip-hop fans revere Daedelus as it was their track 'Experience' that was sampled on 'Accordion' on MF Doom & Madlib's *Madvillainy* album in 2004. A short piece played on the accordion but layered with samples, Daedelus regards it as a piece of electronic music, their playing and producing of the track the culmination of years of work. The piece has also been sampled by global superstar Drake.

Daedelus worked in 2008 with Y Diwygiad (The Revival), a rap duo featuring poet Aneurin Karadog and Ed Holden – who is also a member of Genod Droog with producer Dyl Mei, and a beatboxer with a number of inventive abums to his name as Mr Phormula.

In 2019, Alfred became a founding faculty member at Berklee College of Music in Chicago, one of the world's foremost institutes of music, where their expertise in electronic digital instruments made them an ideal teacher to guidethe next generation of ambitious music-makers.

At times cheeky and charming, at others more bass heavy and unleashed, Daedelus' music has never been boring and they are acclaimed as a leading light in their genre. *Of Snowdonia* is a fascinating collection of tracks. Album closer '*Hiraethus*', drawing on that unique Welsh word that describes a longing for a place, ends the record on a dreamlike note. Once heard, never forgotten, Daedelus' music is like no other, their unexpected affiliation with Wales making it all the more interesting.

daedelus
"of Snowdonia"

CARE CITY
Deyah
(HIGH MILEAGE, LOW LIFE, 2020)

Creating an imaginary, safe world for the purpose of this record, Deyah opens the second track with the words:

> Welcome to Care City,
> a place where your pain is welcome,
> your past is accepted,
> and your future is supported. We hope you enjoy your stay.

Here is an artist who is happy to open up about her troubles and her past, whilst pushing forward by creating art and building her future.

Opening with the dense, claustrophobic production of 'Terminal 7 (Intro)', it's clear that this is an all-encompassing record, a record that demands your full attention. A concept album of sorts that peels back layer upon layer of Deyah's intricacies, *Care City* showcases a gifted lyricist whose quick and hypnotic flow is full of charm and self-reflection.

Deyah's love of hip-hop started young, with her freestyling in school gathering momentum as she arrived in her early twenties. This was the 2010s, when social media, YouTube and a myriad other platforms made it easier than ever to share clips. Deyah made a name for herself online as one to watch, and *Care City* was the first project where everything connected. This was rap music of the subtler kind, ditching bravado and big ideas for self-doubt and zooming in on the little things that make up life. It's an album that wears its heart on its sleeve, appealing to Gen Z music fans who crave something real. This is music to make people feel, as opposed to music made to sell.

Released on Deyah's own High Mileage, Low Life label, its DIY production adds to this record's intimacy, with Deyah's vocals often unaccompanied by beats, making it sound like voice notes left on a phone. Choruses float in and out on beds of rhythms, trippy and dreamlike, interjected with Deyah's stark words of warning: 'Be careful how you treat other people.'

There is a vulnerability here, a sharing of feelings that only somebody who has been through a lot could bring to a record. It is the sound of here and now; of Deyah in confessional, accepting mode, eager to look forward and put herself in the picture. Album closer 'Liquor Lament' calls out to Jesus, with a desperation that rejects peer pressure and asks for acceptance. Deyah knows she has to move on, and this is the sound of that transition.

Care City won the Welsh Music Prize in 2020, a victory for an ambitious, free-flowing and impressive album that was a statement of intent and marked an impressive and important artist arriving.

When the BBC Radio 6 Music Festival took place in Cardiff in 2022, Deyah opened for the Mercury Prize-winning Little Simz at St David's Hall, performing a confident, flawless set to rapturous applause. If *Care City* was her calling card, it was clear the best version of Deyah was yet to emerge.

Deyah has spoken openly in several interviews about the experience of growing up in the outskirts of Cardiff, about drug abuse, and about the importance of religion and her Nigerian roots in her life. Where *Care City* was about looking back and taking stock, the follow-up album would be forward-looking, bold and confident in both its production and its lyrical matter.

She would go on to release *Black Glamour* in 2022, a musically more varied-sounding record than *Care City* that felt like a debut album proper, with crisper production and packing a bigger punch socially.

That we got to hear a snapshot of Deyah's journey before that on the remarkable *Care City* makes her debut release all the more special.

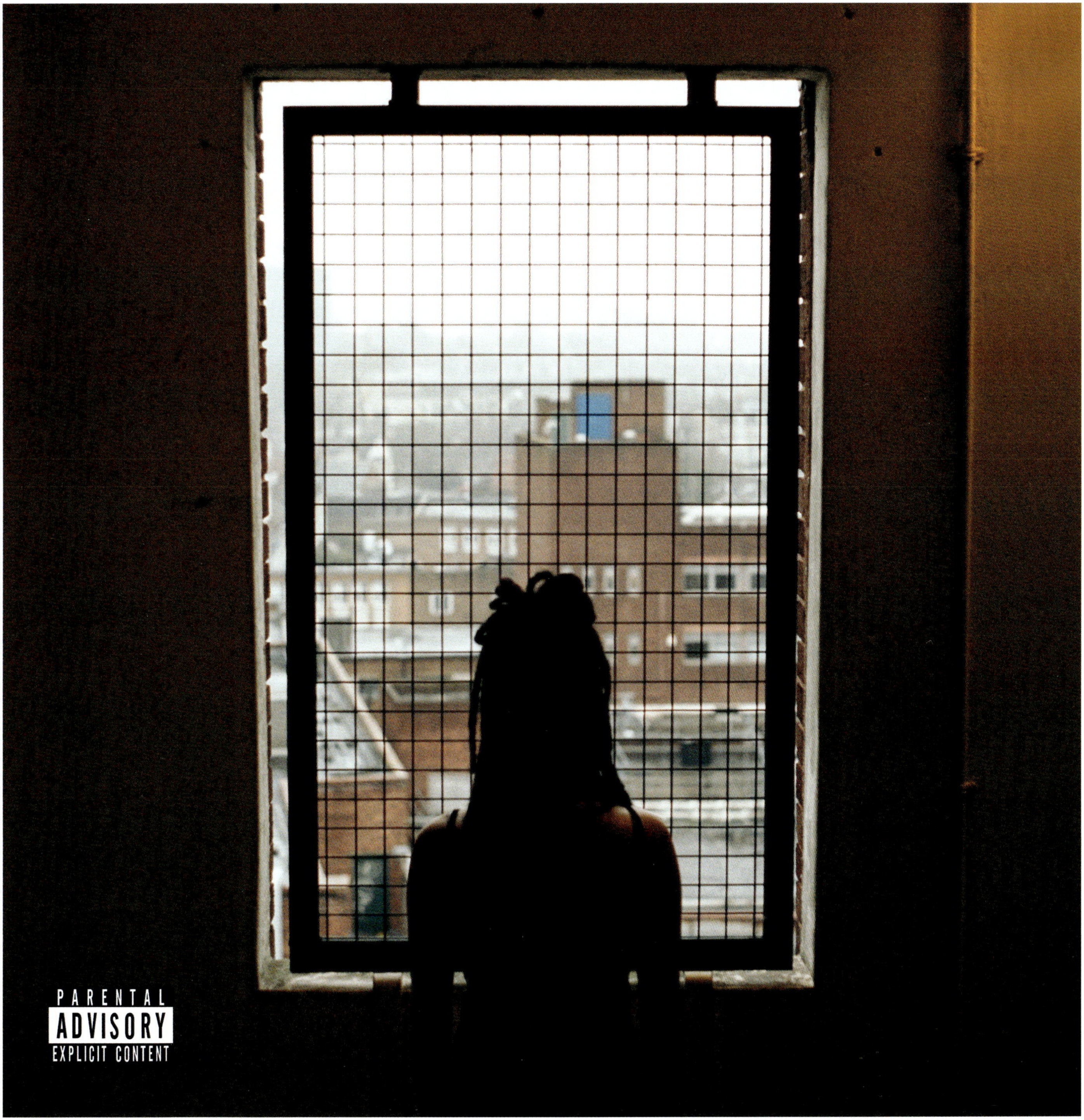
PARENTAL
ADVISORY
EXPLICIT CONTENT

LLAIS SWYNOL
Mary Hopkin
(CAMBRIAN, 1968)

The relatively small town of Pontardawe in Neath Port Talbot can lay claim to one of the most famous singers from Wales.

Search the Welsh-language seven-inch section in a second-hand record shop, and you're likely to find a Cambrian release by Mary Hopkin. Her single '*Aderyn Llwyd*' (Grey Bird) and this EP, '*Llais Swynol Mary Hopkin*' (The Magical Voice of Mary Hopkin), were big hits, with tens of thousands owning a little piece of her majestic voice.

On this EP, her trademark warm, tranquil vocals are in their prime, conveying a purity that made her one of the most captivating vocalists from Wales. Accompanied by her acoustic guitar, it would make Mary one of the most popular singers of the day. For this debut record in Welsh, Mary sings Pete Seeger's song 'Turn! Turn! Turn!' – later covered by The Byrds in 1965 – presented here as '*Mae Bob Awr*' (Every Hour). Seeger's words, from Ecclesiastes in the Old Testament, are in stark contrast to a translation of 'Tammy', a short, simple love song presented as 'Tami'. If ever there was a vocalist who could sing a shopping list and make it sound magnificent, it might be Mary Hopkin.

The release of this EP coincided with a TV appearance on mainstream media that brought her talent to the whole of the UK. 1968 was the year everything changed for Mary when she appeared on the hugely popular *Opportunity Knocks*. It was then one of the most-viewed programmes in the UK, with c.20 million people tuning in each week to see talented performers of all kinds, a postal vote from the public deciding the winner. She won, and landed a record deal with Apple, one of the hippest and most successful labels in the world.

Paul McCartney produced her first single for Apple, the classic 'Those Were the Days', which went to number 1 in the charts and features on her debut album, *Post Card*, also produced by McCartney. The one song in Welsh on the album, '*Y Blodyn Gwyn*' (The White Flower), was a favourite of Mary's – sung by her and a friend at Eisteddfodau in her youth, but recorded on *Post Card* with both parts sung by Mary, to beautiful accompaniment from the harp.

She has two children with her former husband, the legendary producer Tony Visconti, who worked with her on her second album. He produced Bowie's 'Sound & Vision', complete with backing vocals by Mary and Brian Eno. When I spoke to Visconti about his links with Wales, he reminisced about his time visiting the Eisteddfod with Mary and her family, having to have it explained to him that the reason everyone was singing the same song on stage was because it was a competition.

More recently Hopkin has been singing with her daughter, Jessica Lee Morgan, including on the well-received 2023 album *Two Hearts*. A private person who has shunned the limelight since her early success, Mary has, however, found social media platforms to share her thoughts, with generous and supportive messages to her fans and opinions on the matters of the day. Thankfully she continues to sing, her eternally beautiful voice a welcome reminder of both her past and her refusal to wallow in it, as she continues to create. As the closing words on the back of the sleeve of this EP note, some people are born to sing. Mary Hopkin is such a person.

Cambrian

CEP 414

Llais Swynol **Mary Hopkin**

BUKOWSKI
Rheinallt H. Rowlands
(ANKST, 1996)

In the mid 1990s, *Heno Bydd yr Adar yn Canu* (Tonight the Birds Will Sing) on BBC Radio Cymru – a programme hosted by Nia Melville which showcased early incarnations of **Super Furry Animals,** **Gorky's Zygotic Mynci** and **Catatonia** – hosted sessions from the Welsh underground. For their session, Rheinallt H. Rowlands chose to cover Joy Division's 'New Dawn Fades', offering a sprawling, synth-driven take on the iconic band's intense song.

Their debut album, 'Hendaid Brân a Straeon Eraill' (Great-Grandfather Brân and Other Stories), on musician and artist Alan Holmes' Central Slate label, had caught Ankst Records' attention, and soon they'd be joining the influential label's roster, improbable labelmates with bands who would go on to define Welsh music of the time. Rheinallt H. Rowlands joined Gorky's Zygotic Mynci on their *Bwyd Time* album, heard on psychedelic pub lock-in singalong '*Iechyd Da*' (Cheers).

Nothing about Rheinallt H. Rowlands was obvious. Despite the name suggesting an individual singer, they were in fact a duo, with Owain Wright – or Oz to his friends – on guitar and vocals, and Dewi Evans as keyboard player and composer. They'd known each other from growing up in Llanfairpwllgwyngyllgogerychwyrndrobwllllantysiliogogogoch, and bonded over their love of filmic music and enigmatic characters, from Serge Gainsbourg to Ian Curtis. They devised the Rheinallt H. Rowlands character as a mythical stonecutter, intending to hide behind the persona to release their music. Gigs soon meant that the reality of them as a duo became apparent, but the myth was born: Rheinallt H. was here to stay.

Taking in bossa nova, chamber music, harp and their trademark keyboard, *Bukowski* is a beautiful record. '*Merch o Gaerdydd*' (Girl from Cardiff) is a jaunty, carefree song about falling in love by the River Taff. The duo's love of another mysterious, beguiling figure is obvious in the album's title, the image of beat poet and acclaimed writer Charles Bukowski omnipresent on the album. He is immortalised in the album's title track, with Wright making no bones about how he wants to be Charles Bukowski.

Poet Zoë Skoulding, based on Anglesey, contributes lyrics for the English-language songs on *Bukowski*, the western stomp of 'Snow' and the forlorn 'Loved'. The constant throughout is Owain Wright's dense, deeply deadpan yet immaculately romantic, honest vocals.

In 1999 Rheinallt H. Rowlands were involved in an astonishing album called *You Have Just Been Poisoned by The Serpents*, a collaborative collection featuring some 30 musicians, recorded at Bryn Derwen studios in Bethesda and released on Ochre. Author Jon Savage, Ann Matthews, David Wrench, Alan Holmes, Gruff and Dafydd Rhys, John Lawrence from Gorky's Zygotic Mynci and Echo and the Bunnymen's Will Sergeant are some of the contributors to the trippy, mythical record.

Owain Wright died in 2005, his voice and vision leaving an indelible mark, having created one of the most fascinating musical projects in Wales in the 1990s.

Rheinallt H. Rowlands
BUKOWSKI

NOTES WITH ATTACHMENTS
Pino Palladino & Blake Mills
(IMPULSE!/NEW DEAL RECORDS, 2021)

After so long playing with some of the biggest bands in the world, in 2021 it was Pino Palladino himself that was in the spotlight. Born in Cardiff in 1957 into a Welsh-Italian family that still run the Pizzeria Villaggio restaurant in Whitchurch today, his love of music was obvious from a young age. He started playing the fretless bass in his teens, and was soon in demand for his talented playing.

He played on ◉ Endaf Emlyn's 1981 *Dawnsionara* (Slowdancing) album, and was a key member of the bustling rock and blues scene in Cardiff in the 1970s. Moving to London to play in Jools Holland's band, he was soon in demand as a session musician, playing on a Gary Numan record and becoming a full-time member of Paul Young's band. His playing on Young's cover of Marvin Gaye's 'Wherever I Lay My Hat' is instantly recognisable, partly responsible for turning it into a worldwide hit and creating further demand for Pino's skills from musicians worldwide. It also explains the Paul Young plaque on the wall of Pino's family's pizzeria!

The work was constant, with world tours with Simon & Garfunkel, Nine Inch Nails and The Who keeping him busy – the latter coming about after The Who's original bassist John Entwistle died a few days before the start of a big tour, prompting the band to ask him to stand in. Pino told The Roots co-founder Questlove on his podcast that he had only some 48 hours to immerse himself in The Who's music before playing to several thousand Who fans in a stadium gig.

Pino and Questlove have worked together on several projects, including D'Angelo's seminal *Voodoo* album, Pino making his mark in the R&B world – music he loved so much as a young man in Cardiff. He was now in the Soulquarians, whose influence on modern music is enormous. As journalist Dan Charnas wrote in his excellent book *Dilla Time*, Questlove brought Pino and the revered US producer J Dilla together and they connected instantly in the studio, each admiring the other's music and vision and realising they could create something very special. Pino and Questlove reunited with D'Angelo on one of the most eagerly anticipated albums of modern times, 2014's iconic *Black Messiah*, which delighted fans new and old. Another big commitment for Pino was to the John Mayer Trio, joining the phenomenally successful singer in the studio and on the road.

Notes with Attachments is also a collaborative album, made with Californian Blake Mills, a renowned guitarist and Grammy award-winning producer, himself having worked on albums with Bob Dylan, John Legend and Fiona Apple, amongst others. Inspired by West African and Cuban music, the album is a masterclass in jazz playing: intricate, moving and surprising at every turn, a deserving spotlight on a remarkable musician.

Pino Palladino has passed on the music to his son Rocco, also an in-demand bass player, and daughter Fabiana, an emerging singer-songwriter whose self-produced album on XL Records was critically acclaimed.

Down-to-earth and globe-trotting, Pino has made sure the world has sounded exceptional since he first picked up his fretless bass.

NOTES WITH ATTACHMENTS

PINO PALLADINO AND BLAKE MILLS

RECORDED BY JOSEPH LORGE
AT SOUND CITY – VAN NUYS, CA
ADDITIONAL RECORDING BY BEN KANE AND PINO PALLADINO
MIXED BY BLAKE MILLS AND JOSEPH LORGE
MASTERED BY GREG KOLLER
ARTWORK AND DESIGN BY SAM GENDEL
PRODUCED BY BLAKE MILLS

THE FABULOUS SHIRLEY BASSEY
Shirley Bassey
(COLUMBIA, 1959)

Shirley Veronica Bassey was born in Tiger Bay and grew up in nearby Splott, her father Nigerian and her mother from Yorkshire. Her talent was obvious from a young age, her love of singing and dancing encouraged by her family and the tight-knit community she grew up in.

In 1952, she started work in the Currans Steel factory on the banks of the River Taff, having left Splott Secondary Modern School aged 14. The staff would sing together at times whilst working, Shirley's voice booming over the rest. Around this time she had started singing in the local pubs and clubs of Cardiff, where the audience marvelled at the small girl with the big voice. Singing in London, she was spotted by music managers, who took her to meet record companies.

Shirley came back to Cardiff in 1957 with TV cameras capturing the local girl done good, returning to where her remarkable career began. She sang to the children of Butetown's Rainbow Club, a thriving multi-cultural youth club set up to get young people involved in the performing arts, which she herself had once been a member of.

In early 1959 her single 'As I Love You' would become the first number one by a Welsh artist. This, her second album, came out the same year and sees her at the top of her game, backed by a full orchestra. Singing songs from the shows by the likes of Cole Porter and George and Ira Gershwin, her beautiful, powerful voice is also warm and expressive, shining amid the soaring strings and smoky brass. Although these tracks – including 'I've Got You Under My Skin', 'S'Wonderful' and 'They Can't Take That Away From Me' – were well-known already, having been recorded by huge stars such as Frank Sinatra, Fred Astaire, Ella Fitzgerald and Judy Garland, Shirley brings something new to them and succeeds in making them her own.

By now a star on television in the US as well as across Europe, Bassey's work ethos was remarkable, and she released almost an album a year – sometimes two! – until the 1990s. Even then she still created, working with modern-day electronic producers, covering songs she liked from the charts and occasionally looking back at her incredible musical legacy.

Ask people their favourite Bassey number and you're likely to get a different answer each time, such is the extent of her repertoire. The Bond film franchise has been a large part of Bassey's life, with Bond themes 'Goldfinger' in 1964 and 'Diamonds are Forever' from 1971 still regarded as greats from the film world and from Bassey's back catalogue. Years later in 2009 she would work with Bond composer David Arnold on her album *The Performance*, which showcased Bassey's talents singing the words of various songwriters. She sang a James Dean Bradfield and Nicky Wire of **Manic Street Preachers**-penned song, 'The Girl from Tiger Bay' on *The Performance* – possibly the most direct lyrics about her upbringing and actual place of birth she'd ever sung. Other songs on the record were written for Ms Bassey by Pet Shop Boys and Rufus Wainwright.

In later years, Shirley's star quality hasn't diminished, and there have been several greatest hits collections. Her performance at Glastonbury Festival in 2007 has become iconic, the image of the star in her diamante-encrusted wellies making the happy campers even happier with her decades' worth of hits. Her performance at the Electric Proms for the BBC at the Roundhouse in London was outstanding, and in 2019 she was awarded the Freedom of Cardiff. At the Royal Welsh College of Music & Drama there is the Dame Shirley Bassey Scholarship Fund, and after her charitable work raised money for the Noah's Ark Children's Hospital, the road it is based on was renamed Dame Shirley Bassey Way. In 2023, to celebrate her 70th year in music, the Royal Mint issued a series of coins in her honour. A fitting tribute to Welsh music's undisputed queen.

THE FABULOUS SHIRLEY BASSEY **mono**

The fabulous
SHIRLEY BASSEY

COLUMBIA
LONG PLAYING 33⅓ R.P.M. RECORD

DIAL M FOR MERTHYR
Various Artists
(FIERCE PANDA/TOWNHILL RECORDS, 1997)

Fierce Panda is one of the UK's longest running and most respected independent labels. Founded by Simon Williams, an *NME* journalist and fanatical gig-goer, the label was a way for him to take his passion for discovering new bands a step further than writing and raving adbout them, and put out a physical release for them – a real, circular record.

This he did for bands just starting their musical journey, with Coldplay – whose guitarist, Jonny Buckland, grew up near Mold – putting out early release 'Brothers and Sisters' through Fierce Panda. A fan of the bizarre and surreal also, Williams released an interview with Oasis' Gallagher brothers and called it *Wibbling Rivalry*, an unexpected spoken-word almost-chart hit in 1995.

Williams' love of wordplay is evident in the Various Artists EPs he released. *Clooney Tunes* featured a picture of George Clooney, *Cry Me a Liver* featured a plate of liver, *Otter Than July* was a man holding an otter, and the *Mortal Wombat* EP had a picture of The Wombles on the cover. Quips aside, the music featured was always special. On *Dial M For Merthyr*, a 21-track album that tried to capture the excitement of music from Wales in the late Nineties, he featured a picture of Johnny Owen, the Merthyr-born boxer, mid leap on a training run. The joke in the title is a nod to Alfred Hitchcock's film *Dial M For Murder*, has also been used in a book title by Rhondda author Rachel Trezise, and was already the name of a popular football fanzine about Merthyr Town FC.

The compilation brought the obscure and the experimental together, with some of the bands featured already making a name for themselves. **Manic Street Preachers** close the compilation with 'Strip it Down', originally released seven years previously on their *New Art Riot* EP. **Stereophonics** tune 'Looks Like Chaplin' is also on their breakthrough *Word Gets Around* album, and **60ft Dolls**' 'Ballerina' was B-side to their single 'Hair'.

If the label was accused of cashing in on the popularity of Welsh bands, the album opener, 'Welsh Bands Suck' by Teen Anthems, throws the detractors immediately, with its jaunty keyboard and lyrics decrying Welsh bands as a load of rubbish (apart from **Helen Love**). 'They're all so retro, they're all so dated' they sing, a theme they also bring up on their single 'I Hate Oasis (And I Hate The Beatles)'. Swansea's indie-pop heroes Helen Love neatly follow with 'Beat Him Up', a frantic stomper that's an early, thrilling number. Boys with guitars dominate the compilation, with Blackwood's Ether and Carmarthen's Parc Troli contributing memorable tunes. Betws-y-Coed's Melys – led by vocalist Andrea Parker – and the melodic Derrero from Newport, with visual artist Andy Fung on drums and vocals, became favourites on John Peel's late-night slot on BBC Radio 1, their more esoteric approach to music marking them out from the more straightforward indie rock of some of the other contributors. That there are so many Newport bands on this album should come as no surprise: John Sicolo's TJ's venue was the stuff of legend, a mantle taken over by the Le Pub venue now run by Sam Dabb. Her band Disco are included here with a track called 'Ragdoll', as are Novocaine – featuring Richard Jackson, now an in-demand producer working with **Dub War**, who also contribute a track.

This compilation proved that there was a real buzz in the air in Wales at this time; that it wasn't a media-created frenzy. Fierce Panda, together with Welsh label Townhill Records, helped give the artists and the scenes they represented – however diverse – legitimacy. It remains an interesting document of the multitude of young bands creating music in Wales at the time.

• record hir cymraeg gorau yn y byd erioed... mwy na thebyg •

DIAL M FOR MERTHYR

TEEN ANTHEMS • HELEN LOVE • 60FT DOLLS • PARC TROLI • STEREOPHONICS
DOG DAY AFTERNOON • DISCO • CATATONIA • BIG LEAVES • FLYSCREEN • ETHER
NOVOCAINE • CRAC • THE JONAH HEX • MELYS • TRAMPOLINE • ARMSTRONG
DUB WAR • DERRERO • SUZY PEPPER • MANIC STREET PREACHERS

TONY AC ALOMA
Tony ac Aloma
(CAMBRIAN, 1971)

Regulars at the popular *Noson Lawen* talent nights happening around Wales in the 1960s, Tony ac Aloma were portrayed as the golden couple of Welsh entertainment.

Attractive, young and with voices that matched beautifully, their between-song banter was funny, cute and proudly non-highbrow. This was easy-listening music for those who wanted to be soothed, with songs usually about love and never political, and it captured Wales' imagination in a huge way. They sold hundreds of thousands of records, first for Cambrian, then Gwawr and then Sain, in a career that has spanned seven decades.

Proud of their Anglesey roots, songs would often mention Ynys Môn and the pull the island had on them both, such as in their hit '*Caffi Gaerwen*'. By 1968 they were popular names with hundreds coming to see them live, including at the first Welsh-language pop gathering, Pinaclau Pop in Pontrhydfendigaid in Ceredigion. They had a fan club, and TV appearances were demanded by a media keen to show that light entertainment could be done in Welsh – and done exceptionally well too, professionally and note-perfect. As well as singing, comedy routines with special guests were incorporated into their sets, bringing laughs as well as the melodies.

By 1972 their star had begun to fade, and Tony returned to his first love, rock bands, while Aloma sang with ◉ **Yr Hennessys**. But the appetite from the fans was still there, even if they themselves weren't initially keen to get back together, so a reunion a few years later was inevitable, and they continue to attract audiences to this day.

Perhaps the biggest surprise about the duo is that they weren't actually romantically linked. Visitors to their family-run Gresham Hotel in Blackpool would be serenaded by Tony and Aloma, with Aloma's husband Roy playing the keyboards for them. A tight unit, their songs of love and of simpler times keep thrilled audiences happy into the evening, glad to hear Tony ac Aloma still singing in perfect harmony all these years later.

SCENE DELETE
Sasha
(LATENIGHTTALES, 2016)

Sasha was born Alexander Coe in Bangor in 1969.

His partnership with John Digweed made a significant impact on the dance music world, the pair releasing several hugely acclaimed mix albums as Sasha & John Digweed. Emerging from the underground club scene, his remixes of huge tracks for some of the biggest artists in the industry meant he became one of the most in-demand names in modern electronic music.

He was voted the world's Number 1 DJ in *DJ Mag* in the year 2000, when superstar DJs ruled and the world had truly cottoned on to the power of big nights out with famous and respected producers in control of the decks, changing the live music scene and the world's perception of dance music.

Widely regarded as one of the finest DJs of his genre, alongside Paul Oakenfold, Fatboy Slim and Pete Tong, he found a new level of fame. Though perhaps not a household name, he became known as one of the hottest DJing talents on the scene, fusing house music, trance and breaks. He has played residencies across the globe, often headlining enormous club nights and festivals, and has more recently reunited with Digweed – much to the delight of their fans, eager to hear the electricity the partnership bring to their sets.

As well as DJing other producers' music, his early piano lessons stood him in good stead, as he would make himself comfortable in studios throughout his career, creating his own compositions.

Scene Delete is one of a series of albums in the LateNightTales collection. The label invites artists such as Air and Belle and Sebastian to create a compilation of their favourite music, expanding this to encourage artists to release their own compositions. This versatile, spacious album shows a different side to Sasha's musical talents, designed for headphones rather than the club. one for the inevitable comedown after the euphoria of a night on the dancefloor.

Cambrian   CEP473 LP

Tony ac Aloma

SASHA : SCENE DELETE

WE ALL HAD DOCTORS' PAPERS
Max Boyce
(EMI, 1975)

Opening the album with a flamenco-style rendition of '*Sospan Fach*', the announcer begins, 'Ladies and Gentlemen, it's Max Boyce!' The audience immediately begin to sing along, the room erupting into a Max-led 'Oggy Oggy Oggy' at the end of the track, with him proclaiming, 'We're going to have a great night tonight!'

Recognising the melancholy nature of the Welsh all too well and turning that emotion up to 11, mixing it with that unique Welsh humour and a quiet understanding that nothing is more important than sport, Max Boyce was a true one-off.

The difference between Pontarddulais and Gorseinon might not be that familiar to the hundreds of thousands who bought this record, but the audience reaction proves that these things are not only important, but also absolutely hilarious when highlighted and dissected.

This album followed his legendary *Live at Treorchy*, which sold well over half a million copies. That was recorded live from start to finish in one seamless take, no overdubs or post-studio edits interrupting the natural flow of the album. It really does feel like you're sat on a plastic chair in the rugby club with a pint in hand and Max in front of you, giving it his all, a glint in his eye. A great night was most definitely had, caught on record for posterity.

By now Max was a big name and was riding high on success, his audience having taken him to their hearts. They know he's done well, and he mentions his success humbly but proudly, with chat of a £100 coat he'd bought to appear on television 'in London'. But with every near-boast there is always a twist, a laugh that is very much always on Max, the lovable success story.

Max understands sadness. His father, a coal miner, was killed by an explosion underground a month before Max was born. Nevertheless, Max also went to work in the pits when he was 15. He became interested in the protest music of the 1960s, including the music of ○ **Dafydd Iwan**, and TV shows like *Disc a Dawn*, a programme he became a firm favourite on, alongside ○ **Yr Hennessys**, Iris Williams and ○ **Meic Stevens**. He soon started recording in English, and mainstream success followed. Throughout *Doctors Papers* he peppers his sentences with Welsh words and quips: an *yndife?* (isn't it?), a *ti'mo* (y'know), a nod to the miners in 'Rhondda Grey' with their *ni wedi neud ein siâr* (we've done our share).

If '*Duw* it's Hard' on *Live at Treorchy* was a devastating, melancholy ode to Glynneath and the mining community, then 'Rhondda Grey' is guaranteed to bring a tear to the eye – possibly the closest anyone's ever come to explaining the magic of the Rhondda in a song.

Hymns & Arias: The selected poems, songs and stories collected his writing in book form. It incudes a poem he wrote during the Covid pandemic called 'When Just the Tide Went Out', which – like much of his work – struck a chord with the public.

In his 80th year, Glynneath honoured Max with a statue in his hometown. Hundreds gathered as rugby giant Gareth Edwards (himself a labelmate of Max's at Cambrian in the early 1970s) congratulated the singer on the unveiling of the statue. Mark Drakeford, then First Minister of Wales, commented, 'He is genuinely a cultural icon for us.'

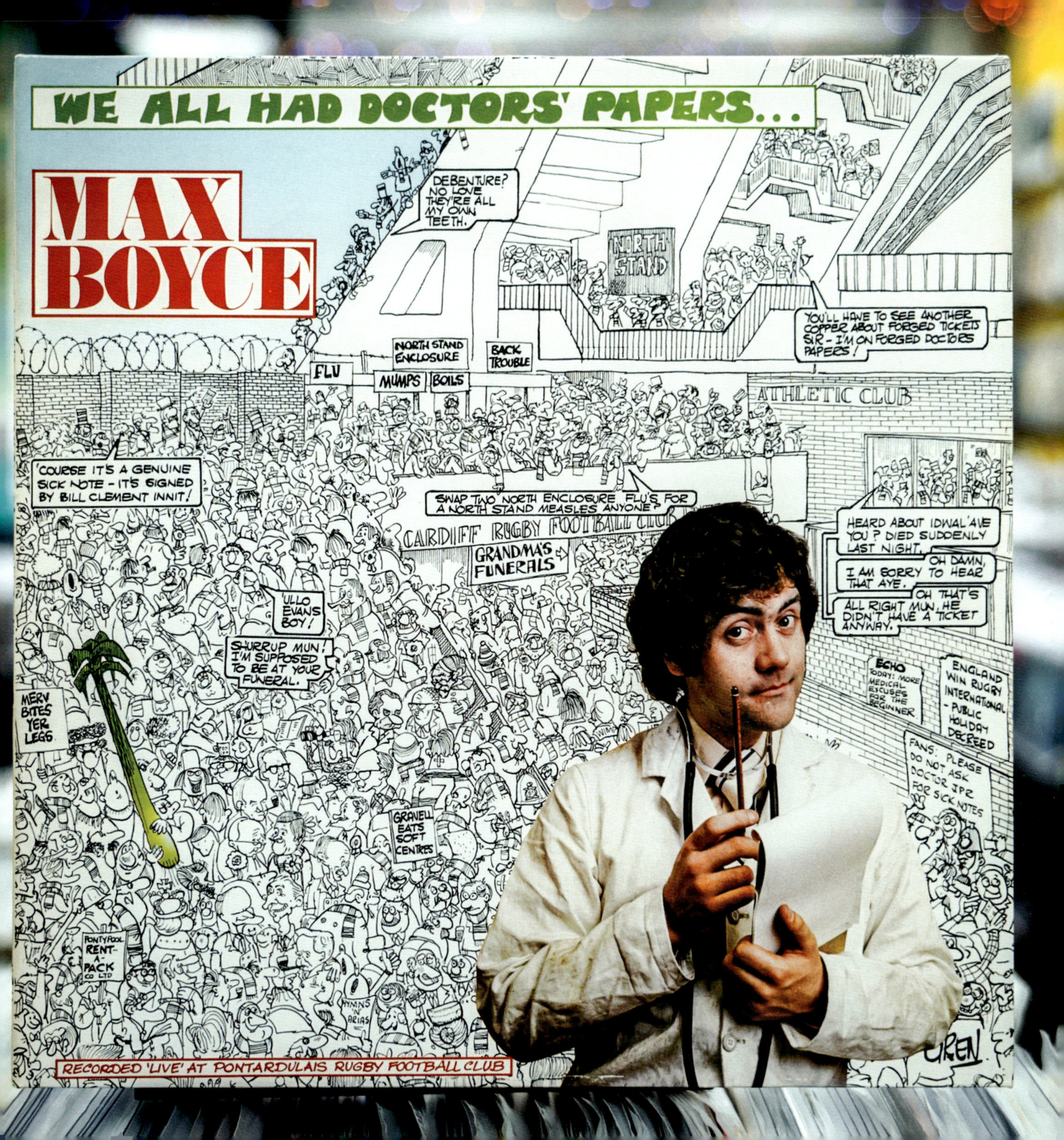

WE ALL HAD DOCTORS' PAPERS...
MAX BOYCE
DEBENTURE? NO LOVE THEY'RE ALL MY OWN TEETH.
NORTH STAND
YOU'LL HAVE TO SEE ANOTHER COPPER ABOUT FORGED TICKETS SIR - I'M ON FORGED DOCTORS PAPERS!
NORTH STAND ENCLOSURE
BACK TROUBLE
FLU
MUMPS
BOILS
ATHLETIC CLUB
'COURSE IT'S A GENUINE SICK NOTE - IT'S SIGNED BY BILL CLEMENT INNIT!
SWAP TWO NORTH ENCLOSURE FLU'S FOR A NORTH STAND MEASLES ANYONE?
CARDIFF RUGBY FOOTBALL CLUB
GRANDMA'S FUNERALS
HEARD ABOUT IDWAL 'AVE YOU? DIED SUDDENLY LAST NIGHT.
OH DAMN, I AM SORRY TO HEAR THAT AYE.
OH THAT'S ALL RIGHT MUN, HE DIDN'T HAVE A TICKET ANYWAY.
'ULLO EVANS BOY!
SHURRUP MUN! I'M SUPPOSED TO BE AT YOUR FUNERAL.
MERV BITES YER LEGG
ECHO TODAY: MORE MEDICAL EXCUSES FOR THE BEGINNER
ENGLAND WIN RUGBY INTERNATIONAL - PUBLIC HOLIDAY DECREED
FANS: PLEASE DO NOT ASK DOCTOR JPR FOR SICK NOTES
GRAVELL EATS SOFT CENTRES
PONTYPOOL RENT-A-PACK CO LTD
HYMNS 'N' ARIAS
UREN
RECORDED 'LIVE' AT PONTARDULAIS RUGBY FOOTBALL CLUB

MY SIDE OF THE BRIDGE
Mace the Great
(MACETHEGREATMUSIC, 2021)

> Cardiff City in the Building!
> Splott Road in the Building!

A talented emcee, there is no doubting where Mace the Great is from, as these opening lines from his 2021 EP prove. A short album at only eight songs in length, there is nevertheless an energy and a spark on this record that perfectly captures Mace's talents.

Performing live, Mace brings the energy, often taking his microphone into the crowd and urging circle pits to form around him, the whole place bouncing.

Title track 'My Side of the Bridge' is a welcome proud and positive track about where Mace is from: a clear and direct message to the world that he is Welsh and not from England. He offers to take the listener on a tour, urging them to understand the difference in geography and what makes his neck of the woods different to what they might have heard before. This in itself is refreshing, but also sounds completely natural.

If some UK emcees were accused in the Nineties of trying to sound American, a new wave of rappers soon changed that by rapping in their own accents. Roots Manuva, Jehst, Skitz and Skinnyman were undeniably English, rapping about things relevant to their lives, and saying it as they saw it. It might have taken a little longer for rappers to rap in English with a Welsh accent and break through. Lews Tunes & Nobsta Nuts, Ralph Rip Shit and ◉ **Astroid Boys** soon changed that, and of course ◉ **Goldie Lookin Chain** were undeniably Welsh, playing up to it in their unmistakably Newport accents.

Mace's debut album is a brilliant calling card, offering a glimpse of this likeable, proud and talented emcee's world. On 'Deeper' there's a nod to Cardiff-based producer ◉ **Minas**, himself a talented musician who has worked with several artists in and around south Wales. Inspirations Kano and Lethal Bizzle get a shout, but it always comes back to Mace's belief in himself.

Of late, platforms like Prendy's *The Shutdown Show*, Radio Platfform, Larynx Entertainment, and the Ladies of Rage collective have been relentless in their support of young artists from Wales making music of Black origin. Welsh rap music has always had its stars and its champions, but it seems that currently the scene is going through a golden period, with Mace's work a testament to this.

Acknowledged by a Triskel Award from the Welsh Music Prize in 2020, reaching the finals of the MOBO UnSung Awards in 2022 and being the first MOBO artist from Wales invited to play a prestigious showcase at South by Southwest, Mace has found his voice and is constantly connecting with new fans, his voice dextrous, thrilling and powerful.

MACE THE GREAT

LL.LL. v. T.G : MC D.R.E.
Llwybr Llaethog v. Tŷ Gwydr : David R Edwards

(ANKST, 1991)

After seeing breakdancers work their magic on the streets of New York and falling in love with hip-hop music and culture, John Griffiths – originally from Blaenau Ffestiniog – returned to Wales and then to London in the mid Eighties, determined to make this music in his own language. If rap music was about commenting on your environment and surroundings, doing that in Welsh was natural to him, and something rap artists from ○ **Tystion** to Sage Todz, Pep le Pew to Dom a Lloyd would later follow him in doing.

Teaming up with his friend Kevs Ford, they chose the name Llwybr Llaethog, meaning 'Milky Way' in Welsh, and released what is regarded as the first Welsh-language rap track, '*Dyddiau Braf (Rap Cymraeg)*' (Lovely Days (Welsh Rap)).

John Peel became a fan of their unique take on the genre, and the '*Dull Di-Drais*' (Non-VIolent Action) EP came out in 1986 on the fledgling Recordiau Anhrefn label, before a string of albums and singles followed, on – amongst others – Ankst Records, the Sain-affiliated Crai and Rasal labels, and their own Neud Nid Deud label. Their own label name sums them up perfectly: it means 'Do, Don't Say', and encapsulates their DIY approach to making things happen. Keen collaborators, they have worked with singers ○ **Geraint Jarman**, ○ **Gwenno** and ○ **Lleuwen** Steffan, and several MCs including Mr Phormula and Rufus Mufasa, and they present a yearly award to someone in the scene they feel deserves recognition for creativity.

On this record they collaborate with Tŷ Gwydr (Greenhouse) – another dynamic duo: Gareth Potter and Mark Lugg. Potter was in punk bands in school, but their love of rave music brought them to form something new, bringing that genre to the Eisteddfod. A continuation of previous bands Traddodiad Ofnus (Fearful Tradition) and Pop Negatif Wastad (Always Negative Pop), this was youthful, modern house music with their 'Reu' slogan capturing the early Nineties music fan's imagination. The 'D.R.E.' here is David Rupert Edwards, enigmatic frontman of ○ **Datblygu**. His musical partner Patricia Morgan is seen on the EP's artwork.

In a documentary on Welsh hip-hop for BBC Radio Cymru, author Llwyd Owen described Llwybr Llaethog as the Welsh Coldcut, commenting on the pick 'n' mix nature of their productions, with samples from bhangra to gabba appearing throughout their discography.

When Emyr Glyn Williams passed away in 2024, his wish was that his Ankstmusik label's last release would be a record of Llwybr Llaethog's Peel Sessions. The award-winning filmmaker was a friend to many, especially Datblygu, Geraint Jarman and Llwybr Llaethog, his love of esoteric art and culture enriching Wales for decades through his work in releasing stunning records.

Hard to define, difficult to pigeonhole, Llwybr Llaethog have been a constant creative and fiercely independent source of musical mischief for four decades, making sure the Welsh-language scene isn't taking itself too seriously, and opening our ears to a world of ideas.

L.L.V.T.G.

MC D.R.E.

THE LEGEND OF LL
Jon Langford & His Men of Gwent
(COUNTRY MILE RECORDS, 2015)

Jonathan Dennis Langford was born in Newport in 1957. Something of a musical enigma, he may have left Wales, but Wales has remained a creative force in his work since his early days.

Newport, in the past described as too Welsh to be English and too English to be Welsh, has produced some incredible lyricists and musicians, every bit a product of the harshness that the city's industrial past had created. Andrea Lewis of The Darling Buds (from nearby Caerleon), Richard Parfitt's ⊙ **60ft Dolls**, Benji Webbe's Skindred and ⊙ **Scritti Politti**'s Green Gartside all became well known with their songwriting. Jon Langford has remained on the fringes of fame whilst finding notoriety in cult circles, writing brutal songs sometimes tinged with sadness, sometimes funny and always with rock 'n' roll running through them.

A student at the University of Leeds in 1977, he was a founding member of punk rock legends The Mekons, originally as a drummer and then as guitarist. But Langford's long music career has seen him not stand still for long – restless, challenging and creative, he has been contributing to culture in every year of his adult life.

He was one of The Three Johns along with Johns Hyatt and Brennan, releasing five albums from 1984–90 before moving permanently to Chicago. There he formed The Waco Brothers, who became heroes in the country-punk scene, and became involved in Bloodshot Records, specialising in alt country records.

Skull Orchard, an album of songs documenting his life in Newport, came out in 1998. *The Legend of Ll*, too, is a record with Wales as its influence through and through, and is the debut album by Jon with a band of friends, The Men of Gwent.

It features a charming singalong cover of ⊙ **Max Boyce**'s '*Duw* It's Hard', with the smell of booze almost wafting over you as you listen, while 'Llamas in Llanyrafon' lists Langford's observations on today's Wales. 'Rebecca Been in a Riot' refers to nineteenth-century protests at tollgates in west Wales, while 'The Ballad of Soloman Jones' documents the Newport Rising. It's Welsh history told through the medium of rock 'n' roll.

2019 follow-up album *President of Wales* was also released on the independent Country Mile Records label, based in Newport and home to many of Langford's other creative endeavours.

A talented painter also known for his portraits of country singers, Langford has written articles, plays and spoken-word pieces that have been well received, presented radio programmes in the US and collaborated with several American musicians, including his neighbour, the acclaimed singer Bonnie 'Prince' Billy.

Recording on the peripheries, singing about his homeland whilst making friends and fans in the US, Langford's discography is an accomplished, fascinating one, awash with musical brilliance and a DIY ethos that continues to shine.

MEN OF GWENT
THE LEGEND OF LL

MILK FOR FLOWERS
H. Hawkline
(HEAVENLY, 2023)

Milk For Flowers is the fifth album released by H. Hawkline, the musical pseudonym of Huw Evans. A beautifully played and produced collection, it is dedicated to his late mother, who plays an important part in the subject matter of the songs on this record. They deal with grief, loss and the acceptance of the departure of someone so dear.

Most of the instrumentation here is played by Hawkline himself, with drums played by Davey Newington of Boy Azooga and the piano by Paul Jones. Jones is one half of Group Listening, an ambient duo with Stephen Black, aka ◉ **Sweet Baboo**, who plays the saxophone on this record. The sax, along with the piano, plays a prominent role on this, Hawkline's most accomplished album to date.

It was released on Heavenly, the highly regarded independent label that brought Hawkline on to the same roster as ◉ **Gwenno** and Katy J Pearson, King Gizzard and the Lizard Wizard, and Confidence Man.

Milk For Flowers was produced by Huw's old friend ◉ **Cate Le Bon**, who, as well as becoming a well-known name on the international avant-garde music scene, has become an in-demand producer. Hawkline's personal lyrics and stripped-back vocals benefitted from being in the studio with Le Bon, the trust between them bringing out the best in Hawkline's ideas and helping to create something very special, . 'Empty Rooms', 'I Need Him' and the title track are album highlights, each a different insight into Hawkline's musical mind.

His first two albums were released on Shape Records, a label run by Mark and Emma Daman Thomas from the band Islet, based in Brecon. Their independent ethos of supporting and nurturing bands, including their own, coincided with events, tours and a supportive community of bands across Wales who played the Gwdihŵ and Clwb Ifor Bach venues in Cardiff, inspired by a spirit of independence in the Welsh scene in the late Noughties.

Huw has played regularly in Cate Le Bon's band, and contributes to recordings and live performances by New Zealand's Aldous Harding and the Venezuelan-American signer Devendra Banhart, bringing a concise and structured playing style to his friends' music. His father Hywel Gwynfryn is a hugely respected radio broadcaster and the longest-serving presenter on BBC Radio Cymru, having broadcast from the station's first day on air in 1977 until the present. Huw's brother Ceri was in Nineties Welsh-language band Hanner Pei. Huw Evans himself has dabbled with presenting, on radio and S4C's *Bandit* series, and while at school in St Asaph was in the band Mwsog with Robin Edwards, who now records as R. Seiliog, and Sam Roberts, now a member of HMS Morris.

H. Hawkline's musical ambition has taken him around the world, his talent for matching the surreal with a distinctly melodic aesthetic hiding under layers of abstract references marking him as a singular talent.

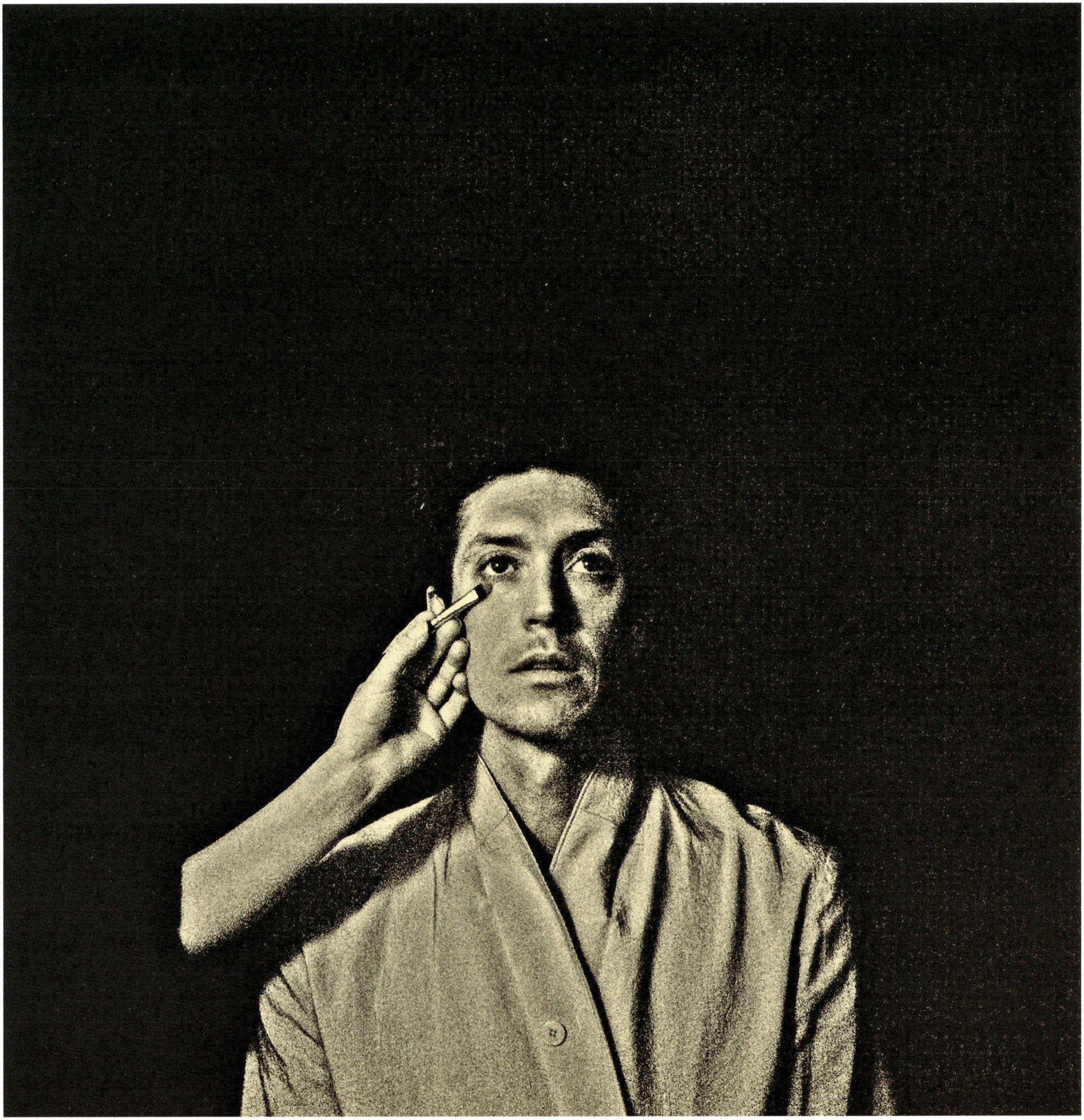

SALEM
Endaf Emlyn
(SAIN, 1974)

Singing and religion go hand in hand when it comes to music from Wales, from hymn-writing to the congregations meeting up to sing them in communities across the country. *Salem* is a record that knows this, and which is eager to delve deeper into these traditions, to personalise them, and create worlds around them.

Raised in Pwllheli on the Llŷn Peninsula, Endaf Emlyn played in the National Youth Orchestra of Wales at the same time as Garnant's **John Cale** and Penclawdd-born early Soft Machine member, composer Karl Jenkins.

Making a name for himself as a television presenter on HTV Wales, Endaf was also making his mark as a songwriter. Parlophone released three singles: 'Paper Chains', 'Goodbye Cherry Lill' and 'Starshine'. His first Welsh-language record was *Hiraeth* in 1972, containing some funky versions of Welsh lullabies as well as Endaf's own songs, like the beautiful opener, '*Hiraeth*' *(Wistfulness)*. Here was a calm, introspective voice – a thinker and a romantic. His next album landed in 1974, and *Salem* is now regarded as a Welsh-language classic.

The cover is based on a painting from 1908 by Sydney Curnow Vosper, an English painter who had a long fascination with Welsh imagery. It depicts a real woman, attending a service in Salem Chapel in Pentre Gwynfryn, Gwynedd, glorious in her Welsh hat amongst the prayers. Siân Owen was a regular chapelgoer, but the image has gained notoriety and become iconic because some see the face of the devil in her traditional Welsh shawl (on her left arm). Vosper denied this, and the painting became a household favourite across Wales. Siân is immortalised also in a song named after her here, as is the chapel deacon in '*Y Gŵr o Gae'r Meddyg*' (The Man from the Doctor's Field) and the young boy, 'Evan Edward Lloyd'. The album, regarded as the first concept album in the Welsh language, is a nod to the chapel past of Wales, the language and community dependent on it – but also a look to the future as the chapel plays a less important role in society.

Emlyn's third solo album, *Syrffio Mewn Cariad* (Surfing into Love) brought in his funk influences, a genre that the supergroup he joined along with Caryl Parry Jones (later of **Bando**) and others, Injaroc, played at the end of the 1970s. His next band, Jîp, also played funk but his solo album *Dawnsionara* (Slowdancing) in 1981 went for a more restrained, easy-listening sound, and featured renowned bassist **Pino Palladino**.

Endaf Emlyn has become a mysterious figure in the vast Welsh-language music landscape, possibly because of a lack of new music in subsequent years. He didn't gig as much as **Meic Stevens** or **Geraint Jarman**, preferring to concentrate on other projects instead, mostly his successful career as a television and film director. A short documentary was made on him by Kliph Scurlock, the American drummer who has settled in Wales and drums in Gruff Rhys' band, ending with Kliph meeting Endaf in a suburban Cardiff garden.

His music is heard on the longest-running soap on UK television: S4C's *Pobol y Cwm* still uses the Endaf Emlyn theme tune, albeit updated from its 1974 original version. His records have become hugely sought-after collectors' items thanks to their limited runs when first pressed, each one sounding fresh and regularly gaining a new following thanks to their musicianship and vision.

SALEM
Endaf Emlyn

EVERY VALLEY
Public Service Broadcasting
(PLAY IT AGAIN SAM, 2017)

Coal and the mining industry might at first seem like a strange concept for a record.

In the hands of Public Service Broadcasting however, the subject becomes a thing of beauty, their music elevating the tales of ingenuity, community and despair to soaring new heights.

Led by J Willgoose Esq., Public Service Broadcasting take on different subjects for each of their albums and bring them alive using archive voices and samples. *The Race for Space* (2015) took us on the infamous US-Soviet space missions of the 1950s–1970s, while *This New Noise* (2023) commemorated a hundred years of the BBC.

Every Valley is their ode to coal mining, an industry that fascinated Willgoose. It was recorded on location in the former South Wales Coalfield at Ebbw Vale Institute, the band wanting to record as close to the subject matter as they could. They would play launch shows at the same venue when the album was released by the Play It Again Sam label in 2017.

Starting in the 1950s, we hear on 'The Pit' and the boastful 'People Will Always Need Coal' how reliance on coal was reported and sold when the future of coal mining seemed secure. Tracyanne Campbell from Scottish band Camera Obscura sings on the joyful 'Progress', but by the heavy 'All Out', the tale of coal is changing.

James Dean Bradfield from **Manic Street Preachers** guests on 'Turn No More', adapting the words of Idris Davies' poem '*Gwalia Deserta*' – another part of which can be heard adapted in **The Byrds**' 'The Bells of Rhymney'. The industry is in decline, and Wales detects trouble, James' soaring voice bringing Davies' words alive. **9Bach** vocalist Lisa Jên Brown sings beautifully in both Welsh and English on 'You + Me', joined by Willgoose – the first time he had sung on his own band's work. Tender and caring, the song encapsulates the sense of love and support the miners' families showed those affected by pit closures, which kept communities together in times of hardship and through horrendous scenarios. The voice clips of miners in 'Mother of the Village' are devastating, in the realisation and acceptance that a way of life, livelihoods and the very essence of the South Wales Valleys was gone for ever. It is melancholy and quite emotional.

By the time the Beaufort Male Choir's voices sing in harmony on album closer 'Take Me Home', we are back in the present day, aware of what has been before, the changing face of this area of Welsh soil.

Every Valley is an unusual record in that it is a history lesson which takes you on an astonishing journey. The use of Welsh voices from across the decades makes it an intimate listen, with Public Service Broadcasting's masterful, subtle and sympathetic music creating a personal and close-to-the-bone telling of a hugely significant part of Wales' history.

PUBLIC SERVICE BROADCASTING   EVERY VALLEY

WAY BEYOND BLUE
Catatonia
(BLANCO Y NEGRO, 1996)

When Y Cyrff (The Bodies) disbanded in 1992, many hoped Mark Roberts would continue his remarkable songwriting. Having met singer-songwriter Cerys Matthews on the Cardiff scene, hanging out at Clwb Ifor Bach's Juice Joint night and other gig venues, they started composing songs together. Interest from S4C's iconic *Fideo 9* programme, and from the late-night *Heno Bydd yr Adar yn Canu* (Tonight the Birds Will Sing) on BBC Radio Cymru, led to Rhys Mwyn hearing the band and inviting them to record for the Crai label, a subsidiary of Sain for which Mwyn was charged with nurturing new talent. If that was the job description, then you could say he struck gold with Catatonia.

The songs 'For Tinkerbell' and 'Sweet Catatonia' made it from that first Crai EP to this, their debut album. Their slow/heavy style was held together by Cerys' charming voice, at times otherworldly and ethereal, at other times commanding and not-to-be-messed-with. This was a formula that would become Cerys' vocal trademark: a force of nature that would deliver lyrics with an astounding power, demanding that you listen and bringing rousing choruses alive. Mark and Cerys' songwriting was dreamlike with the odd dose of reality thrown in for dramatic effect. Their music was classy but never pretentious, a striking mix of the desperate and the luxurious.

There are indie dancefloor-fillers here: 'Bleed', 'Sweet Catatonia' and 'You've Got a Lot to Answer For' are all fizzing with energy, undiluted mini guitar anthems that are super-catchy, with the latter becoming the band's first taste of the top 40 singles chart. But there are softer moments too: 'Infantile', 'Dream On' and the title track show a poignancy and an emotional depth that remained throughout the band's albums.

Equally melodic and subtle, *Way Beyond Blue* might have been a progression from their early EPs, but it is also in many ways the calm before the storm.

Catatonia would go on to become bona fide chart stars, play to large audiences and be a welcome breath of fresh air on the bloated Britpop scene of the mid to late Nineties. After a particularly muddy outdoor gig at Margam Park in 1999, the front page of *Wales on Sunday* read 'Splatatonia!' They really were all over the front page. Their commercial success was considerable, but in 2001, the band called it a day. Cerys Matthews is an inquisitive and highly regarded broadcaster whose popular show on BBC Radio 6 Music, *Add to Playlist* show on BBC Radio 4 and *The Blues Show* on BBC Radio 2 bring tunes of all flavours from an international playlist to a huge audience every week, her extensive knowledge and relaxed style striking a chord with musically curious listeners. Mark Roberts has released albums as Y Ffyrc (The Forks) and MR, and has toured across Wales, with the odd Cyrff classic making an appearance, in a band featuring his Catatonia friends Owen Powell and Paul Jones. Drummer Aled Richards is a music technology lecturer.

The beautiful painting on the cover of *Way Beyond Blue* is by renowned artist Elfyn Lewis, originally from Porthmadog. A friend of the band for many years, his striking artwork across the various formats of *Way Beyond Blue* and its accompanying singles helped bring the songs on this special album together as a whole.

This was the end of one chapter in the band's history, their DIY and independent days over, and a major new chapter unfolding, their star about to shine its brightest.

Catatonia
"Way Beyond Blue"

THE COLLECTIVE
Various Artists
(ROUNDA RECORDS, 2000)

As hip-hop entered the 2000s, independent labels and a hands-on DIY approach continued to be the way to get things done in Wales.

Rapper Little Miss (aka Sophie Barras, whose brother Will designed the artwork for this release) founded Rounda as a support service for artists, aimed at showcasing the creative energy in the Welsh capital at the time. DJ Jaffa (aka Jason Farrell), a highly regarded DJ on the scene since the 1980s, was one of the emcees, producers and beatmakers in the collective. This compilation by the label is a reflection of the scene in Cardiff at the turn of the millennium, and just one release in Jaffa's fascinating discography.

Jaffa started as a scratch DJ in his teens in Eighties Cardiff, encouraged by the Grassroots studio to get involved in music. Teaming up with his friend Eric Martin, they formed rap duo Just the Duce. The success of their tunes 'Special Request' and 'Ease Off' on a Jive compilation, *Def Reggae*, in 1989, was the culmination of hard work, friendship and a love of the culture, with both their talents at play. While Eric joined Technotronic and recorded as **Me One**, Jaffa has been a vital nurturer of talent in Cardiff, bringing new music to many platforms. His contributions here are epic, moody tracks, reminiscent of DJ Shadow, James Lavelle and their Unkle project.

Erban Poets featured Nay'tan Tha Watcha, a gifted Rastafarian emcee who collaborated with Green Man Festival founders Jo Bartlett and Danny Hagan, his mesmerising flow bringing something new, conscious and exciting to the Welsh scene, teaming up with vocalist Kari.

Little Miss joins forces with Kevs Ford, one half of esteemed production duo **Llwybr Llaethog**, and Sir Doufus Styles, aka Kris Jenkins. Kris' contribution to music from Wales is enormous – with his own band Bench, his work with **Super Furry Animals**, and his production on music by **Cate Le Bon**, Hanner Pei and **Geraint Jarman**, amongst others.

Jaffa became a member of Welsh-language hip-hop crew **Tystion**, appearing on the front cover of their album *Hen Gelwydd Prydain Newydd*, and playing with them at Maida Vale for a John Peel session on BBC Radio 1. He was the tour DJ for Manchild and formed Bronx River DJs with his friends Paul B and Cuz, who appears on this compilation. His latest project is Xenith, with Dregz and Johnny B rapping over Jaffa's beats.

He attempted a world record in 2003 for the longest continuous DJ set, achieving a remarkable 70 hours. His love and appreciation for Cathays Community Centre also saw him raise money for the space by DJing for 24 hours for them in 2021. He DJs internationally, and regularly in Cardiff nightclubs, with residencies at weekly nights, from disco sets to specialising in hip-hop and R&B, and always showcasing new music from the Welsh R&B and rap scenes on his *This, That & the Third* show on Raptz radio. His support for the music scene in Wales is unparalleled, focusing on quality from singers, rappers and producers.

The Rounda *Collective* was compiled by Sophie Barras, who continues to work in music – she has been a director of product management for the Universal Music Group for the past decade.

ROUNDA PRESENTS

Rounda records

little miss · that i am
dj jaffa · erban poets
cuz · mac

THE COLLECTIVE

JOIA!
Carwyn Ellis & Rio 18
(BANANA & LOUIE, 2019)

Carwyn Ellis is an international man of many musical talents. His playing with Scottish indie legend Edwyn Collins, a slot on Soho Radio which showcases his vast musical tastes, and a number of records as Colorama have all kept him remarkably busy, his musical compass set to recording, touring and remaining constantly inquisitive.

Whilst touring the world playing stadium gigs supporting Genesis as keyboardist in the Pretenders, singer Chrissie Hynde suggested to Carwyn that he met some Brazilian musician friends of hers, and proposed that they record in Welsh. The results are a trio of extraordinary albums: *Joia!*, *Mas* and *Yn Rio*. With the album titles next to each other, they translate to 'Enjoy!' 'Out', 'In Rio'. And it does sound like Carwyn had a lot of fun making these bright, musically free-flowing albums.

Joia! contains a few undisputed bops: the sunshine-drenched '*Duwies y Dre*' (Goddess of the Town) & '*Tywydd Hufen Iâ*' (Ice Cream Weather) in particular stand out as perfectly encapsulating a lazy afternoon in a sunny square, or the simple pleasure of an ice cream by a beautiful ocean. Vocalists throughout the album are sisters Mared and Elan Rhys from the popular folk band Plu – a band Carwyn had admired enough to collaborate with on an album called *Bendith* in 2016. Whilst that was a stunning folk record, the Brazilian influences run throughout *Joia!*, *Mas* and *Yn Rio*, and they run freely, rich in their musical dexterity and infectious nature.

Carwyn's a romantic soul, his knack for observing the simplest act of love captured in songs like '*Gwên*' (Smile) and '*Diolch Amdani*' (Thanks for Her).

At the Green Man Festival in 2022, Sunday afternoon on the main Mountain Stage opened with the BBC National Orchestra of Wales tuning up before Carwyn Ellis & Rio 18 joined them to perform selections from the three albums, but particularly from the last, *Yn Rio*. Recorded with the orchestra as a lockdown project for BBC Radio Cymru, it was a stunning session that culminated in the release of the record. With the fine orchestra at their best, the result was a plusher album compared to *Joia!*, with Carwyn's delicate, warm vocals and the Rio 18 instrumentation. I was lucky enough to be in the session when Carwyn and the Orchestra played, in my role as presenter, and it was a hugely emotional experience – having had so many months without concerts or being in the same room as musicians.

Joia! closes with Carwyn thanking those that have made this album, his musical life and the path it has taken possible. Every thanks is followed by *obrigado*, the Portuguese for 'thanks' – the perfect closer to this first fascinating, brilliant musical adventure with Rio 18.

Carwyn Ellis & Rio 18

JOIA!

FASTER THAN THE SPEED OF NIGHT
Bonnie Tyler
(CBS, 1983)

By 1983, Bonnie Tyler had released four albums. Her 1977 debut, *The World Starts Tonight*, featuring the hit 'Lost in France', was a striking record, letting the world know that Bonnie meant business, but none of her albums had yet charted in the UK. That was about to change.

Born Gaynor Hopkins in Skewen, Swansea in 1951, she first renamed herself Sherene Davis before settling on Bonnie Tyler, and was signed by RCA Records after being spotted singing in the clubs of her home city. By the early Eighties, Bonnie had been grafting for some time as a recording and touring artist, but her deal with RCA had run out. But the best was yet to come.

Bonnie's instinct was to team up with renowned songwriter and producer Jim Steinman to make her next album, and her instinct was right. Steinman's trademark sound is evident throughout this blockbuster record. He'd made his name as a versatile songwriter who'd begun working with Meat Loaf in the early 1970s, a partnership that would be resurrected quite regularly until both of their passings in the early 2020s.

Steinman presented Tyler with a new song in his apartment, a song that would be the centrepiece of this album. When 'Total Eclipse of the Heart' was released, it went straight to number 1 in the UK chart, and went on to become one of the biggest singles of all time, with an astonishing six million copies sold and over a billion views on YouTube. Steinman also wrote the album's title track, full of crashing drums and fast-paced piano, his trademark sound matching Tyler's distinctive vocals perfectly. Other big names have a connection to the album too: playing on the title track were members of Bruce Springsteen's E Street Band, and 'Straight from the Heart' is a cover of a Bryan Adams song, one that Bonnie loved. Her voice, husky and bruised, is perfect for baring her soul and showing the emotion in these songs.

Talking on Tim Burgess's popular *Tim's Twitter Listening Party* in 2020, she recalled her enjoyment in making this album, working with Jim and duetting with Frankie Miller. 40 years after the album was released, Bonnie called it "a big risk that paid off massively," and said that she was "so grateful for everything that followed".

Bonnie Tyler went on to release a further 13 albums, plus several greatest hits compilations. She was asked to represent the UK in the Eurovision Song Contest in 2013, and was made an MBE in the Queen's last Birthday Honours List in 2022. She also received an Honorary Degree from the University of Swansea in 2013 for her services to music.

For all her global success and constant travelling, she still calls Swansea home, her house on the Mumbles a stone's throw from the university. From humble beginnings to international fame, Bonnie documents her life in an open and honest way in her autobiography, *Straight from the Heart*, chronicling a remarkable life in music.

As North America witnessed the solar eclipse in 2024, Bonnie's 'Total Eclipse of the Heart' was clearly the soundtrack for many watching it, as it leapt up streaming charts the world over. Bonnie has sung it at every concert she's played since its release, and her incredibe delivery continues to bring people out of darkness today.

Bonnie Tyler
Faster Than The Speed Of Night

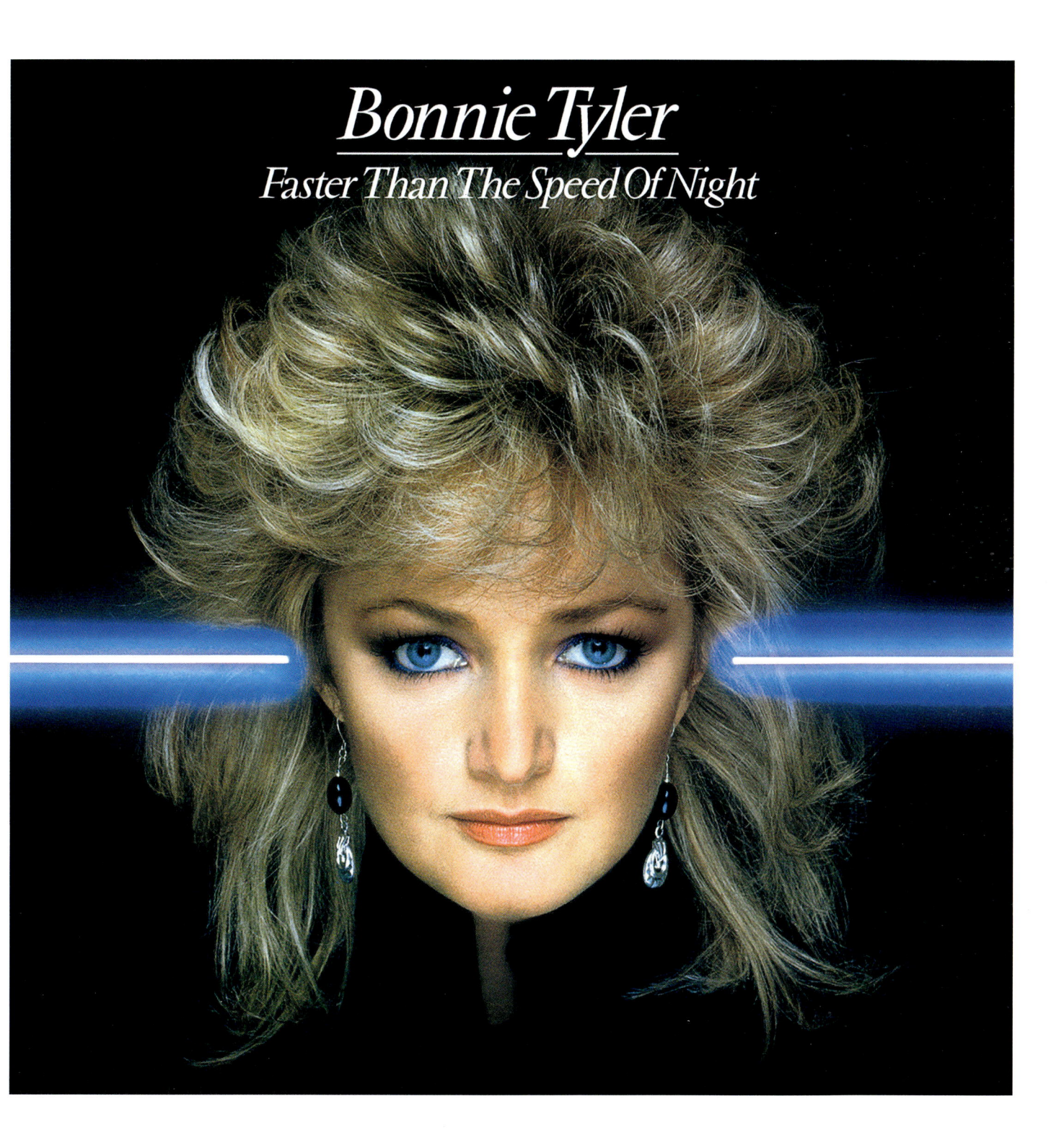

HAPPY SHOPPER
60ft Dolls
(TOWNHILL RECORDS, 1994)

In the mid 1990s, young bands from Wales were being taken notice of, and taken seriously. After decades of Welsh music stereotypes pushed by the media, young Welsh bands were finally breaking through into the mainstream, and not irregularly. If each band was a product of their environment – with ◎ Catatonia singing about city life in Cardiff, the ◎ Super Furry Animals bringing rural and city life together with traditional and electronic influences, ◎ Gorky's Zygotic Mynci a west Wales psych juggernaut, and the ◎ Stereophonics portraying small-town life on their debut – then 60ft Dolls were every bit the Newport grit they were portrayed as. Unglamorous, proudly working-class purveyors of unpretentious romantic poetry, tied up in rip-roaring riffs and licks.

Learning their craft on the stages of The Legendary TJ's and the original incarnation of the Le Pub venue, 60ft Dolls were a three-piece that spat out their lyrics and played no-nonsense rock 'n' roll with vigour. A bustling indie DIY scene in Newport was captured on Frug! Records' *I Was a Teenage Gwent Boy* compilation in 1994, bringing the Dolls, Novocaine, Flyscreen, Five Darrens and The Jonah Hex together. Soon music journalists dubbed Newport 'the New Seattle', referencing the post-industrial American town and the abundance of bands coming from there, most notably Nirvana and the Sub Pop roster. Legend has it that it was journalist Neil Strauss who coined the term after the 60ft Dolls showed him around Newport, commenting that it felt like Seattle did when Nirvana broke.

Steeped in musical history, Newport has given us some outstanding rock stories. The famous Stone Roses cherub can still be seen on the Newport bridge, as it sits above the city's coat of arms, and the city's iconic Transporter Bridge features in 60ft Dolls' video for 'Talk to Me'. A young Joe Strummer worked in Newport as a gravedigger, the Clash frontman's guitar now taking pride of place in the Diverse Vinyl record shop in town. ◎ Jon Langford was born in Newport and formed punk heroes The Mekons, now playing more country-influenced music with his band The Waco Brothers. And ◎ Dub War were making a name for themselves with their blending of punk and reggae, a winning formula which sees them smashing stages to this day.

The band's early singles 'Happy Shopper', 'Talk to Me' and 'Stay' were short, sharp bursts of pure punk euphoria, sizzling with charm in each groove of their seven-inch vinyl. 'Happy Shopper' – their debut single, released on Swansea's Townhill Records by their manager Huw Williams – was a prelude to the buzz that was to come. Soon signing to Indolent Records in the UK and Geffen in the US, the Dolls' excitement was caught beautifully on their debut album *The Big Three*, which still sounds as vital and essential today as the day it was released.

Drummer Carl Bevan's father was a pastor and much was made of the contrast between that profession and his son's rock 'n' roll antics in the music – and more mainstream – press. The band loved this attention, and released Ray Bevan reading a sermon as a limited-edition track. Carl went on to produce other bands, including Exit International, and is now a popular visual artist. Singer Richard Parfitt continued to write, releasing a solo album, *Highlights in Slow Motion*, in 2002. He wrote songs for ◎ Duffy, and played guitar for McAlmont & Butler. His novel *Stray Dogs* was published by Third Man Books in 2023.

Although The Dolls perhaps didn't reach quite the commercial success of other tight rock groups from south Wales, they certainly made a lasting impression on the alternative scene.

60FT DoLLS

HAPPY SHOPPER

SIR FÔN BACH
Llio Rhydderch
(FFLACH:TRADD, 2019)

Popular in Italy in the 1600s, the triple harp is now synonymous with Wales. It's a beautiful instrument to look at and to listen to, with three rows of strings: the semitones are in the middle row, with the two outer rows tuned to the diatonic scale. Travelling musicians brought the instrument to Wales, where it was quickly adopted, embedding itself in the Welsh tradition ever since.

Nansi Richards (1888–1979), known as *Telynores Maldwyn* (the Montgomeryshire Harpist), was seen as the queen of the triple harp. Llio Rhydderch was her pupil and became her friend, travelling with her to perform in the United States in the early 1970s and continuing Nansi's legacy from her own home on Anglesey. Llio's playing is stunning and transcendental; both subtle and soaring, intricate in its delivery, but warm and welcoming in its beauty. Its calmness has found her a new audience, keen to embrace this stunning, quieter music, steeped in such history. She received particular support early on from BBC Radio 3 and world music publications.

Coming from a long lineage of triple harp players, from a young age Llio won every prestigious prize on offer when it came to the harp. She worked in the world of education, teaching from Splott to Porthaethwy, and found fame as a recording artist later in life, signing to the fflach:tradd label, who were keen to take her expertise and talent to a new audience. Her debut release was *Telyn* (Harp) in 1997, at the age of 60. *Sir Fôn Bach* (Little Anglesey), her sixth album, was recorded with Gorwel Owen at his Ofn studio on Anglesey, and is a collection of tunes Llio researched from manuscripts kept in the National Library of Wales, Aberystwyth and Bangor University, where she was awarded an honorary fellowship.

The album was produced, like all of her albums, by Ceri Rhys Matthews, an accomplished folk musician from Swansea, whose band Fernhill with vocalist Julie Murphy have had several gorgeous releases. Ceri compiled an album for Smithsonian Folkways called *Blodeugerdd: Song of the Flowers*, a highlight of which was a collaboration between Llio, Christine Cooper and ⊙ **Max Boyce** on the song '*Hiraeth*' (Wistfulness).

Llio's craft may date back hundreds of years, traditional to its very core, but her playing technique and forward-thinking ideas have made her a hero in her world, keen as she is to accommodate new ideas. She played with ⊙ **John Cale** in his *Camgymeriad Gwych/Beautiful Mistake* collaboration film in 2000, and collaborated with young Welsh jazz band Burum on tour. She has played several times in Europe, including Italy for Celtic Connections in 2001, across the UK and Ireland, and in every major concert hall in London – four times at the Royal Albert Hall in the 1950s.

Llio has passed on the playing of the triple harp to young pupils, who in turn take it to a new generation themselves, bringing new ideas to the world of the instrument. There are several younger musicians who have embraced the harp and aim to push forward their music and the instrument's image. One of them is another triple harpist, Cerys Hafana, who has a distinct style and is unafraid to push the boundaries of how music played on the instrument can sound, delighting audiences with her beautiful, stark music.

Another friend of Llio's is the Aberystwyth-born, Swansea-based Rhodri Davies. His experimental albums have gained a reputation for themselves as bold, challenging works. In a varied career, he has played with Charlotte Church, and formed the psychedelic band Hen Ogledd with Northumberland singer Richard Dawson.

Llio Rhydderch has dazzled audiences at many Eisteddfodau, performing with her gang of triple harpists playing in unison, lost in the moment but very much keeping a tradition alive. It's a remarkable sight: Llio in her element, making magic.

llio rhydderch
sir fôn bach

MWNG
Super Furry Animals
(PLACID CASUAL RECORDINGS, 2000)

The stark black and white image of a goat, drawn by long-term collaborator Pete Fowler, is perhaps an indication of the more sombre mood contained in this special album by Super Furry Animals, in stark contrast to their colourful previous records.

There is a melancholia to *Mwng* (Mane) – in the sparse, relaxed tone of '*Nythod Cacwn*' (Wasps' Nests), '*Y Gwyneb Iau*' (Liverface) and '*Gwreiddiau Dwfn*' (Deep Roots) – with only a few glimpses of the frantic style of their earliest EPs for the Ankst label. The album was recorded at their old friend Gorwel Owen's Ofn studios in Llanfaelog, Anglesey, where the band had recorded their earliest work. Gorwel had been in Eighties synth-pop band Plant Bach Ofnus (Scared Little Children) and continued to sing with his wife, poet Fiona Owen. Their homely, relaxed studio was the perfect setting for making *Mwng*, the lo-fi production sounding as warm and welcoming as the studio where it was recorded.

This is the sound of a band taking stock: a deep intake of breath amidst the madness of a rock 'n' roll schedule, and bringing it back to their roots. Sung entirely in Welsh, and – thanks to a new freedom in being able to release this – on their own Placid Casual label, the record was a mainstream chart success for them, reaching No.11. To this day, it is the bestselling Welsh-language album of all time. It was commended in the Houses of Parliament by Elfyn Llwyd MP, as proof that 'the Welsh language is re-establishing itself as a central part of popular youth culture'. In retrospect, perhaps *Mwng* was the turning point in making Welsh-language music sound not only acceptable but popular, finding an audience around the world.

But singing in Welsh was completely natural for the Furries, who had done so in previous bands. Guto Pryce and Huw Bunford were in Cardiff punks U Thant and Anglesey's Cian Ciarán in electronic project Wwwzz with his brother Dafydd Ieuan – who was also an early drummer for ◉ Catatonia, and previously a co-founder of Ffa Coffi Pawb with Bethesda's Gruff Rhys. When Super Furry Animals came together, their first EPs were sung in Welsh, before they recorded their first three albums in English. Their contract with Creation Records took them on tour to far-flung countries and they became one of the most celebrated new bands in the world.

There are rays of sunlight on *Mwng*, not least on the sundrenched '*Ysbeidiau Heulog*', itself a song about sunny intervals. '*Y Teimlad*' (The Feeling) is their take on a ◉ Datblygu song. Originally recorded in the early 1980s, it would be the Furries' cover that would bring this simple, stripped-back song about the mystery of love to a new audience.

'*Nythod Cacwn*' is a warning against pulling a wasps' nest onto your head, while '*Dacw Hi*' (There She Is) was written by a young Gruff Rhys about his junior school teacher. The haunting, disparately chiming guitars on '*Sarn Helen*' are an ode to the visionary Roman roads of Wales, connecting the country from north to south. The same could be said of Super Furry Animals, a fascinating, layered band of members from across Wales. Bassist Guto Pryce went on to form Gulp, with guitarist Huw Bunford recording as Pale Blue Dots. Cian's project was Zefur Wolves and Daf's The Peth (with actor Rhys Ifans) and The Earth – featuring Mark Roberts from Catatonia and vocalist Dionne Bennett. The four of them went on to form Das Koolies, their debut album released in 2023. Frontman Gruff Rhys has released ten solo records – his first, *Yr Atal Genedlaeth* (as with many of Gruff's titles, a playful one which could mean 'The Stuttering Generation' or 'The Contraceptive Generation'), recorded with Gorwel Owen in the same studio as *Mwng*.

The energy, vision and combined talents of Super Furries made being a fan of theirs a continually surprising, exhilarating ride, of which *Mwng* was an essential part.

mwng

BRÂN
Brân
(GWAWR, 1974)

Released on the Gwawr label, this was the first time this talented young band were heard on record.

Singer Nest Howells remains one of the great Welsh-language vocalists. She occasionally sang with folk heroes Pererin, but has remained away from the limelight for most of her life. Her daughter Elin Fflur is also a singer, with several hugely successful Welsh-language releases to her name, and her son Gwion Llŷr Llewelyn is a drummer who has played with Race Horses and Villagers, amongst others. John Gwyn from Brân would make his name as an in-demand TV producer, working on Channel 4's *The Tube* amongst his many credits, and was instrumental in forming supergroup Jîp with ⊙ **Endaf Emlyn**, Arran Ahmun, Richard Dunn and Myfyr Isaac. Gwyndaf Roberts plays harp and bass guitar here, and was also a founding member of ⊙ **Dafydd Iwan**-collaborating Celtic renaissance band Ar Log, as well as playing in Yr Atgyfodiad with the drummer on this record, Keith Snelgrove.

The song '*Tocyn*' (Ticket), a celebration of having a ticket to be able to escape from a girl called Gwenan, became a favourite of Ffa Coffi Pawb and was a staple in their live sets. It was later covered by Manchester psych band Whyte Horses.

Brân's last album was *Gwrach y Nos* in 1978, preceded by *Hedfan* in 1976. But it's their 1975 debut *Ail-Ddechra* that has truly become the stuff of legend amongst rare record collectors. It changes hands for hundreds of pounds, and has become one of the most sought-after Welsh-language records ever pressed. It has also been given an unexpected mention by Hollywood actor Elijah Wood, who mentioned his fondness of the band whilst eating hot sauce, in an interview seen by millions of viewers.

Although only together for some four years, Brân's wonderful music and legacy remains, having created a huge impression both then and now, delighting fans in Wales and around the world.

HELL FOR CERTAIN
Gwenifer Raymond
(TOMPKINS SQUARE, 2020)

Taken from her second album, *Strange Lights Over Garth Mountain*, this mesmerising piece is played on the acoustic guitar. It's an instrumental, like all of Gwenifer's tracks, and a striking single in both pace and playing.

Born in Cardiff before moving to Taff's Well aged 3, Gwenifer became enamoured with American grunge bands, most notably Nirvana, and started to play in public around the Valleys in punk bands. Kurt Cobain's band's cover of Lead Belly's 'Where Did You Sleep Last Night?' piqued her interest, and she turned her attention to the great guitar pickers, John Fahey most notably. She took a keen interest in Appalachian music, picking up the acoustic guitar and the banjo and starting to shred.

A computer game designer by trade, and living in Brighton, her distinctive style has taken Gwenifer to many venues across Europe and mainland USA. She found fans in US-based radio stations, and captured the attention of Tompkins Square Records, a label specialising in American primitive guitar music, who loved her work so much that they signed her for the first album, *You Never Were Much of a Dancer*.

Gwenifer's brother is the artist Casey Raymond, whose work with ⊙ **Cate Le Bon**, ⊙ **Sweet Baboo** and ⊙ **H. Hawkline** has seen him team up with Tregaron animator and filmmaker Ewan Jones Morris several times, and he has made distinctive videos and artwork for John Grant and The Lovely Eggs, amongst others. Their mother Jennifer directed the video for this single, with Gwenifer playing next to a table containing a wedding cake and other intriguing objects.

The Garth Mountain in the title of the album this piece of music is taken from is not far from where Gwenifer was raised in Taff's Well, and overlooks Cardiff and the beginning of the Rhondda Valleys. It was the inspiration for the novel (and later film) *The Englishman Who Went Up a Hill but Came Down a Mountain*, and is a very pleasant climb.

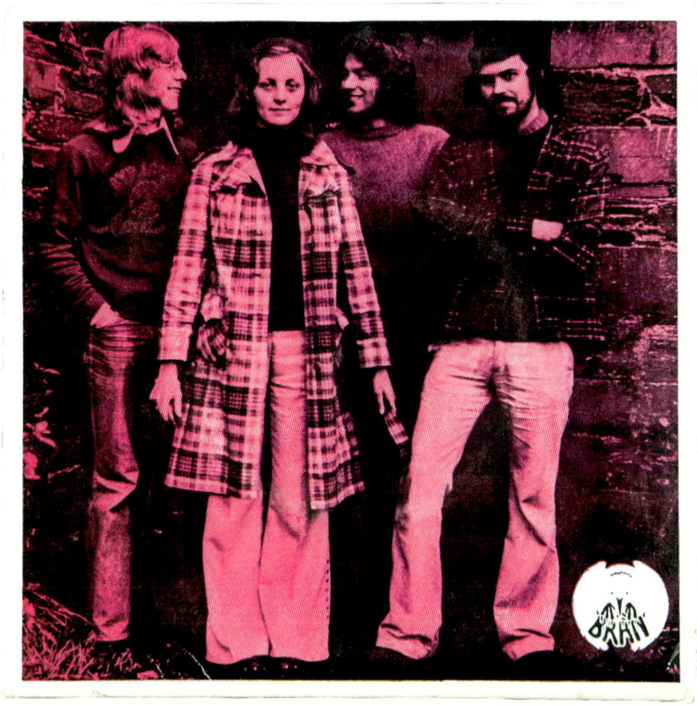
BRAN

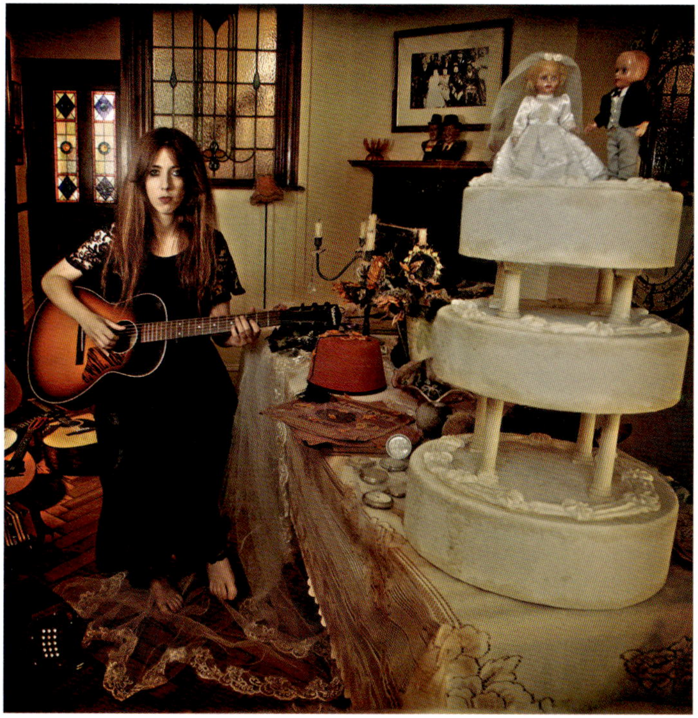

GWN GLÂN BEIBL BUDR
Lleuwen
(SAIN, 2018)

Gwn Glân Beibl Budr sounds like an album that had to be made. It was released unexpectedly, and welcomed by an audience who realised a huge talent was at work here.

This was the third solo album by Lleuwen, the follow-up to *Penmon* (2007) and 2011's *Tân* (Fire). Her father is the singer-songwriter Steve Eaves, who has several acclaimed albums in Welsh to his name. His songs are political and steeped in blues music, and Lleuwen would regularly sing backing vocals with him, along with her sister Manon Steffan Ros and singer Jackie Williams. Manon is better known now as an author, her novel *Llyfr Glas Nebo/The Blue Book of Nebo* becoming a sensation in the literary world, being translated into several languages and winning the Yoto Carnegie Literary Medal in 2023.

Gwn Glân Beibl Budr translates to 'Clean Gun Dirty Bible', the striking title indicating from the off that this is no ordinary album. The confessional stylings of Lleuwen's vocals here are remarkable. She ponders, prays and looks for hope throughout, our guide on a journey that tries to make sense of life.

There are traditional songs, hymns and Welsh favourites that are given a whole new lease of life here. 'Cwm Rhondda', John Hughes' famous hymn, is performed here with beauty and grace, instrumentation brought to the fore, turning the rousing hymn into an intricate and almost flamencoesque structure. Lleuwen's delight in these reinterpretations is clear: they are from the heart and performed with respect and grace, whilst confidently showing a new side to these huge songs.

'Bendigeidfran' is an original song, named after the giant in the *Mabinogion*'s ancient Welsh folk tales, noting that we need bridges like his more than ever. 'Caerdydd' (Cardiff) is another original, a tender love story with the city of 346,000 inhabitants and its streets as the central character. The density of the music and the purity of Lleuwen's vocals create an ambience that is breathtaking.

Soon we are back in Lleuwen's natural habitat, with '*Mynyddoedd*' (Mountains) celebrating Eryri's landscape. Near the end of the album, Lleuwen notes on the impressive '*Y Don Olaf*' (The Last Wave) that everyone leaves in the end. This is an album in a state of flux, epitomising the push and pull between the acceptance of the traditional and the continual craving to evolve and seek new things. Here it sounds as if Lleuwen has come to if not a happy place, then a comfortable place of finding herself. She sings of her frustration at there not being an emoji that expresses *hiraeth*, which for me is the line that sums the album up perfectly: an old Wales which commands deep respect seen through the eyes of a confused, caring modern human being.

Her most recent release, *Tafod Arian* (Silver Tongue), is a collection of forgotten Welsh hymns which never made it into the hymn-books of the time – some by female writers excluded by all-male committees. The result of a project she started by delving into the archives at St Fagans National Museum of History, by tracing the writers' descendants and performing the pieces in 50 chapels across Wales, Lleuwen has given these hymns new life.

GWN GLÂN BEIBL BUDR

WESTGATE UNDER FIRE
Dub War
(EARACHE, 2022)

Benji Webbe remains one of the most captivating frontmen Wales has ever seen. In the mid Nineties when Britpop and Cool Cymru ruled the airwaves, Benji and his friends in Dub War were forging their own, heavier, sound, often on the stage of The Legendary TJ's, the fabled Newport venue. Mixing metal and punk, genres which their home city was known for, with reggae and ragga, which it mostly wasn't known for, Dub War were an anomaly that stood out in their immediate crowd. Their distinctive sound found them an appreciative audience in the larger scheme of things, with both the indie and rock press celebrating them.

After a couple of releases on Words of Warning, a small independent label, Dub War signed to the respected heavy music label Earache, founded in Nottingham by Digby Pearson and home to experimental boundary-pushers Napalm Death. Dub War instantly connected with a fanbase which loved their no-nonsense approach to guitars, rhythm and lyrics, and the experience of seeing them live was not to be forgotten. Not seeing Benji exhausted and in a pool of sweat at the end of a gig was unthinkable: here was a band who gave it their all onstage. Mikee Gregory played drums, Jeff Rose was on guitar and Richie Glover on bass, with Benji up front bringing his conscientious lyrics to the youth.

However, after two albums on Earache in 1995 and 1996, the millennium ended with Dub War no more. Luckily, another project, Skindred, had already come to fruition, with Benji fronting this new band, still hungry to create. Skindred found their audience, playing in the US and on main stages at festivals around the world. Their 'Newport Helicopter' at live gigs is the stuff of legend, with fans rotating their shirts above their heads. They went on to release eight albums, including the impressive *Roots Rock Riot* and *Union Black*. Skindred's latest album, 2023's *Smile*, found an even bigger audience thanks to the band's readiness to fuse yet more melody into their music. Skindred became the first Welsh artists to win a MOBO Award, for Best Alternative Act, in 2024.

But Dub War hadn't been wiped out completely. During the Covid period, Benji entered the rehearsal space with original members Jeff and Richie and set about recording new songs. Writing in the city where the Newport Rising took place in 1839, their comeback album is named after the Westgate Hotel, where the Chartists fought and many were killed.

Producer Richard Jackson, a Newport music stalwart, worked with the band to record *Westgate Under Fire* at their homes. Six different drummers joined Mikee Gregory on the album: Dub War fans from established bands, including Stone Sour, Faith No More and Killing Joke. The image of the mosaic on the album cover is from the Chartist mural designed by Kenneth Budd and unveiled in Newport in 1978. It was removed from its home in a busy underpass in 2013 as part of building work in the city, much to the dismay and anger of many. An album highlight is a version of Max Romeo and The Upsetters' *War Inna Babylon* featuring the late, great vocalist Ranking Roger of The Beat. It's a celebratory record, proud of its Newport heritage – another bold entry in Benji Webbe's extraordinary back catalogue.

WESTGATE UNDER FIRE
Child War

WEEK OF PINES
Georgia Ruth
(GWYMON, 2013)

The title track of this collection of work is a sprawling piece of music that sets the tone wonderfully for this magical, warm record.

Georgia Ruth conjures a sense of the coast and the sea, and of an artist on the move, throughout *Week of Pines*. The music might well be on the peripheries, not quite sure of its place in the mainstream, but happy to be discovering itself on the edges of creativity. '*Codi Angor*' (Raising Anchor) is from the sea-shanty tradition, Georgia's warm tones set beautifully against the reed organ. Musicians on the album are her husband Iwan Hughes, from Cowbois Rhos Botwnnog, and his brothers Dafydd and Aled Hughes. Georgia has spoken about how their band, from the village of Botwnnog on the Llŷn Peninsula, helped her forge her own musical path – her sound previous to this album taking a more traditional tone, with Georgia accompanying herself on the harp. The harp is still key to *Week of Pines*, her exquisite playing at the album's core, and central to the heartbreaking 'Winter', which closes the album. ◉ **Lleuwen** Steffan joins Georgia on vocals throughout the album too.

Georgia's way with words cannot be denied, her lyrics at times simple and longing, at others doused in mystery and pure poetry.

The drums, dragging and occasionally distant, play an important role here, marking a shift in Georgia's musical journey. The production here is perfect, with Georgia's voice cutting through. The album was recorded at Bryn Derwen studios in Bethesda, which hosted some remarkable sessions over the years. Owner Laurie Gane built a residential studio that was used by bands on the Welsh scene, as well as ones from further afield. Sadly, it has now closed down.

The in-house engineer there and the producer on this album was David Wrench, who brought a unique production touch to his work. A founding member of the band Nid Madagascar as well as a solo artist, Wrench has gone on to become one of the most respected sound mixers in the world, working on albums by Frank Ocean, The xx, Blur and many more. He has brought out the best in so many of the records he's worked on, not least this beautiful collection.

Originally released in 2013 by Sain imprint Gwymon – a label named after the ◉ **Meic Stevens** album and inspired by its folk sounds – it went on to win that year's Welsh Music Prize. *Week of Pines* was given a new lease of life in 2023 by the Bubblewrap Records Collective, who issued it on vinyl for the first time to commemorate ten years since the release of this dazzling, warm and very special album. Along with ◉ **9Bach** and ◉ **Carwyn Ellis**, Georgia was heralded as an artist emerging from the folk scene in Wales, but doing something different with the music – possibly upsetting some purists along the way. Not that this mattered to Georgia, who was keen to create something new and forge her own path. Her vision paid off, the album gaining her new fans in those intrigued by her novel takes on traditional songs.

A slight change of direction followed, as Georgia aligned herself with less folky influences and moved towards more modern instruments. The results have been no less wonderful, her voice weaving a rich tapestry throughout all that she does. She duetted with James Dean Bradfield on 'Divine Youth' on ◉ **Manic Street Preachers**' *Futurology* album, her powerful but contained vocals adding a clarity to the band's Eurocentric opus.

Georgia Ruth is also a cherished radio presenter, her weekly show on BBC Radio Cymru focusing mainly on new sounds from Wales, but with an international outlook to her musical choices too.

GEORGIA RUTH
WEEK OF PINES

HYSBYSEBION
Maffia Mr. Huws
(PESDA ROC, 1983)

This self-financing four-track EP was released by Bethesda band Maffia Mr. Huws in conjunction with Bethesda's Pesda Roc festival, but the title is more than just the name of a song.

The record's artwork is made entirely of adverts (*hysbysebion*), the names of local businesses covering almost the entire cover and inner sleeve. This DIY-style way of funding the EP gives us a historical document recording which businesses existed in the town at the time. Pesda Roc co-organiser Gwynfor Dafydd organised the disc's business model, inspired by a Howdy Boys release he came across in Manchester when Maffia Mr. Huws gigged there with The Frantic Elevators (featuring a pre-Simply Red Mick Hucknall). Emyr Pierce designed the sleeve, his eldest son Cai pictured on the cover. Richard Morris produced it in his then brand-new studio in Cwmtwrch Isaf, complete with sheep wandering into the recording space. The record was mistakenly pressed as a seven-inch originally, before being released as a twelve-inch.

Maffia Mr. Huws' members also periodically played with many other bands, such as Offspring (not the American one!), Llwybr Cyhoeddus (Public Footpath), **Anhrefn** and Celt. Fellow Offspring member Les Morrison, a hugely influential and much-loved producer and studio owner in Bethesda, who nurtured several bands throughout his lifetime, would also occasionally play with the band. When Hefin Huws temporarily left in 1984, Neil Williams became the lead singer for Maffia Mr. Huws, with founding members Deiniol Morris, brothers Siôn and Gwyn Jones, and later Alan Edwards (who died in an accident in 1987 whilst on tour) making up the band.

Maffia, as they were known, were big names on the scene and won the best rock band category in both 1983 and 1984 at the hugely popular *Sgrech* Awards in Corwen – a spin-off of the magazine of the same name, which championed Welsh music. They became friends with **Geraint Jarman**, touring with him in 1986 and releasing a collaborative cassette EP, *Taith y Carcharorion* (Tour of the Prisoners).

Maffia's manager and sometime trumpet player Dafydd Rhys was also involved with *Sothach* magazine, a popular new music magazine in Welsh that gave underground bands a much-needed platform. The magazine was part of a rock journalism and information system that included *Y Sgrin Roc* on televisual information pages, an early outlier to what would become the internet. His brother Gruff Rhys was inspired by Maffia to form the band Machlud, in which he played the drums, and later Ffa Coffi Pawb and **Super Furry Animals**.

The original Pesda Roc festival happened in 1983. Brought back in 2003, it fell on the centenary of the Great Penrhyn Strike, and was headlined by a then hugely popular Super Furry Animals. A young Four Tet played, and local heroes Celt, Mim Twm Llai from Blaenau Ffestiniog and Cerys Matthews of **Catatonia** were also on the bill. Today Neuadd Ogwen is a successful independent venue and community space in the heart of Bethesda, welcoming artists such as Richard Hawley and Arrested Development to play there, and it has been hosting the Ara Deg festival since 2018. Maffia have played several more Pesda Rocs, the festival they hold so dear.

Maffia Mr. Huws released four albums and a handful of singles, their star burning brightly through the 1980s, bringing a much-needed bolt of heartfelt rock to the Welsh scene.

Maffia Mr. Huws

Pesda Roc R001   GORFFENNAF 2il 1983

HYSBYSEBION

Rhyddhawyd record gan Maffia Mr. Huws ar y cyd a Pesda Roc, gwyl roc ar faes Clwb Rygbi Bethesda, ar Orffennaf yr ail, 1983.

Noddwyd y record gan gwmniau, cymdeithasau, a mudiadau amrywiol. Prynodd bob un ohonynt ofod hysbysebu ar y clawr.

CANEUON

Y prif gan ar y sengl 12" yw 'HYSBYSEBION'. 'BYTH ETO' yw teitl yr ail gan ar yr ochr gyntaf, a 'TRI CHYNNIG I GYMRO' ac 'YR ADDEWID' yw'r ddwy ar yr ochr arall.

Y RHAI AR FAI

Gwyn Jones chwaraeodd y drymiau, a chwaraewyd y gitar fas gan Deiniol Morris sydd hefyd wedi cyfrannu i'r lleisiau cefndir ar 'Tri Chynnig i Gymro'. Hefin Huws yw'r prif leisydd, a Sion Jones chwaraeodd y gitarau, yn ogystal a chanu llais cefndir ar 'Yr Addewid', can a'i recordwyd a chyfraniad ar y blastar gan Dafydd Rhys. Cynhyrchwyd a pheirianwyd y recordiad gan Richard Morris (er Gwaethaf ymdrechion Gwyn) yn stiwdio newydd 16 trac y Bwthyn. Cynlluniwyd a chysodwyd y clawr gan Gwynfor ac Em.

DIOLCH

Dywedodd y grwp yr hoffent ddiolch i Dewi, Gwynfor, Dafydd, Ems, Christine (am y bwyd da) Nia, Tex? Nona Wyn (noson goffi),Pesda Roc, ac hefyd i bawb oedd mor garedig a noddi'r record.

Sgrech

PABELL SGRECH AR FAES YR EISTEDDFOD YN CYNNWYS ARDDANGOSFA O LUNIAU SGRECH DROS Y 5 MLYNEDD DIWETHAF. CEYSAU T A BATHODYNNAU. PENBLWYDD SGRECH YN 5 OED.
HEFYD KRIFYN ARBENNIG PENBLWYDD SGRECH AR WERTH YN Y STEDDFOD
ADLONIANT SAM — GWYLIWCH ALLAN AM Y POSTERI YN CYNNWYS MANYLION AM DDAWNSFEYDD ROC/GWERIN SAM.
MWYNHEWCH Y STEDDFOD YNG NGHWMNI SGRECH
CYLCHGRAWN POP CENEDLAETHOL CYMRU

SGRECH YN STEDDFOD LLANGEFNI '83
SESIYNNAU SGRECH
DYDD MERCHER (AWST 3ydd)
DYDD GWENER (AWST 5ed)

Gwasg Gwynedd
Argraffu a Chyhoeddi
Cibyn, Caernarfon.
Ffôn: Caernarfon 4486

SIOP ALMO
24 Hen Farchnad, Caernarfon, Gwynedd
ARGRAFFIR TRA'N DISGWYL
CLYBIAU • TAFARNDAI • MOEITHASAU • YSGOLION
ANSAWDD GORAU — GWASANAETH GORAU
Waunfawr 637 (ar ôl 6.00)
Holwch am brisiau
MAUREEN GRIFFITH

ORIEL David Windsor
Delwyr Celfyddyd Gain
Adferwyr Arluniau
Glanhau a Fframio
Hen Papiau a Phrintiau
201 Stryd Fawr, BANGOR
Bangor 4639

SATCOM
PEIRIANNWYR LLOEREN
C. GILLIAM · W.N. JONES
2, TY'N RHOS, GAERWEN,
YNYS MON - 024877-891

Disgo'r Corwynt
Ffôn Bangor 362095

Adfer
UN IAITH I'R FRO

Y DDRAIG GOCH
Esgidiau o'r ansawdd gorau
4 Stryd Porth Mawr
CAERNARFON   Ffon (0286) 2739
Scipiau   Arfon
YMGYMERIR A CHLIRIO SBWRIEL O BOB MATH, ADEILADWYR, CARTREF A DIWYDIANNOL, SCIPIAU ISEL HAWDD I'W LLWYTHO
Ffôndydd: Caernarfon 2322 Sul/nos: Llanberis 872236

Dowch am ginio, a pheint neu ddau i'r Babell Glên
Y 'COACH HOUSE'
tu ôl i'r BWL,
LLANGEFNI
12 – 2
Drama, cerddoriaeth, rifiw, a llawer mwy.

Gwasg Ffrancon
ARGRAFFWYR BETHESDA a'r CYLCH
'STAD COED PARC
BETHESDA
Ffon: Bethesda 601669

siop flodau SWAINS
Stryd Fawr, Bangor.

CAFFI'R CEI
6 Stryd Porth Mawr
Caernarfon
Croeso Cynnes bob tro.

bonwm   HON DIN E.F.

Adloniant Y CYMRO
A YDYCH CHI YN EI GAEL BOB WYTHNOS?

gwasg CARREG GWALCH
POB MATH O WAITH ARGRAFFU
CYFFREDINOL AC ARBENIGOL
AR Y PEIRIANNAU DIWEDDARAF
Hefyd nifer o lyfrau didorol ar werth a dewis helaeth o ddramau byrion —
DANFONWCH AM EIN CATALOG

TATAY
Gorky's Zygotic Mynci
(ANKST, 1994)

Gorky's Zygotic Mynci, possibly the band with the name that's caused the most head scratching in Welsh music history, met when they were students at Bro Myrddin school in Carmarthen, with siblings Euros and Megan Childs, Richard James and John Lawrence travelling from Pembrokeshire for their Welsh-language education. The band formed when the boys were just 15, their love of the music played on the John Peel programme and in their parents' collections inspiring them to create their own esoteric, hard-to-pigeonhole tunes.

The first results were two self-released cassettes, *Allumette* (Matchstick) and *Peiriant Pleser* (Pleasure Machine), with some of the songs resurfacing over the years on future albums. Nia Melville of the influential *Heno Bydd yr Adar yn Canu* (Tonight the Birds Will Sing) programme on BBC Radio Cymru invited them to the Cardiff BBC studios to record a session, a boost of encouragement for the young experimentalists from west Wales. Those at Ankst were keen listeners of the programme, and fell in love with Gorky's lawless music. The *Patio* EP came out on the label in 1993, with live recordings and selections from the cassettes made available on vinyl and CD for the first time.

Tatay was the band's first studio album – a fantastic collection of songs that really managed to capture the fledgeling Gorky's magic.

From sublime, softly sung beauties like 'O Caroline', a bilingual version of the song by Robert Wyatt – a big influence on the band – and '*Gwres Prynhawn*' (Afternoon Heat), to the downright ridiculous in '*Beth Sy'n Digwydd i'r Fuwch*' (What's Happening to the Cow) and 'When You Hear the Captain Sing', it's clear that this band is ambitious, refusing to be restrained by any musical rules, and unlike any of their contemporaries. Album closer 'Anna Apera' is a song in four parts, partly narrated by violinist Megan Childs and Euros, containing some knockout melodies and a dreamlike musical soundscape.

Alan Holmes' influence on the band is obvious on *Tatay*. A member of idiosyncratic rock band Ectogram, and previously Fflaps with vocalist Ann Matthews (both signed to the Ankst label), he is responsible for the psychedelic artwork for *Tatay*, complete with a portrait of himself in a yellow hoodie. Alan co-produced the record with the band, recorded in Gorwel Owen's Ofn Studios in Llanfaelog. The use of this studio and Alan's artwork and friendship would last for several EPs after *Tatay*.

Pentref wrth y Môr (Village by the Sea), *Llanfwrog* and *If Fingers were Xylophones* were all EPs released on Ankst before the band's second album *Bwyd Time* (Food Time), which brought them more attention. Dressed in druid costumes mid-ritual, there's a dark, haunting undertone on *Bwyd Time*, mixed with a surreal and playful energy, not least in a radio jingle-esque 45-second album opener, letting us know it's 'Bwyd Time!'

The magic of Gorky's was that they could make the offbeat and peculiar sound organic and natural, never wacky or jovial for the sake of it, and although they had plenty of influences, they sounded like no one else. Their back catalogue is remarkable, with later albums *Barafundle* and *Spanish Dance Troupe* amongst their best work.

Gorky's called it a day in 2006. Euros Childs has gone on to release a solo album every year since, and now plays with Scottish band Teenage Fanclub. Richard James released four solo albums and still records from his home in Pembrokeshire, while John Lawrence made music under the name Infinity Chimps. Their musical legacy remains, with an avid fanbase online sharing images of memorabilia and gig photos, almost as if to convince themselves that it wasn't all a wonderful dream.

gorky's zygotic mynci

TATAY

TRANSATLANTIC EXCHANGE
Paul Robeson & The Treorchy Male Voice Choir
(N.U.M., 1957)

Paul Robeson's huge voice matched his huge figure both physically and spiritually, his bass-baritone vocals enrapturing audiences in every one of his concerts film and stage productions. Born in New Jersey in 1898, Paul Robeson was an extremely charismatic figure, talented in many fields, and was undeniably a man who broke down barriers.

He won an academic scholarship and became the only African-American student at Rutgers College, where he was elected class valedictorian, as well as showing great promise playing American football.

His love of acting and singing brought him to the stage, and to London in 1928. This is where Wales and the Welsh enter Robeson's life, creating a special bond that has thrilled and fascinated audiences ever since. After performing in the West End musical *Show Boat* one evening, Robeson heard a choir of men singing on the streets. They were from the Rhondda valleys, down in London to march and protest at the hardship caused by mines closing and the poverty their families were living in. Intrigued, he joined them, sharing that famous voice of his. And so began a beautiful friendship, with Robeson soon singing in Eisteddfodau and concerts around Wales, and Wales and Robeson's stories were interlinked from then on.

In 1934 an explosion at the Gresford Colliery in Wrexham killed 266 men, prompting Robeson, then on a tour of Wales, to contribute a substantial sum of money to the miners' families.

One of Robeson's many films, *The Proud Valley*, was released in 1940 and filmed in Llantrisant and Tonyrefail. He plays a sailor arriving in Cardiff's Tiger Bay, where he soon joins a male voice choir and gets a job at the pit, the miners extending the hand of friendship to this man with the remarkable voice – something that of course had happened in real life over a decade earlier.

An engaged activist and supporter of civil rights, Robeson came under scrutiny from the McCarthy-era US authorities in the 1950s, and was refused a passport to travel outside his country. This was Wales' time to stand up for Paul, as he had done for them so many times.

The 'Let Paul Robeson Sing!' campaign gathered momentum, and the result was this hugely powerful, political record. Robeson is in New York with his wife, son and two grandchildren, unable to travel. The miners and the Treorchy Male Voice Choir are in Porthcawl at the Eisteddfod with their families and friends, hanging on Robeson's every word, coming to them via telephone from across the Atlantic.

Will Paynter, President of the South Wales Miners, begins, declaring their support for him. 'We'll Keep a Welcome in the Hillside', he says, is dedicated to Robeson. Then Robeson speaks, sending his 'Warmest greetings to the people of my beloved Wales'. He goes on, 'All the best to you, as we strive toward a world where we all can live abundant, peaceful and dignified lives,' before performing a remarkable short set of songs, including an English-language version of 'Hen Wlad fy Nhadau', simply titled 'Wales'.

The record was on Qualiton Records (though they are noted here as Cwaliton), who were based in Pontardawe, but released on behalf of the National Union of Miners, with proceeds going to the cause. **Manic Street Preachers** paid tribute to him in 'Let Robeson Sing' on their *Know Your Enemy* album, which features the miners' applause for him towards the end of the song. Robeson left a phenomenal legacy, his close ties with Wales an important part of his story.

MLP 3001

MANUFACTURED FOR
N.U.M. (SOUTH WALES AREA)
BY CWALITON RECORDS
(WALES) LTD.

TRANSATLANTIC EXCHANGE

★

Paul Robeson IN NEW YORK

THE MINERS' EISTEDDFOD AT PORTHCAWL
SATURDAY, OCTOBER 5th, 1957

PAUL ROBESON singing
DID'N MY LORD DELIVER DANIEL? · ALL THROUGH THE NIGHT
THE LITTLE LIGHT OF MINE · ALL MEN ARE BROTHERS
SCHUBERT'S LULLABY

THE TREORCHY MALE VOICE CHOIR singing
Y DELYN AUR · WE'LL KEEP A WELCOME IN THE HILLSIDE

N.U.M. | LONG PLAYING RECORD

LOST BOYS
The Flying Pickets
(10 RECORDS, 1984)

Starting with the jolly 'Remember This', a Flying Pickets original by Rick Lloyd – also a founding member of the first ever Welsh-language rock band, ○ **Y Blew** – you could be fooled into thinking that The Flying Pickets were your average barber shop quartet-style band, their a cappella voices harmonising with a joyful stride and a beaming style, maybe the odd jazz hand in the air. But wait! There was nothing average about The Flying Pickets.

The name itself was a nod to the picket lines formed around that time by striking miners and steel workers – picket lines the part-time acting members themselves had previously been a part of and knew all too well. Brought together by Ebbw Vale's Brian Hibbard, the a cappella style of his band caught the audience's imagination. The structures of the song really stand out when sung without instrumentation, the male voice choir stylings of the Valleys a possible influence on the group, shining a light on the song and also their vocal prowess.

On this debut studio album, the song choices make it obvious that The Flying Pickets had their fingers on the pulse of what was exciting musically. The cool sounds of the late Seventies and early Eighties are represented. 'Psycho Killer' by Talking Heads is a surprising song they decided to take on, turning the funky New York band's classic into something altogether more dramatic. Eurythmics' 'Who's That Girl?' is deconstructed and played up, the song possibly benefitting from the acting talents of the Pickets.

Some real classics also make the cut. Marvin Gaye's 'I Heard it Through the Grapevine' is stripped back to a chugging, lovelorn song of epic proportions. 'You've Lost That Lovin' Feeling', originally by The Righteous Brothers, is given a refresh and, as with so many of the band's covers, a new tenderness is unearthed.

Ideas of this being a novelty record or even a novelty band, however, are put to rest by the closing track, the striking 'Masters of War' by Bob Dylan. The closing lines, hoping for a man's death, imagining following his casket and making sure he is dead whilst standing at his graveside, is a sorrowful, sombre and impeccably dark closing to a strange, unique record.

The big hit on the record is a song that has followed the band around for the duration of the project. The success of 'Only You', a cover of Yazoo's song, took them into the public consciousness. Still heard often on Christmas playlists, the band's performance on *Top of the Pops* is a treat, their suits and facial hair – particularly Hibbard's famous sideburns – instantly recognisable.

Hibbard was a respected actor, who died in 2012. He starred in long-running S4C soap *Pobol y Cwm* and *Coronation Street*, as well as appearing on stage in various productions. Perhaps he is best known for his portrayal of Dai Reese in *Twin Town*, a film set in Swansea with an excellent soundtrack featuring ○ **Catatonia**, ○ **Super Furry Animals**, ○ **Manic Street Preachers** and Petula Clark's 'Downtown'. Despite his departure, The Flying Pickets have constantly welcomed new members into the line-up, and are still touring today. A band full of spirit and defiance, singing songs in their own inimitable way.

The Flying Pickets

Lost Boys

DIAL-A-POEM and CLYWCH-Y-BARDD
Various Artists
(WREN RECORDS, 1971)

In 1970 the Welsh Arts Council, keen to promote the work of young poets from Wales, committed to a novel idea for people to hear poems by emerging wordsmiths. The public would call a special number (Cardiff 45144), where a recording of a poem could be heard being recited by the poet themselves, down the phone line. It was called *Dial-a-Poem*, and proved popular, according to the sleeve notes receiving 40,282 calls during the year.

These stylish seven-inch EPs, one in Welsh and one in English, were released simultaneously. *Clywch-y-Bardd* (Hear-the-Poet) features works by the renowned poets Gerallt Lloyd Owen and Nesta Wyn Jones, with a young ◯ **Geraint Jarman** reciting his work for the first time on record. *Dial-a-Poem* features John Tripp, Sam Adams, Gwyn Williams and Gillian Clarke, all of whom became established and respected names in poetry from Wales.

The Welsh Arts Council published several records of poetry, including *Anglo-Welsh Poetry 1470–1970*, featuring Siân Phillips and Rhydwen Williams reading poems by Brenda Chamberlain, Idris Davies and Alun Lewis, amongst others.

The *Poets of Wales* series brought the works of Glyn Jones, Roland Mathias and David Jones to an audience eager to hear recitals of their work at home. *Cyfres yr Ysgol a'r Aelwyd* (the School and Home Series) on Wren Records/Recordiau'r Dryw brought the works of literary greats such as Gwenallt, Cynan, Kate Roberts and Gwyn Thomas to a new audience, with suitably psychedelic sleeve artwork befitting of the early 1970s.

Even Dafydd ap Gwilym, the great medieval poet, had his work read by a professional and packaged up as a twelve-inch record.

Several recordings of Dylan Thomas remain popular, most notably his own narration of *Under Milk Wood* and *A Child's Christmas in Wales*. More recently, a lovely seven-inch called *Under Dubwood* set Richard Burton's dulcet tones to dub music.

Poetry and rock 'n' roll have long been congenial bedfellows, of course. Twm Morys led the charge in blurring the lines between poetry and music with his band ◯ **Bob Delyn a'r Ebillion**, and more recently, Jack Jones from Swansea band Trampolene will often recite his poetry on stage in between songs. Blackwood's Patrick Jones – brother of ◯ **Manic Street Preachers**' Nicky Wire – is another poet showcased on vinyl, his latest album a collaborative one with punk musician John Robb. On BBC Radio Cymru, *Talwrn y Beirdd* travels Wales with groups of poets competing against each other to compose the sharpest, most poignant or simply most impressive poem. The more raucous Stomp is a less formal, generally more alcohol-soaked version of *Talwrn*, inspired by poetry slams. Former *Bardd Plant Cymru* (Welsh-language Children's Laureate of Wales) Casi Wyn also creates music, and Connor Allen, another former laureate, has many references to hip-hop in his thrilling work.

Dial-a-Poem and *Clywch-y-Bardd* have always fascinated me, as they were made possible by my father, the writer Meic Stephens, then the Literature Director at the Welsh Arts Council, whose specialism was writing from Wales in English. A trip to Friesland in the Netherlands inspired him to open the Oriel bookshop in Cardiff, publish these records and bring many other then radical ideas to fruition.

His and my mother's record collection is full of music and spoken word in several languages, including Breton, Gaelic, Welsh and English, and these beautifully designed spoken-word seven-inches, released on Wren Records/Recordiau'r Dryw from Llandybie, are fascinating artefacts from the era.

Dial-a... POEM

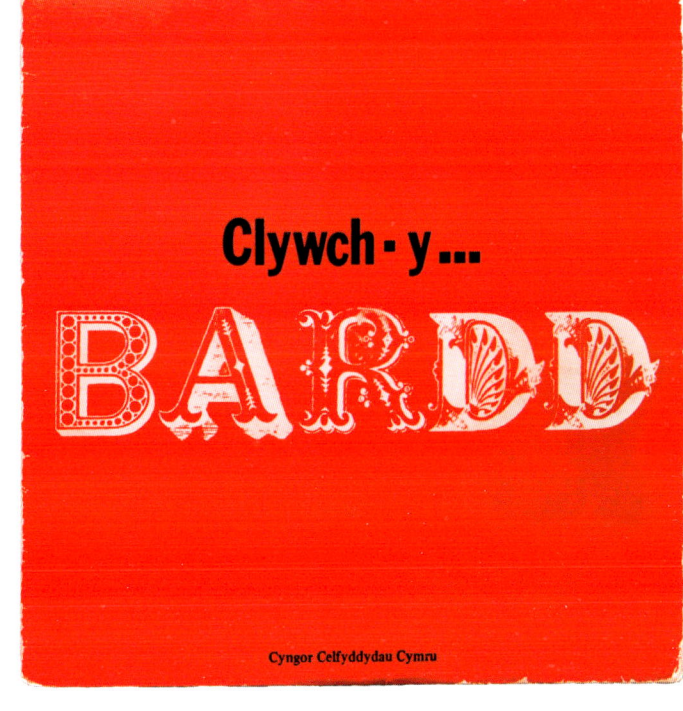

Welsh Arts Council

WRE 1110

John Tripp	Elegy for England
Tom Earley	Too Soon
Sam Adams	Onion Sellers & St. Pol de Léon
Gwyn Williams	Aspects of Now
Gillian Clarke	Blaen Cwrt
J. P. Ward	Mission Completed (Prague)

On this record you will hear some of the poems commissioned and read on the Welsh Arts Council's Dial-a-Poem service. The scheme was launched in February 1970 by the Literature Department in association with the G.P.O. Each week, on Cardiff 45144, a new poem in Welsh or English could be heard. A total of 40,282 calls were received during the year and the service proved extremely popular. A record of some of the Welsh poets who took part is also available.

JOHN TRIPP born 1927, Bargoed. Educated at Whitchurch Senior School. Worked in London for many years for the B.B.C., Indonesian Embassy and the Central Office of Information. Now lives in Cardiff where he is a free-lance writer and journalist. Has published four volumes of poetry: DIESEL TO YESTERDAY (Triskel Press 1966), THE LOSS OF ANCESTRY (Christopher Davies 1969), THE PROVINCE OF BELIEF (Christopher Davies 1971), BUTE PARK (Second Aeon 1971).

TOM EARLEY born 1911, Mountain Ash. Educated at Trinity College, Carmarthen. Now lives in London where he is a teacher of English. Has published two volumes of poetry: WELSHMEN IN BLOOMSBURY (Outposts 1966), THE SAD MOUNTAIN (Chatto & Windus 1970).

SAM ADAMS born 1934, Gilfach Goch. Read English at University College, Aberystwyth. Now lives in Monmouthshire where he is a lecturer at Caerleon College of Education. Reviews editor of POETRY WALES. Has co-edited a volume of short stories THE SHINING PYRAMID (Gwasg Gomer 1970) and a collection of essays on Welsh and Anglo-Welsh literature TRISKEL ONE (Christopher Davies 1971).

GWYN WILLIAMS born 1904, Port Talbot. Educated at Port Talbot, Aberystwyth and Oxford. Has spent most of his working life in the Near East, as Professor of English. Now lives near Aberystwyth. Has published two novels, a volume of poetry INNS OF LOVE (Christopher Davies 1970) and three volumes of translations.

GILLIAN CLARKE born 1937, Cardiff. Read English at University College, Cardiff. Still lives in Cardiff and is the Reviews editor for THE ANGLO-WELSH REVIEW. Has published a volume of poetry in the TRISKEL POETS series (Christopher Davies 1971).

J. P. WARD born 1937, Felixtowe. Went to Canada in 1952, finally going to Toronto University before returning to Cambridge and England in 1959. Now lives in Swansea where he is a lecturer in Education at University college, Swansea. In addition to writing poetry, he has contributed painting and visual poetry to various exhibitions. Has published one volume of poetry, THE OTHER MAN (Christopher Davies 1969).

This record was produced with the support of the Welsh Arts Council.

WREN RECORDS   RECORDIAU'R DRYW
Llandybie, Carms., Telephone: Llandybie 303

Printed and made by C. E. Watkins Ltd., Green Dragon Lane, Swansea.

Clywch-y... BARDD

Cyngor Celfyddydau Cymru

WRE 1111

Eirian Davies	Chi a Fi
Geraint Jarman	Pan ddaw'r Dydd
Gerallt Lloyd Owen	Etifeddiaeth
	Tir Iarll
John Hywyn	"Black Power"
Nesta Wyn Jones	Dychwelyd
Meirion Pennar	Dirfod

Ar y record hon fe glywch rai o'r cerddi a gomisiynwyd ac a ddarllenwyd ar wasanaeth Cyngor Celfyddydau Cymru, "Clywch-y-Bardd". Cychwynnwyd y cynllun ym mis Chwefror 1970, o dan ofal yr Adran Lenyddiaeth, mewn cydweithrediad â Swyddfa'r Post. Bob wythnos, ar lein Caerdydd 45144, gellid clywed cerdd newydd yn Gymraeg neu yn Saesneg. Derbyniwyd cyfanswm o 40,282 o alwadau yn ystod y flwyddyn, a bu'n wasanaeth poblogaidd dros ben. Mae record o rai o'r beirdd Eingl-Gymreig a gyfrannodd ar gael hefyd.

EIRIAN DAVIES ganed 1918, yn Nantgaredig, Sir Gaerfyrddin. Bellach yn weinidog gyda'r Presbyteriaid Cymraeg yn yr Wyddgrug. Awdur cyfrol o gerddi:- AWEN Y WAWR (Gwasg y Druid).

GERAINT JARMAN ganed 1950, yn Ninbych Myfyriwr yng Ngholeg Drama Caerdydd am gyfnod; wedi actio llawer gyda Chwmni Theatr yr Awyr Agored ym Mharc y Rhath, a chanu hefyd, gyda'r grwp pop "Bara Menyn". Ei gyfrol gyntaf yw EIRA CARIAD (Llyfrau'r Dryw).

GERALLT LLOYD OWEN O'r Sarnau, Sir Feirionydd. Am gyfnod yn athro yn Ysgol Glyndwr, yn awr, yn paratoi deunydd darllen ar gyfer plant. Enillodd gadair Eisteddfod yr Urdd yn 1962 a 1965. Cyhoeddiadau – UGAIN OED A CHERDDI ERAILL 1966, CERDDI CYWILYDD 1971.

JOHN HYWYN ganed 1947, yn Aberdaron. Trefnydd yr Urdd yn Sir Feirionydd, ar ôl blwyddyn fel athro yn y Rhondda. Cadair Eisteddfod Genedlaethol yr Urdd, 1968. Cyhoeddiadau yn "Cerddi '69", "Llên y Llannau 1969" a nifer o fân gylchgronau.

NESTA WYN JONES ganed 1946, yn Abergeirw ger Trawsfynydd. Astudiodd Gymraeg ac athroniaeth ym Mangor. Ar ôl cyfnod gyda Chwmni Theatr Cymru, nawr yn ymchwilydd ym Mangor. Buddugol yng nghystadleuaeth Cyngor Celfyddydau Cymru i feirdd ifanc ym 1969. Cyfrol o gerddi CANNWYLL YN OLAU (Gwasg Gomer 1969).

MEIRION PENNAR ganed 1944 yng Nghaerdydd. Cafodd ei addysgu yng Ngholeg y Brifysgol, Abertawe ac yna coleg yr Iesu, Rhydychen; bellach, yn darlithio yng Ngholeg y Brifysgol, Dulyn. Awdur cyfrol o gerddi:- SYNDOD Y SÊR (Llyfrau'r Dryw 1971).

Cynhyrchwyd y record hon gyda chymorth Cyngor Celfyddydau Cymru.

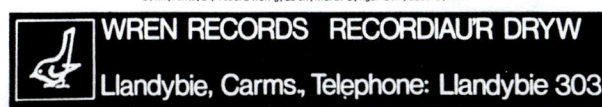

WREN RECORDS   RECORDIAU'R DRYW
Llandybie, Carms., Telephone: Llandybie 303

Printed and made by C. E. Watkins Ltd., Green Dragon Lane, Swansea.

DUBNOBASSWITHMYHEADMAN
Underworld
(JUNIOR BOY'S OWN, 1994)

Search the internet for evidence of pre-Underworld music from its founding members Karl Hyde and Rick Smith, and you'll find their second project Freur playing on stages, including one in an HTV Wales TV studio introduced by Caryl Parry Jones (of ⦿ Bando). Freur's biggest hit was the unusual sounding 'Doot-Doot', from the album of the same name in 1983. Early indications of Underworld's warm, textured electronic sensibilities can be heard here, mixed with the New Romanticism of the early 1980s and the minimalism of Krautrock. But Freur weren't to last, with Hyde and Smith's greatest musical project yet to come.

They met having both moved to Cardiff to study. Inspired by the city's clubs, art scene and affordability in the early Eighties, hanging out in Chapter Arts Centre and Howard Gardens gave the duo the sense of community and experimental drive that would take them and their music around the world.

Technically their third long player, 1994's *Dubnobasswithmyheadman* is an album that twists and turns, blending light and shade to create an evocative and thrilling listen. It was released on Junior Boy's Own Records – a dance label born out of a fanzine, which captured the spirit of illegal raves and DIY club culture perfectly, and where they were labelmates with The Chemical Brothers. With Darren Emerson having joined the band, all elements of club music are here, from throbbing techno to playful house, glimmers of sparkling sunshine bursting through dense clouds.

From the anticipation of a beat dropping to the submergence of getting lost in a wall of blissful sounds, it works as a headphone record with nuances and intricacies as effective as the record's mass dancefloor appeal. The single 'Cowgirl' captures their sound perfectly, with Hyde's repeating of the 'Everything, everything' lyric matched with a brooding, simple melody and a frenzied breakdown – the perfect hook to reel in curious dance music fans.

Later, Darren Emerson would depart the band, leaving the two-piece to create even more successful and engaging electronic music albums. *Barbara Barbara, We Face a Shining Future* and *A Hundred Days Off* would sit as some of their finest work, blurring the lines between hedonistic rave music and headphone cult classics.

Rick Smith was born in Ammanford and worked in a bank before moving to Cardiff, meeting Karl Hyde and forming The Screen Gemz, their pre-Freur band. It was the perfect meeting of minds. Karl emerged as one of the great dance music frontmen with his twisting and writhing and frantic, pulsating moves effortlessly in time to the music, and he was the perfect accompaniment to Smith's shyer, more reserved nature.

Karl's love for Wales takes him to remote parts of the country for new ideas. Wales remains an important source of inspiration for Underworld, as does Essex, which Karl beautifully documented in his book *I am Dogboy: The Underworld Diaries* in 2016. I've often thought of Karl's lyrics as works of art, cryptic and mysterious, striking in their starkness. This is a constant in their music, his vocals weaving their way through Rick's rich, beautiful beats.

The inclusion of their song 'Born Slippy .NUXX' on the *Trainspotting* soundtrack in 1996 brought Underworld to a whole new mainstream, global audience. A favourite on dancefloors, radio and forever synonymous with the hedonism of the late Nineties, it remains a captivating live favourite. Underworld's performances have become unifying, memorable events, with fans coming together to get lost in their mesmerising music, Rick lost behind rows of samplers, synths and sequencers, and Karl up front like a man possessed.

Latterly, Underworld remain a powerful creative force. Playing live shows around the world, they are still one of the most revered live electronic music acts. Their *Drift Series* ensured that their new songs could be released regularly and independently without the time or label constraints of traditionally released albums.

dubnobasswithmyheadman
underworld
naked
and angel
for a perfectstar
she was beautiful god
she was beautiful god
she was beautiful god
and in walks this girl
real lolita
just groan chemical
derail me every time.
of bass m.e.
dubnobasswithmyheadman
underworld
dubnobasswithmyheadman

SURROUNDED BY TIME
Tom Jones
(EMI, 2021)

Tom the Voice.

A nickname that big doesn't come to you lightly.

Since he found fame in the 1960s, Tom Jones – born Thomas Jones Woodward in Trefforest, near Pontypridd – has achieved what most popular singers can only dream of, from touring to collaborating, working with idols, hosting hugely popular entertainment shows, tasting success globally and becoming a true icon in his field. A huge fan of music and those who sing the songs, he has reinvented the public's perception of him several times, whilst remaining true to his roots and the music he holds so dear. His success has been unparalleled – his name synonymous with Wales, his big hits heard the world over.

After fronting Tommy Scott & The Senators in the clubs of south Wales, he was spotted by Trealaw musician turned manager and songwriter Gordon Mills, who suggested a name change. Tommy Scott and The Squires made the move to London, but it was a solo and newly named Tom Jones who signed the deal with Decca Records. Countless hit singles followed, from 1965's number 1 'It's Not Unusual' to 1988's 'Kiss', a cover of the Prince song.

His 1999 album of covers, *Reload*, which saw him collaborating with his friends ◯ **Stereophonics**, James Dean Bradfield, Cerys Matthews, Van Morrison, Pretenders and more, brought him to a new, younger audience, as did 2002's *Mr Jones*, with Fugees' Wyclef Jean on writing duties. But by 2010, it was time for the next phase in Tom's musical story. For his 38th studio album, he teamed up with producer Ethan Johns at the Real World Studios near Bath, and took it back to the songs of his youth. *Praise & Blame* was a collection of songs Tom admired: some he'd sung in chapel in Trefforest, others gospel numbers he'd admired as a young man. Sister Rosetta Tharpe's 'Strange Things' and the traditional song 'Didn't It Rain' brought the stomping blues to Tom's live shows, while 'Nobody's Fault But Mine' and Bob Dylan's 'What Good Am I?' showed Tom in a reflective mood. It was a winning combination and the album was critically acclaimed and well received by the public, with Tom commenting in his autobiography that it changed his life.

After two further albums with Ethan Johns at the controls, the partnership continued on *Surrounded by Time*, recorded partly at Monnow Valley Studio, next to Rockfield near Monmouth, and partly at Real World. An album of interpretations of songs that Tom had a deep affinity for, it again shows him in contemplative mode. 'I Won't Crumble with You If You Fall' sets the tone for this masterful record, recorded shortly after his wife died. The album's centrepiece is its first single, 'Talking Reality Television Blues', originally a country song by Todd Sneider. Tom's version is perhaps the most surprising-sounding record he's made. It's a dense, twisting, menacing track which, at six and a half minutes long, is unlike anything he's recorded previously. 'I'm Growing Old' was given to Tom by Bobby Cole when Tom was in his early thirties and kept until an apt time came to record it, and the resulting recording is nothing short of spine-tingling.

But for me the stand-out track from these sessions appeared on the extended version of this album, the Hourglass Edition of *Surrounded by Time*. 'One Hell of a Life' is a song by Welsh-Breton artist ◯ **Katell Keineg**. Sung by Tom Jones, the lyrics take on a new poignancy as he sings the words of sorrow, of regret and of looking back at One Hell of a Life.

Tom Jones Surrounded By Time

TINCIAN
9Bach
(REAL WORLD RECORDS, 2014)

Singer and actress Lisa Jên met Martin Hoyland, a former member of rock band Pusherman, in London through mutual friends. Soon they would set up home in Lisa's hometown of Bethesda, the slate quarry town in Gwynedd, near Bangor. The town, also known as Pesda, has a rich cultural history, and is steeped in the Welsh language, Lisa's mother tongue.

The meaning of 9Bach's name is slightly ambiguous, with '9' pronounced the same way as *nain*, a word for 'grandmother' in Welsh. The literal translation of *bach* is 'small', and brought together, *nain bach* can be a term of endearment. So a love of words and of a play between meanings in Welsh and English is characteristic of the band.

Lisa's Bethesda roots play an important part in the band's music and vision. She has often spoken about tensions between local and international affairs that affect each other, how communities at home and worldwide are under immense social pressures, and how a sense of pride in her roots coupled with an eagerness to look outward are important to her.

The album's release through Real World Records, the label set up by musician Peter Gabriel, meant that these songs would be heard by ears which might previously have missed a Welsh-language band. Welsh folk music had come of age, with the work of Trac – the folk development agency for Wales' traditional music – and several other organisations and individuals having come to fruition. Welsh folk music could be brave, forward-thinking and experimental, yet remain true to the original songs. Welsh artists would look beyond Wales for collaborative projects, such as 9Bach working with Australia's Black Arm Band collective. ◯ **The Gentle Good**'s Khasi-Cymru collaboration with north-east Indian musicians and his *Bardd Anfarwol* album with Chinese musicians, and Cerys Hafana's progressive harp playing would keep the Welsh traditional music flame alive, whilst being unafraid to bring in musical elements not always within the Welsh trad world. This might upset some purists, but it would excite a lot more who are unafraid of breaking the 'rules', or maybe even unaware that rules exist within the tradition.

Loops and intricate playing mix to create an otherworldly atmosphere on *Tincian*. Côr y Penrhyn contribute their stunning vocals to '*Ffarwel*' (Farewell) – the choir tracing its roots back to the 1880s, when small choral groups which had formed on the galleries in the famous Penrhyn slate quarry united to form one choir. The influence of slate mining and the stunning surroundings of the quarry can be heard throughout *Tincian*, an intimate and moving album. The closing song is '*Asteri Mou*' (My Star), sung in Greek: the language of Lisa's father's family. A beguiling remix by Gruff Rhys – a long-time collaborator of Lisa Jên's – appeared on an EP by the band, testament to their willingness to shake things up and look to the future whilst respecting and recognising the past that got them here.

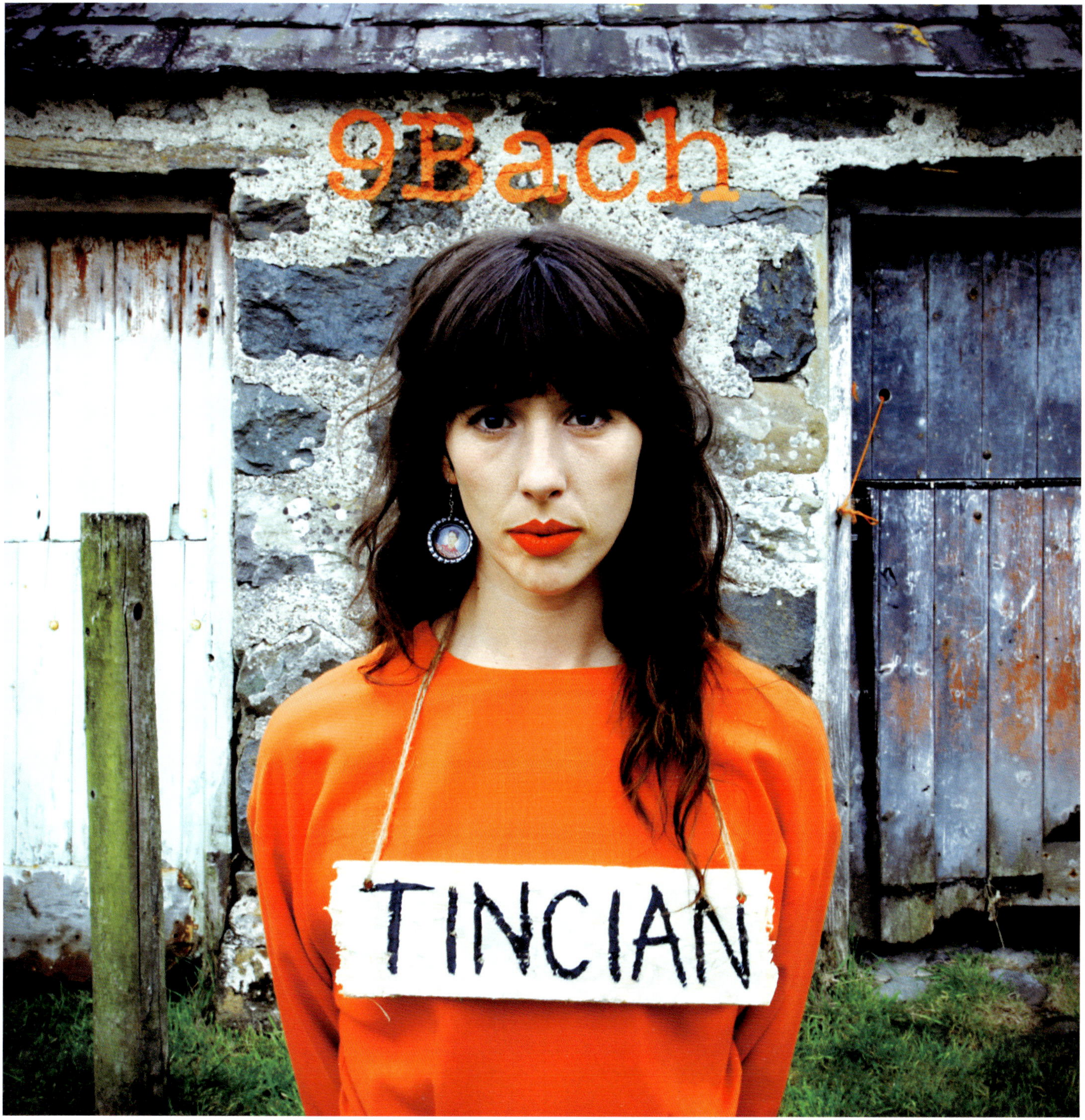
9Bach
TINCIAN

THE GOWER NIGHTINGALE
Phil Tanner
(VETERAN TAPES, 2003)

The Gower Nightingale. It conjures up many images, but it was singer Phil Tanner who earned the name.

Born in 1862 in Llangennith on the western edge of the Gower Peninsula, Phil Tanner was born into a family of weavers, when Gower had many mills. His adoption of the Gower dialect was inevitable: it was in his blood; and his singing of folk tales sung in and around the Gower made him stand out. He became known as one of the most highly regarded British folk singers, his English style of singing a delight to those that heard his charming renditions.

The English Folk Dance and Song Society released his singing, as did Columbia and Folktracks Records. This compilation was released by Veteran Tapes, and includes a BBC documentary on Tanner by Wynford Vaughan-Thomas from a series called *Amiable Eccentrics*, which celebrated Tanner's life and legacy. Its full title is *Ballads, Songs and Mouth Music from South Glamorgan recorded in the 1930s & 40s*.

In the archive of St Fagans National Museum of History there are plenty of examples of this kind of singing: songs passed on from generation to generation all around Wales, performed in front of fires in houses and pubs, barns and streets, long before the mass commercialisation of the recorded voice. Roy Saer began working there as a research assistant in 1963, collecting and studying Welsh folk songs for future generations to discover and enjoy. His work, and that of several others there, is regarded as highly important, and Saer became a scholar on the history of the Welsh folk song.

Cerys Matthews included Tanner on her excellent *Ultimate Guide to Welsh Folk*, alongside a who's who of singers from Wales who made huge contribution to the cultural and musical life of their locality and country as a whole.

Luckily for us, Phil Tanner's distinctive voice was recorded and has endured to this day – a glimpse of Pembrokeshire past, there for future generations to hear and learn from.

JOEY RAMONEY
Helen Love
(DAMAGED GOODS, 1993)

Dayglow luminous indie-pop never sounded so vibrant, essential and so much fun as it did when Helen Love decided to emerge from the Welsh underground in 1992. Formed in Cardiff before relocating to Swansea, they are anomalies in the indie music scene, mostly unknown but adored by those enamoured with their thrilling lyrics and unashamedly pop melodies.

The long-haired New York punk rocker is the subject of this 1993 single, released on cult label Damaged Goods, also responsible for an early ⊙ **Manic Street Preachers** single. Another single, 'Debbie Loves Joey' is an homage to young love – and in turn to Debbie Harry, lead singer of Blondie, and Joey Ramone, lead singer of the Ramones.

But this wasn't a one-way love affair, as Joey declared himself a fan of Helen Love's music, later duetting with them on the song 'Punk Boy', and introducing their BBC Radio 1 session for Steve Lamacq's *Evening Session* in 1998.

Live Helen Love performances might be rare, but a dedicated fanbase make sure they are warmly received every time they do decide to play onstage. Although notoriously mysterious and uninterested in any sort of limelight, radio sessions for Peel and Lamacq brought them to a bigger audience in the 1990s. The patronage of presenter Adam Walton on his legendary BBC Radio Wales show has been long-running, with Adam calling them 'the best thing to come out of Swansea since ⊙ **Badfinger**, so therefore The Greatest Welsh Band of my period in office.'

Rock 'n' roll good times do make way for the realities of life, as 'Clearing Out Mum's House' on their 2022 album *This is My World* perfectly demonstrates – an honest and poignant song that swirls with keys and emotions. But they're guaranteed to bring a smile with their infectious tunes.

The Gower Nightingale

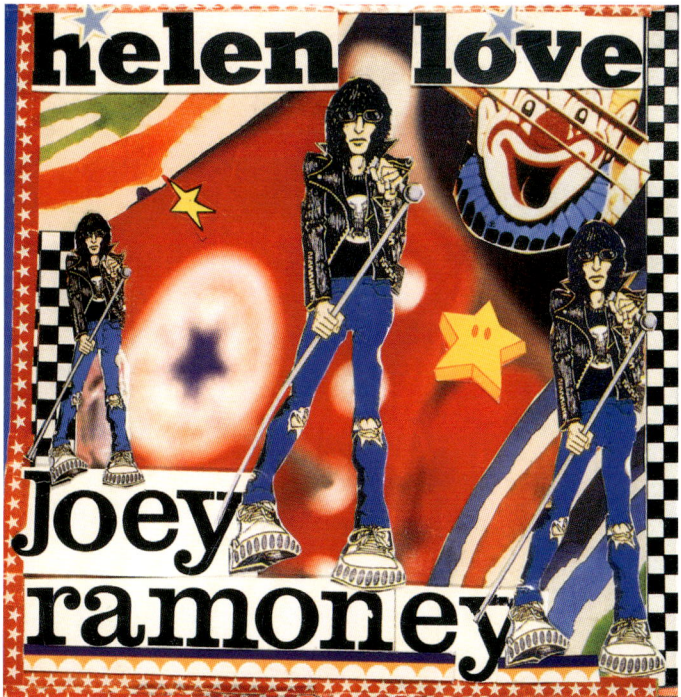

ballads, songs and mouth music
from South Glamorgan
recorded in the 1930s & 40s

Phil Tanner

with an introduction by
Wynford Vaughan Thomas

VT145CD

helen love
joey ramoney

GREATEST HITS
Goldie Lookin Chain
(ATLANTIC, 2004)

It's a brave band who call their first nationally released album *Greatest Hits*.

Knowingly childish, constantly swearing and featuring some of the most in-jokes on record, this is a document of a strange time in music history. The early Noughties saw a crew of Newport friends break through into the mainstream, causing confusion, mayhem and delight in equal measure. 'You Knows It' became one of the most popular phrases of the time, purely thanks to Goldie Lookin Chain, a crew of men who wore gold-looking chains everywhere they went.

When performing live, the Goldie Lookin Chain experience can be somewhat chaotic – the members, and occasionally additional friends also wearing full tracksuits, continually moving around on stage, each member working their way to the front if it's their time to rap. At festivals, including a main-stage slot at Reading in 2005, they would play to some devoted fans, but mostly bewildered punters awaiting that evening's headliners. It would be hard not to be amused by what GLC stood for, however.

Although a left-field, niche idea on paper, the reality was very different. Once signed to the major label Atlantic, you could hear these Newport rappers on daytime BBC Radio 1, making the playlist with several of their surreal singles, like 'Half Man Half Machine' and 'Guns Don't Kill People, Rappers Do'. It should be said that not many, if any, rap records from Wales made it to these playlists prior to Goldie Lookin Chain's unlikely rise to fame. Some would feel it a shame that it was a comedic take on Welsh culture that was embraced by a wider audience, while others felt that GLC were doing something distinctively Welsh and true to themselves: the sound of their immediate environment in Newport.

As reality television boomed, the public became used to seeing themselves reflected in the arts, and GLC's success was possibly a by-product of this. Hip-hop culture, which had been around for nearly three decades, wasn't just the preserve of professional rappers – anyone could have a go. It really shouldn't work, but somehow it did. Led by P. Xain (Rhys) and Billy Webb, Eggsy and Mike Balls, Adam Hussain and 2Hats, puns and slang are present throughout this silly, tongue-firmly-in-cheek album that deals with drugs and boredom in equal measure. On 'The Maggot', we get to know the tallest member of the band, a sort of Fagin figure who delights in stealing your possessions. There are slower moments too, 'You Knows I Love You' chosen as a single from the album to show the band's romantic side.

What started as a joke between friends caught music fans' imaginations, on a scale that even the GLC members themselves found surprising. They took the life they truly knew in Newport, warts and all, to an audience who hadn't heard it represented on record before. Years later they are still making music, self-releasing albums and videos and playing on the live circuit. In 2024 they embarked on the *420 Tour*, celebrating 20 years of the band with 20 shows, playing 20 songs for a £20 ticket. They're still enjoying every minute of rapping their lyrics to fans of the weird and wonderful.

goldie lookin chain
greatest hits

MAE 'NA OLAU
Pedair
(SAIN, 2022)

Pedair is the feminine version of the Welsh word for 'four', the perfect name for this remarkable four-piece.

Gwenan Gibbard, Gwyneth Glyn, Meinir Gwilym and Siân James are the four voices here, each with their own remarkable back catalogue of music.

Showing promise as a multi-instrumentalist, Siân James from Llanerfyl studied music at Bangor University, formed the folk-rock band Bwchadanas, and went on to release nine solo studio albums. She also collaborated with Rhys Mwyn of ◉ **Anhrefn** on the 1995 album *Hen Wlad fy Mamau* (Land of My Mothers), which blended drum and bass with traditional sounds.

Gwyneth Glyn from Llanarmon is also a successful solo artist, with four albums released and a number of books for adults and children. Her song '*Adra*' (Home) was a big hit in the Welsh-speaking world, and she sang it at the funeral of one of Wales' most-loved rugby players, the late Ray Gravell, who, it is said, was moved to tears whenever he heard it.

Meinir Gwilym from Llangristiolus found fame in the early Noughties with her EP *Smôcs, Coffi a Fodca Rhad* (Smokes, Coffee and Cheap Vodka), which she recently revisited for its 20th anniversary. It won fans with its account of what it was like to be young, skint and Welsh, bridging the gap between young and older audiences. Meinir is also a popular television presenter, appearing on gardening programmes.

Gwenan Gibbard from Pwllheli is an expert on *Cerdd Dant*, a specifically Welsh form of music where the words are sung over a harp melody. She has won the main prizes for the harp and singing at the National Eisteddfod, and she specializes in breathing new life into this ancient tradition. Studying the ◉ **Meredydd Evans** and Phyllis Kinney archive for inspiration for her latest solo album, her reinterpretations of old Welsh songs bring them to life, thrilling those hearing the songs for the first time. She is also Artistic Director of Sain Records, on which she releases her music.

By joining forces and therefore bringing their deep knowledge and respect for Welsh traditions together, they are reminding themselves of each other's strengths and bringing different perspectives to the songs featured here. '*Dawns y Delyn*' (Harp Dance) celebrates the harp, an instrument close to their hearts. '*Teg Oedd yr Awel*' (The Wind Was Fair) is a sea shanty, reimagined from the J Glyn Davies collection, while '*Philomela*' brings to life tales of the Greek gods. The four voices blend beautifully, with humour and fun intertwining with sorrow and sadness.

Welsh folk and traditional music has enjoyed a renaissance since the early 2000s, and this album is a perfect introduction to a part of Welsh music history, delivered by four supremely talented keepers of the flame who live and breathe the art form.

pedair

mae 'na olau

SHABOO STRIKES BACK
Don Leisure
(FIRST WORD RECORDS, 2022)

With his friend Earl Jeffers, Don Leisure made music as Darkhouse Family, thrilling audiences with their soulful, masterful jazz-influenced music. As Don Leisure he has delved deeper into his passions, creating sonic soundscapes that bring his obsessions and ideas to life in the most beautiful fashion.

Born Aly Jamal in Aberdare before moving and settling in Cardiff, Don Leisure is one of the most fascinating and enigmatic producers to have emerged from Wales in recent years.

Shaboo Strikes Back is a 25-track album which has the feel of a mixtape. Tracks are presented here as mini nuggets of musical brilliance: a loop, a beat or a theme tune turned into a short, sharp sonic delight. This style, preferred by beatmakers as a way to make a continually flowing record that showcases beats and ideas without committing to a full conventional song, owes a lot to the Detroit musician J Dilla, who sadly passed away in 2006, aged 32. A hugely influential producer in life and untimely death, J Dilla's unusual time structure in music had a remarkably wide-ranging influence on popular music, still felt today. *Shaboo Strikes Back* can sit next to Dilla's seminal *Donuts* album quite comfortably, both records the sound of young producers keen to cultivate something radical and brilliant from the vaults. On *Shaboo Strikes Back*, Asian beats sit side by side with hip-hop, synths and sequencers make way for reggae grooves, while entertaining radio infomercials or jingles – an audio genre much loved by producers over the years – are peppered throughout the album. The beats here take a side step, they twist and turn, finding their own rhythm from track to track. And yet there's nothing disconcerting about *Shaboo Strikes Back*: it's an album that flows naturally and organically, creating its own sonic universe as it goes.

Multi-instrumentalist Davey Newington from the excellent Cardiff band Boy Azooga joins Don Leisure on drums for 'The Balcony', while acclaimed LA-based free-jazz musician and educator Angel Bat Dawid plays some magical swirling harp on 'All Praises Due'.

Like so many other cratediggers, Jamal became obsessed with the back catalogue of Sain Records, becoming friends with Gruff Rhys and Andy Votel and often DJing with them, swapping rare records as they searched for that elusive beat or sample. Gruff sings on 'Neon Drizzle (Hotel Shaboo)', a play on words and a nod to Gruff's own *Hotel Shampoo* album from 2011. Don Leisure in turn remixed Gruff's track 'Loan Your Loneliness', from his album *Seeking New Gods*.

Don Leisure's 2017 precursor to this album, simply titled *Shaboo*, was a similarly themed record, drenched in delicious samples and a myriad of looped beats. A tribute to Don Leisure's late uncle, Bollywood actor Nasser 'Shaboo' Bharwani (who features in the artwork for both records), both albums are musical journeys that are personal tributes to a much-missed family member.

Released on First Word Records, *Shaboo Strikes Back* became a favourite with leftfield DJs and producers around the world, gaining airplay on specialist radio stations including Gilles Peterson's Worldwide FM, LA-based KCRW, and BBC Radio 6 Music, where Lauren Laverne named it one of her favourites of the year.

Don Leisure collaborated in 2023 with Welsh harpist Amanda Whiting on a beautiful record called *Beyond the Midnight Sun*. He also began working on a beat tape made up of samples frrom the extensive Sain back catalogue from their Llandwrog studios – a space used by working musicians today, as well as a treasure trove of the label's history.

MUSIC:
DON LEISURE

SHABOO STRIKES BACK!

STEREO TOTAL

TAKE ONE!
Shakin' Stevens
(EPIC, 1980)

When Shakin' Stevens was declared the winner of a BBC Radio Wales poll in 2015 to find Wales' Greatest Living Voice, it might have surprised a few to see the singer take the top spot ahead of Bryn Terfel, **Shirley Bassey** and **Tom Jones**. It wasn't a surprise to the Shakin' Stevens fan club, who voted for him in their thousands – their hero where he belonged, top of the charts once again. Shaky has achieved more number one singles than any other Welsh artist or band, and was the UK's biggest-selling singles act of the 1980s, ahead of the likes of Madonna.

Take One! was the first album released after Shaky signed to Epic Records in 1978. Centred around the hit single 'Hot Dog', it came out almost a decade after Shaky had started to release albums, and two years after going solo. There are some brilliant musicians joining him here, with pedal steel guitar from London's acclaimed B J Cole and piano from Geraint Watkins of Abertridwr, an in-demand musician who has played with Paul McCartney, Nick Lowe and Dave Edmunds, amongst others.

Stevens was born Michael Barratt and grew up in the Ely area of Cardiff, the youngest of 13 brothers and sisters. In a noisy household he fell in love with rock 'n' roll, and caught the bug for singing it live. Spotted by music manager Paul Barrett (father of acclaimed drum 'n' bass producer Lincoln Barrett, aka **High Contrast**) when singing with The Denims, Michael Barratt would soon be fronting Shakin' Stevens and The Sunsets; a band name he had coveted as a young boy playing in the streets of Ely.

Released in the same year as seminal new wave albums by Visage and OMD, *Take One!* is an unashamed rock 'n' roll record, aimed at the fanbase that Shaky had been cultivating. As success looked set to come his way, there was no chance of turning his back on a musical style that gave him great pleasure, a genre embedded in his DNA since he had started singing. Sticking to his musical guns for several decades since then, his hard work has made him one of the most evergreen singers in Britain today.

Could 'Is a Bluebird Blue?' be a nod to his love for Cardiff City Football Club? I like to think so. As with Tom Jones, his knowledge and love of great rock 'n' roll ballads and his way of making them his own are the keys to his success. Full of tracks penned by American songwriters including Buck Owens and Tennessee Ernie Ford, and the Buddy Holly song 'I Guess I Was a Fool', this album was a sign of things to come in the story of Shaky.

More big hits would soon follow, among them 'Green Door', released in 1981, and 1985's 'Merry Christmas Everyone' – produced by fellow Cardiff musician Dave Edmunds and still a recurrent favourite come December time. Several 'best of' compilations and themed albums have been released over the decades, concentrating on his love of blues and country music. His most recent albums, *Echoes of Our Times* and *Re-Set*, have received some of the best reviews of his career and attracted a new audience, while retaining his loyal fanbase. Shaky remains popular on the international and UK touring circuits, securing return gigs in his home city of Cardiff. These are jubilant, celebratory nights, his fans happy to welcome home one of the city's most truly popular sons.

SHAKIN' STEVENS take one!

stereo

SHAKIN' STEVENS take one!

WYAU
Datblygu
(RECORDIAU ANHREFN, 1988)

When David R Edwards died in 2021, Wales lost an important and unique lyricist.

Born in Cardigan in 1964, disillusioned by school and inspired by local band ○ **Ail Symudiad** and electro musician Malcolm Neon, he soon started recording his fascinating lyrics with friend T Wyn Davies, and Datblygu was born. Later Patricia Morgan also became a long-serving member of the band. An array of musicians and producers, most notably Gorwel Owen, joined them at various times across their musical life, releasing their music on the seminal Ankst label following a few early appearances on Casetiau Neon, Ofn and Recordiau Anhrefn.

David's lyrics speak for themselves: a disaffection with the Wales of the time, a hatred of the middle classes, his anger at what he saw as hypocrisy in several areas of Wales. But scattered throughout Datblygu's back catalogue there are occasional rays of sunshine. A light-hearted lyric sitting next to a deep thought, a pun that David knew was so good he sounds gleeful in spitting out the words. '*Y Teimlad*' (The Feeling), later covered by ○ **Super Furry Animals**, remains one of the sweetest love songs on tape, and is a highlight of the Furries' *Mwng* album.

On this, Datblygu's debut album proper, album opener '*Gwlad ar fy Nghefn*' (Country on my Back), David sings, '*Byw yng Nghymru; ru'n peth a syllu ar y paent yn sychu, ar y gwair yn tyfu lan. Tyfwch lan.*' (Living in Wales is the same as watching paint dry, or grass grow. Grow up.) '○ *Dafydd Iwan yn y Glaw*' finds David observing the folk singer and political activist sitting in the Plaid Cymru stall at an Eisteddfod, the rain dripping through the roof onto his head. The calmest song here is '23', which sees David reflecting on turning the grand old age, whilst angrier moments come in '*Fanzine Ynfytyn*' (Idiot Fanzine), which repeats the title more than once – a David R Edwards speciality on many of his records.

Patricia Morgan's minimal electronics chimed with experimental music fans the world over, her beats and rhythms the driving force for David's lyrics. If his words were intriguing for those not fluent in Welsh, Patricia's music was the international sound that made Datblygu cross so many borders. She was born in a vicarage in Llandybie, and in her teens was in Y Cymylau (The Clouds), a traditional-sounding band who sang pretty songs, but everything changed when she heard Datblygu. She fell for the music so hard she eventually joined the band for their most prolific era. Later, as David's ill health meant less music from Datblygu, Patricia would work with harpist Rhodri Davies on a musical project, and record as Canolfan Hamdden (Leisure Centre) with ○ **Gwenno** Saunders and Jakokoyak (Rhys Edwards), making music with a thriving Welsh underground she had helped shape and create.

In 2020, she and David surprised the world with a final album, the well-received *Cwm Gwagle*, released on Ankstmusik. A retrospective compilation featuring 60 tracks from bedroom demos to their most well-known songs, *Terfysgiaith 1982–2022*, was released after David's death. His lifetime work was prolific, only singing in English in his later years.

Datblygu's patronage from John Peel not only brought their music to an international audience, but made those in Wales who previously just didn't get it pay attention. David was hellbent on singing the truth, on never conforming, on truly following his own map. He did so throughout his life, refusing to play anyone's games, and creating a musical legacy that is truly remarkable.

DATBLYGU

WYAU

NO DICE
Badfinger
(APPLE RECORDS, 1970)

Few bands from Wales have reached as mythical a status as Swansea's Badfinger.

Previously working as The Iveys, the band had changed their name to Badfinger and released their *Magic Christian Music* album in 1970. They became the first band signed to The Beatles' Apple label, and success came fast, with that debut album selling well and creating a big hit in the Paul McCartney-penned single 'Come and Get It'. The association with The Beatles would last long after the relationship with Apple ended, the press continuing to compare them to the Fab Four thanks to their own remarkable songwriting skills and powerful harmonies. Paul McCartney studio produced them, and was a fan of their composing and sound.

'No Matter What', 'I Can't Take It' and 'Love Me Do' (not that one), are power-pop highlights on *No Dice*, a glimpse into the driving guitar sound that took Badfinger on countless tours, particularly across north America. The sixth song on *No Dice* turned out to be one of the most powerful, forlorn and heartfelt love songs of all time. 'Without You' was initially dismissed by the band members as a little too soft for them to really push and release as a single. American singer Harry Nilsson had different ideas when he heard the song, and released his own version in 1972. It became a multi-million-selling hit, with Mariah Carey's version becoming an even bigger smash for the soul singer in the early 1990s.

For the *No Dice* album, new member Joey Molland had joined the band – he is now the only surviving member from the original Badfinger line-up. The band's story is a turbulent one, with lawsuits and money matters engulfing them in complicated and long-lasting legal wrangling. Singer and guitarist Pete Ham and later bassist Tom Evans would both end their own lives due to the fallout of the issues surrounding the band.

A blue plaque has been put up in Swansea for Ham, a wonderful and gifted songwriter. There is also a plaque for Ham and the band in Swansea train station, placed not far from where The Iveys would rehearse in their early days, on Ivey Place, the street they named themselves after. It was unveiled by his daughter, born a month after he died in 1975, on what would have been his 66th birthday in 2013. The plaques serve as a reminder of Badfinger's music, which is still being discovered by music fans today. James Dean Bradfield of **Manic Street Preachers** is a big fan, and told *The Guardian* in 2014, 'If you delve into their back catalogue, there are songs that are masterclasses in empathy and full of the most beautiful, human, plaintive tones.'

Their song 'Baby Blue' was used in the final scene of popular drama series *Breaking Bad*, with Vince Gilligan (the cult series' creator) insisting on using the powerful, beautiful track in the closing scenes to devastating effect, bringing a new generation of fans into Badfinger's rich world. Their story is undoubtedly a tragic one, but Badfinger's music has stood the test of time, with *No Dice* rightly considered a classic album.

NO DICE
BADFINGER

THE BELLS OF RHYMNEY
The Byrds
(COLUMBIA, 1965)

Idris Davies was born in Rhymney in 1905, and made his name writing about the coal faces surrounding him, mining disasters, strikes and World War II. *Gwalia Deserta* was his first published collection of work, and included 'Bells of Rhymney', the poem he is best known for. T S Eliot and Dylan Thomas were admirers of his work, and it was thanks to the famous Swansea poet that folk singer Pete Seeger found Idris Davies' words. Published shortly after Thomas' death, radio transcripts of Dylan Thomas heaping praise on 'Bells of Rhymney' brought the poem notoriety. Thomas called it 'one very simple and moving song'. When Seeger read the words, he fell in love with them and turned them into this piece.

Based on the rhythm of well-known nursery rhyme 'Oranges and Lemons', Idris' words are from the viewpoint of the bells of Welsh towns, each couplet bringing its viewpoint alive.

In Seeger's version of the song, Rhymney is mostly pronounced correctly, in a sparse, thoughtful version that lets Davies' words breathe, with Seeger's guitar playing only erupting towards the end of the recording.

Seeger's popularity took the song to many ears, and other artists would include their own versions in their sets, bringing the tale of Wales to a huge audience.

Bursting from the café-culture folk scene, The Byrds were a remarkable band that formed in 1964. They took 'The Bells of Rhymney' to the next level, including the song in their live set and on their debut album, *Mr Tambourine Man*. Their pronunciation of Rhymney would set the precedent for future versions – 'Rimney', as opposed to 'Rhumney', the natural pronunciation in Wales. As the popularity of recorded music soared, it meant even more would hear the song, and subsequent versions stuck to The Byrds' take on the place name – though Merthyr, Blaina, Cardiff and even the Rhondda mostly escaped a Byrds revision of their names.

It's a remarkable poem and song: a real celebration of Welsh place names from Cardiff to the Wye, bringing the history of Newport and the Rhondda – amongst other locations in Wales – alive with just one short line each.

As the folk-rock boom continued, other artists covered this well-travelled song. There is a jangly version by Cher on her debut album *All I Really Want to Do* from 1965, which closes with 'Blowin' in the Wind'. Bob Dylan himself recorded a version of 'The Bells of Rhymney', with The Band in 1967, as did Dylan's son Jakob with Beck in the 2019 documentary *Echo in the Canyon*. Welsh rock band ◍ **The Alarm** have a thoughtful version too, the song fitting perfectly with Mike Peters' love of Wales and understanding of its intricate politics.

Whilst 'Green, Green Grass of Home' is an American song that has often been taken to be from Wales, these are lyrics from Wales that most have heard through American voices, their tale an internationalist one that many have connected with.

THE BYRDS
Chimes Of Freedom
The Bells Of Rhymney

COLUMBIA

S 160
PV 72861

SONGS OF IGNORANCE
Murry the Hump
(TOO PURE, 2001)

Named after a Chicago gangster with Welsh heritage, Murry the Hump were a band whose kooky view of the world won them many fans.

Those searching for a nostalgic play of Tom Jones' 'Green Green Grass of Home' on streaming sites might be in for a surprise if they come across a similarly named song by much-loved early Noughties indie sensations Murry the Hump. It's a song about an altogether different kind of grass: the song's subject is scoring some marijuana, the deceptively pleasant harp making way for a darker sound as singer Matthew Evans recites the tale of meeting his dealer, who lives by the sea. It sets the tone beautifully for this album chronicling misspent youth, friendship, love and everyday life.

The influence of Britpop continued into the first few years of the early Noughties with some sweet and innocent melodic indie tunes being recorded – not yet making way for the day-glo tendencies of what was soon to come.

Guitarist Gwion ap Siôn Rowlands had been in the Fflach-signed Tips Wyn Gruffydd with Dylan Ebenezer, who many will now know as a BBC newsreader and football commentator. After meeting Matthew Evans, bassist Curig Huws and drummer Bill Coyne, they formed Murry the Hump. Lots of gigging locally in the pubs of Aberystwyth – of which there were plenty – under their belts, they soon decamped to Cardiff and signed a deal with Too Pure Records, with the *NME* and John Peel quickly falling for their irresistibly charming hooks and lo-fi tales of Welsh life.

All student life is here, from the self-explanatory 'Booze and Cigarettes' to 'Vodka and Wine', while 'Don't Slip Up' features an amusing line about having a TV that can only be tuned to S4C. Though throwaway quips and the odd internal rhyme would bring them attention (this was the band, after all, that sang 'Kebab or Shag'), it's not all instant brashness and novelty couplets.

There are deliciously accomplished moments here too. 'The House That Used to Be a Ship' and 'Thrown Like a Stone' are proud of their perfect pop, stand-alone singles that showed the band's potential. *NME* called the album 'one of the lost greats'.

Matthew Evans was born in Resolven, near Neath. With friends El Goodo, the band would find themselves on the gigging circuit in Cardiff, bringing a much-needed sense of melody and fun to a sometimes slightly po-faced world of indie bands. El Goodo continued to release records until their last live appearance at 2022's Green Man Festival, the perfect setting for a band so influenced by international psych sensations like Neutral Milk Hotel and Olivia Tremor Control. El Goodo and Murry the Hump were particularly fond of Beulah, a band from San Francisco who had such a strong following in Resolven that they came to play a gig with their Welsh contemporaries there, stopping off for a photo at nearby Beulah.

A year after the release of this album, Murry the Hump were no more. Thankfully Matthew Evans and Gwion ap Siôn Rowlands continue to make music today as Keys. Matthew Evans is also a Senior Lecturer in Music and Sound at the University of South Wales.

murrythehump
SONGS OF IGNORANCE

RYAN
Ryan
(WREN RECORDS, 1971)

The story of Welsh entertainment cannot be told without including the story of Ryan Davies.

A true showman, he exuded charm in all that he did onstage, and when he sang, it was almost possible to hear the twinkle in his eyes.

Ryan was born in Glanaman in 1937. This early EP brought his wide repertoire to vinyl, with a version of Lennon & McCartney's 'Yesterday' as *Ddoe Mor Bell* (Yesterday So Far Away), traditional numbers and his own compositions.

He found fame with his friend Ronnie Williams, appearing as double act Ryan a Ronnie up and down Wales in person, as well as on the emerging light entertainment television formats. The duo were a huge hit, their routines hilarious – mocking themselves as much as the audience, and always from a place of kindness. Comic sketches would leave audiences in stitches, making way for moments of reflection as Ryan sang from his extensive repertoire in both Welsh and English. The duo would eventually part ways, but Ryan's star refused to be diminished.

His talents were a hit in London, with audiences mesmerised by his voice and comedic stories, but also by his dancing and serious acting skill. He took a starring role in *Fo a Fe* (Him and Him), one of S4C's most cherished comedy programmes, Ryan playing the *Hwntw* from south Wales, in a programme that celebrated the different accents of Wales.

A live recording of his set at the Top Rank nightclub in Swansea became the bestselling 1975 long-player *Ryan at the Rank*, probably his most iconic album. It showcased his humour, his warmth and his voice, captured perfectly in the emotional, heart-tugging Welsh ballad 'Myfanwy'. For many, Ryan's version of this sad, sad song was the definitive one.

He died at the age of 40 whilst in New York. A truly iconic Welsh entertainer, gone far too soon.

VERSIONS
The Anchoress
(DROWNED IN SOUND, 2023)

Catherine Anne Davies is The Anchoress. A producer, vocalist and musician who has released several enchanting and individual-sounding records, her solitary image and distinctive-sounding records are both arresting and captivating.

Born in Glynneath before moving to Australia and then to England, her first two studio albums were *Confessions of a Romance Novelist* and *The Art of Losing*, both critically acclaimed.

Having been a member of Simple Minds' live band, Catherine had always been an admirer of another Celtic rock group. 🔵 **Manic Street Preachers** themselves heard her music and were keen to work with her, inviting her to sing with them on some of their most-loved songs.

Her first recording with the Manics was 'Dylan & Caitlin' for their *Resistance is Futile* album, telling of the tumultuous relationship between Dylan Thomas and his wife Caitlin. It would be the first of many songs Catherine and James Dean Bradfield would duet on on stage – seeing them sing *The Holy Bible*'s 'This is Yesterday' to an enamoured crowd at a particularly hot Glastonbury festival in 2023 was a highlight of the weekend for me.

This album, *Versions*, is a glimpse into her musical inspirations and influences. It features the Manics, of course, alongside The Cure's 'Friday I'm in Love', New Order's 'Bizarre Love Triangle' and Depeche Mode's 'Enjoy the Silence', all given an Anchoress makeover, and they are as striking as they are soothing. There is a theme here, with stunning songwriting and lonely, solitary storytelling from cultural outsiders given space to breathe and find solace. It was released on Drowned in Sound, an influential music website turned record label.

That The Anchoress does the songs on *Versions* justice and brings something new to them says a lot about this committed, bold artist.

RYAN

WREN EP

PWY SY'N GALW?
Big Leaves
(CRAI, 1999)

Beganifs from Waunfawr, Gwynedd, formed at a remarkably young age, starting to jam and compose when they were just 11. They found a home on the Ankst label, then based in nearby Penygroes, who liked their tunes and vision. These early Nineties releases were baggy-influenced melodies, a loose sound with some poetic lyrics poured over the beats.

By the time this debut album was released, Beganifs had become Big Leaves and must have played every venue standing, particularly across north Wales. Welsh groups riding high in the mainstream charts gave Welsh labels and bands a shot of adrenalin that was infectious, and although not everyone got signed by major labels, the more DIY scene at home was spurred on.

It's occasionally noted that there's a glass ceiling in Wales when it comes to bands singing in Welsh, with headlining the Maes B gigs at the National Eisteddfod being a pinnacle, although several artists like ◯ **Adwaith** and ◯ **Gwenno** have proved that theory wrong. Big Leaves headlined Miri Madog in 1999 and were a familiar name on the Welsh and UK-wide circuit, their singing in English taking them down new avenues, including a slot on the New Bands stage at Reading and Leeds Festival that year.

Richly poetic lyrics married with immaculate melodies, this was indie rock 'n' roll that would sit on BBC Radio Cymru's daytime playlists as well as thrilling the kids at night. The band were clad in flares and shades, which proved handy when trying to conceal the odd hangover.

For all their musical talent and popularity, Big Leaves never quite reached the giddy heights of contemporaries ◯ **Super Furry Animals** or ◯ **Catatonia**. They supported both bands on tour many times, but a breakthrough record proved elusive. If the Furries' success proved one thing, it was that bands didn't *need* to sing in English to reach a large audience, but if breaking out was to be accomplished, it certainly helped. Bilingual rock came naturally to Big Leaves, and they released a couple of singles, 'Sly Alibi' and 'Racing Birds', on BBC Radio Wales presenter Adam Walton's Whipcord Records, getting them Single of the Week on Mark Radcliffe and Marc 'Lard' Riley's show on BBC Radio 1. Another single, 'Electro Magnetic Pollution', was put out on Boobytrap Records, which found airplay on Peel's show. Their second album, *Alien and Familiar*, released in 2004, would be their last.

Pwy Sy'n Galw was covered in its entirety by Band Pres Llareggub, the 9-piece brass band bringing in guest vocalists such as popular singers Yws Gwynedd and Kizzy Crawford to reinterpret the record, something they also did with Super Furry Animals' *Mwng*.

Big Leaves vocalist Rhodri Siôn and keyboard player Osian Gwynedd formed a new band, Boi, and released an album, *Coron o Chwinc*, in 2021. Osian and his brother Mei Gwynedd formed Sibrydion soon after Big Leaves, and Mei is a popular solo artist on the Welsh-language scene, re-recording the Urdd youth movement's official single in 2019, and running his own studio and label, Jig Cal, in Cardiff. Kev Tame was a member of electronic producers Acid Casuals, who released several majestic techno and dance albums, including the beautiful *Omni* in 2006.

Big Leaves' melodic, youthful, sundrenched songs soundtracked endless summers for thousands of music fans, holding a special place in the memories of many.

BIG LEAVES

PWY SY'N GALW?

THE WRECKAGE
Sweet Baboo
(AMAZING TAPES FROM CANTON, 2023)

From the musical mind of Stephen Black, Sweet Baboo has been a celebrated breath of fresh air on the Welsh music scene for over a decade.

Starting life as demos in Black's bedroom after he started composing in Trefriw while still at school, Stephen's songs of love and innocence have charmed indie fans, with his flair for writing witty and poignant words combined with some magnificent floating melodies. Here was a songwriting talent who worshipped Daniel Johnston and Paul McCartney, his meandering, relaxed lyrics and knack for writing a cracking tune making his charming pop songs irresistible. Celebrated by a music press previously enamoured with Stateside artists Adam Green and The Moldy Peaches, Sweet Baboo fit into this world of anti-folk seamlessly, but with a depth and longevity that has served him well.

Sweet Baboo's eighth album, *The Wreckage*, signalled a shift in Black's songwriting, with a maturer sound emerging. There were fewer observations on the minutiae of life, concentrating instead on bigger subjects and themes, with strong imagery used on songs such as the title track. Davey Newington – usually the composer in Cardiff band Boy Azooga – plays drums, with **Georgia Ruth** singing backing vocals throughout the album. Accompanied by a piano on 'Left Out the Door', Steve is at his most yearning, whilst the piano on 'The Worry' is the jolliest sound on this record. Having previously released his music on Shape Records and then Moshi Moshi, *The Wreckage* came out on his own label, Amazing Tapes from Canton, after a five-year hiatus from releasing music as Sweet Baboo. He wrote it at home in Penarth and recorded most of it at StudiOws in west Wales, with the majority of the instruments – from the flute to the wurlitzer – played by himself.

Emma Daman Thomas from the band Islet was the photographer for the album cover's striking image, an homage to a 1920 photograph of the actor and comedian Buster Keaton.

In the five years he was writing this album, Steve was also busy collaborating and refocusing his attention on his work with Gruff Rhys, **H. Hawkline**, Euros Childs and **Cate Le Bon**, playing live and touring with them.

Steve's other musical outlet is the duo Group Listening, with Paul Jones on piano, joining his clarinet. Their covers and reinterpretations of the work of avant-garde heroes and visionary composers Arthur Russell, Robert Wyatt and Cardigan's Malcolm Neon are delightful. They made an EP with Cate Le Bon, *Here It Comes Again*, honing their meditative and minimalistic style, a joyful wander through their musical ideas. As with his own albums as Sweet Baboo, their records too have been critically acclaimed, with many a review commentating on Black's ability to write and perform songs, making them seem effortless.

SWEET BABOO

THE WRECKAGE

THE BIG ROAR
The Joy Formidable
(ATLANTIC RECORDING CORPORATION/CANVASBACK, 2011)

The Big Roar begins with the sound of balloons popping – a nod perhaps to a moving on from their previous, debut EP, *A Balloon Called Moaning*. Independently released, that record certainly got The Joy Formidable noticed, but as with so many bands, the back story of a hard slog to get to that point was inevitable.

Making music together as Tricky Nixon and gigging in and around Manchester originally, Rhiannon Bryan – or Ritzy, as she is known – and Rhydian Dafydd met in their hometown of Mold in Flintshire, north Wales while at school. Hailing from so near the border with England, a move to Manchester was attractive, with the city's bustling music scene proving irresistible to these young songwriters who were desperate to gig as much as they could. Tricky Nixon became Sidecar Kisses, pausing for Rhydian to release a solo EP as Stitches on the Peski label, and then they settled on The Joy Formidable with drummer Matt Thomas completing the three-piece band.

Their early days of gigging and struggling to get an audience would serve them well in years to come as they became an incredibly busy band on the road, unafraid of dauntingly long tour schedules across north America and Europe. They would go on to play the main stage at Reading Festival, and in 2011 and in 2018, after Dave Grohl heard them on the radio and loved them, he offered them huge tours opening arena shows for his band Foo Fighters, one of the biggest rock bands in the world. Sometimes good things do happen.

Lyrically dense, the pent-up frustration conveyed by Ritzy throughout this album is impressive, matched with huge riffs and a penetrating beat. Similar perhaps to the ◉ **Manic Street Preachers**, despite circumstances and geography, the band's ambition is enormous, as captured in the album's title, while the themes are personal and the band are not afraid to engage emotionally with the listener.

The artwork for *The Big Roar* is by Rhydian Dafydd, who has been behind the sleeves for most of his band's output. Both Ritzy and Rhydian are Welsh-speakers and they have recorded the entirely English-language *A Balloon Called Moaning* in Welsh for the record's tenth anniversary. Welsh-language versions of huge radio hits like 'Austere', 'Cradle' and 'Whirring' have been released, and a compilation called *Pen Bwy Gilydd* (From Start to Finish). Keen to promote new music from Wales as well as their own Welsh-language recordings, they set up their own Aruthrol singles club in 2014, putting out double A-side vinyl singles with tracks by We Are Animal and Colorama on one side and the Joy Formidable's Welsh-language songs on the other side, and holding gigs to celebrate the releases.

Splitting their time between Utah, USA and Mold, Wales, The Joy Formidable have created their own community of fans brought together by their powerful, moving music.

The Big Roar

SOBIN A'R SMAELIAID I
Sobin a'r Smaeliaid
(SAIN, 1989)

Most countries have their own music phenomenon, someone who's a star in their native language, but finds it hard to get noticed outside their own world. Bryn Fôn is one of these artists.

A member of Crysbas in the late 1970s and singer on their hit, '*Draenog Marw*' (Dead Hedgehog), Bryn was also a popular actor, playing the role of Tecwyn in football comedy *C'mon Midffîld* (Come on, Midfield) – still regarded as a high point in S4C's output. But Bryn continued with his singing and became a huge hit with a mainstream audience on television, radio and most importantly on the live Welsh-language circuit.

Using the made-up name of Sobin a'r Smaeliaid for his new group in the late 1980s, he drew on his acting experience to create a musical moniker that he could hide behind. The band told stories of everyday life and memorable nights out in songs like '*Mardi Gras ym Mangor Ucha*' (Mardi Gras in Upper Bangor), namechecking pubs like the Belle Vue and Globe. '*Meibion y Fflam*' (Sons of the Flame) is a reference to the Meibion Glyndŵr movement of the 1980s and the burning of holiday homes in predominantly Welsh-speaking communities. '*Mae rhywun yn rhywle'n gwybod lawr yn dre*' (Someone knows, down in town) goes the upbeat song, commenting that someone must know who the firestarters were, but no one's willing to say. Bryn himself would be arrested for involvement in the organisation in 1990, but released without charge, making a documentary on his arrest and the movement several years later. Patagonian-born singer René Griffiths duets on '*Ynys y Meddwyn*', while '*Ar y Trên i Afonwen*' is a hugely popular middle-of-the-road song that rouses audiences without fail.

As Sobin, Fôn gigged constantly, playing student nights, locally arranged gigs and festivals from the National Eisteddfod to the Royal Welsh Agricultural Show in Llanelwedd, as well as countless smaller festivals and agricultural shows. He was a stalwart of Cymdeithas yr Iaith (the Welsh Language Society) gigs, organised by an energetic and devoted crew to bring Welsh-language culture alive, connecting with a young audience.

When he rested the Sobin name, Bryn Fôn continued to be a hit, in rural Welsh-speaking Wales especially, occasionally playing the bigger cities like Cardiff and Swansea. He didn't change his style to fit in with musical trends, but stuck to romantic, heart-rending ballads. He would sing about pubs and places that his audience drank in and knew well; these were beautiful, popular songs that spoke to real people, showing the singer's pride in north Wales and its place in the world. That they were melodic and accessible made Bryn a huge hit on the live circuit.

Released initially on cassette and then in the shiny new format, the compact disc, this album went on to sell tens of thousands of copies, earning them a silver disc from the ubiquitous Sain Records. Several solo albums would follow, Fôn's popularity not dwindling in the 2000s when it came to live performances – indeed, as well as appealing to a new audience who love his songs, there is now an element of nostalgia that brings audiences together.

SOBIN A'R SMAELIAID · I

CLYCHAU DIBON
Catrin Finch & Seckou Keita
(ASTAR/MWLDAN, 2013)

In his excellent book *Major Labels*, writer Kelefa Sanneh opens with a touching tale of playing the *Clychau Dibon* album to his dying father – who grew up in the Gambia, not far from Keita's native Senegal – in hospital in the US. The Welsh harp and Senegalese kora proved to be a soothing balm to him in his final days. Such is the power of this music; it is destined to travel, to find new ears in every corner of the world, and to evoke memories.

Wales has long been proud of its harp tradition, and Catrin Finch is generally regarded as the greatest classical harp virtuoso of her generation.

The first of her family to take up the instrument, she showed exceptional promise when she started playing age 6, growing up in Llan-non, Ceredigion. A pupil of renowned harpist Elinor Bennett, Finch would travel to Bennett's home every week for her lessons, a journey of several hours from west to north Wales. She would go on to study at the Purcell School and the Royal Academy of Music in London, where in 2022 she became a Visiting Professor of Harp.

Seckou Keita also showed immense talent at an early age, and went on to become a master of his craft. He plays the kora – a traditional Senegalese stringed instrument made from a gourd – which he was brought up around in Casamance, as well as the drums. He relocated to the UK in 1999, and has continuously collaborated and found new ways to work, much like Catrin. They met when Toumani Diabaté had to pull out of a 2013 tour with Catrin and Seckou stood in, and it was the beginning of a beautiful musical relationship.

Released by Astar and Cardigan-based Mwldan Records, the label based at Aberteifi's theatre, *Clychau Dibon* was critically acclaimed and hailed as an extraordinary album by the music press, *The Guardian* calling it 'an elegant, gently exquisite set'.

The magical sound of Seckou's 22-stringed double kora and Catrin's 47-stringed harp have been brought together twice more on record, for *Soar* in 2018 and *Echo* in 2022. Weaving Western and African song traditions together, *Soar* was inspired by the osprey and its migrations between Africa and Europe. *Echo* is another stunningly haunting and striking record, from its very first note. This is transportative, otherworldly music that should probably be prescribed, it is so freeing and good for the soul.

Catrin's work with a Colombian group, Cimarron, was well received when they took their infectious fusion of up-beat harp-focused joropo music on tour. Her most recent project is with Irish fiddle player Aoife Ní Bhriain, weaving Welsh and Irish trad melodies into each other and composing new pieces, free from the classical worlds they have both excelled in. This latest album is another fascinating collaboration in Catrin's restless quest for musical creativity.

CATRIN FINCH
SECKOU KEITA
CLYCHAU DIBON

Y BARDD ANFARWOL
The Gentle Good
(BUBBLEWRAP RECORDS, 2013)

This unique-sounding album marries the folk traditions of Welsh and Chinese music to devastating effect, to tell the story of poet Li Bai, known as 'The Fallen Immortal'. Thought to have been born in 701, around a thousand of his poems are known today, and are famous for their beauty and their depiction of life in the Tang Dynasty era in which he lived.

His work intrigued Gareth Bonello, a passionate and masterful musician who records using the name The Gentle Good, whose own work had become highly regarded on the Welsh folk scene. Inspired by the finger-picking of Bert Jansch and ◉ Meic Stevens, he'd made a name for himself on the live circuit since he started playing in earnest in 2005. In 2011 he travelled to the city of Chengdu in China to take up a six-week artistic residency with the Chengdu Associated Theatre of Performing Arts. Organised by The British Council and the PRS Foundation, its aim was to encourage music between nations, and Gareth embraced the opportunity with passion and eloquence.

He seized the chance to explore Chinese folk music and literature and collaborate with local traditional musicians. The album is a fascinating, relaxed listen – unusual at first, if unfamiliar with Chinese instrumentation – with new sounds melting into each other.

His restrained, beautiful vocals appear throughout, as do the sounds of the guitar, essential to the track '*Bore Braf*' (Lovely Morning), a short instrumental piece near the end of the album. He is replaced on '*Marwnad Chang-Khan*' (Chang-Khan Elegy) by Lisa Jên from ◉ 9Bach, her warm, lilting vocals sounding majestic. Birdsong appears on the album too, recorded in China by Gareth, himself a keen birdwatcher.

Li Bai's life is chronicled, from his attempt to become a military strategist to ageing and embracing his white hair. If there is a sleepy, nocturnal feel to this album, it is probably because of Li Bai's fascination with the moon, a constant theme in his work. It would be the end of him, the legend goes, as he drowned trying to embrace the moon's reflection in water. This is captured in the song '*Afon Arian*' (Silver River).

It was recorded partly with musicians from Chengdu during Gareth's visit to China, partly home in Wales with producer Llion Robertson, arranger Seb Goldfinch and the Mavron Quartet, and partly in London with the UK Chinese Ensemble.

Y Bardd Anfarwol (The Immortal Poet) won the inaugural *Albwm Cymraeg y Flwyddyn* (Welsh-Language Album of the Year) prize, a new award that the National Eisteddfod launched in 2014 to highlight and praise albums released in Welsh. Gareth's 2016 release *Ruins/Adfeilion* was an album of original material that won the 2017 Welsh Music Prize, and in 2023 he released *Galargan* (Elegy), a collection of traditional Welsh songs including '*Nid Wyf yn Llon*' (I Am Not Happy), which Gareth found in ◉ Meredydd Evans and Phyllis Kinney's archive at the National Library of Wales. Many of his albums have been released on Bubblewrap Records, an excellent independent label run by Rich Chitty, with ◉ Georgia Ruth, HMS Morris, early Boy Azooga and Buzzard Buzzard Buzzard on the roster.

Gareth would travel again in 2019 to record another remarkable album, '*Sai-thaiñ Ki Sur* (The Weaving of Voices), this time as one of the founders of Khasi-Cymru Collective with artists from the Khasi community of north-east India. Exploring the legacy of a Welsh Methodist mission to the region, it brings Welsh and Khasi words and sounds together effortlessly, to create another memorable, unique record.

THE GENTLE GOOD + Y BARDD ANFARWOL

(IF PARADISE IS) HALF AS NICE
Amen Corner
(IMMEDIATE, 1969)

Could this perhaps be the catchiest single ever to emerge from Wales?

Like the triple harp, which at first glance appears to be from Wales, the song actually originates in Italy, written by Lucio Battisti, a singer-songwriter who grew up in Rome. A young Amen Corner recorded the English-language version in late 1968, seeing it fly to the Number 1 position in the charts in February 1969. They were the first Welsh band to achieve this chart status, paving the way for the ○ **Manic Street Preachers** and ○ **Stereophonics** a few decades later. Amen Corner's previous big hit was 'Bend Me, Shape Me' – another cover, and a Number 3 hit in 1968.

Amen Corner had formed in Cardiff nightclubs in 1966, swept up in the rock 'n' roll explosion, before moving to swinging London to sign to Decca Records. Renowned producer Andrew Loog Oldham soon signed them to his Immediate record label, and they released *The National Welsh Coast Live Explosion Company* album in 1969. The crowd's screaming throughout this live album speaks volumes about the band's young fanbase. They were a phenomenon, riding on the coat-tails of The Beatles – a handsome, young and talented band who seemed to be up for a good time and were taking this new-found fame in their stride.

Singer Andy Fairweather Low, originally from Ystrad Mynach, went on to have a successful solo career, releasing several records and playing with Paul Weller, Eric Clapton and Bill Wyman's Rhythm Kings, amongst others. Although he acknowledges his past success, he has continually made sure he pushes forward and has constantly created new music, toured relentlessly, and is widely regarded, along with ○ **Pino Palladino**, as one of the finest session musicians in the world.

SICK BOI
Ren
(THE OTHER SONGS, 2023)

Ren Eryn Gill's story is one of bravery, defiance, creativity, perseverance and rhymes laid bare. His self-reflective lyrics matched with a keen sense of humour have created something very special that has taken Ren to both people's hearts and the top of the charts.

Raised in Dwyran, Anglesey, Ren was a beatmaker when he was in his early teens, before moving to Brighton. There he joined rap crews and started busking, honing his style and perfecting his craft. After years of ill health, he was finally diagnosed with the debilitating Lyme disease.

Ren began showcasing his music on platforms including YouTube, where he continues to amass millions of views, his music and visual aesthetics a huge hit globally. Talking openly about his mental health and his severe illness with self-deprecating affability, his mesmerising style of rapping has gained him a solid fanbase that can identify with the honesty in his lyrics. His album *Freckled Angels*, released in 2016, is dedicated to a friend who took his own life aged just 19. In 2023, Ren raised thousands for Beaumaris RNLI to thank them for trying to find his friend.

The title track from this album unveils the pain Ren has been through in understanding and coming to terms with his own illness, and is a celebration of his independence, defiance and success against the odds.

Ren surprised the music industry and himself as this album hit No. 1 in the UK album charts, while Ren was in Canada receiving treatment for his rare illness. The opening lines of the album, in Welsh, are sung as if Ren had died and is mourning himself. Varying the mood and themes on this impressive record, Ren's versatility as a rapper and producer is striking. Hard and heavy tracks 'Animal Flow', 'The Hunger' and 'Wicked Ways' flow into more comical and knowing tunes 'What You Want' and 'Loco'.

Ren's fanbase made sure this independent artist was top of the charts, and the *Sick Boi* album he had poured everything into had made the history books.

IMMEDIATE
Cyril Shane
Music Ltd.
ALL RIGHTS OF THE
SOLD IN U.K. SUBJECT TO
RESALE PRICE CONDITIONS,
SEE PRICE LISTS
© 1969
(If Paradise Is) HALF AS NICE (2.50)
(Battisti, Fishman)
AMEN CORNER
A Shel Talmy Production

GOBAITH MAWR Y GANRIF
Geraint Jarman
(SAIN, 1976)

Born in Denbigh in 1950, Geraint Jarman and his family made Cardiff their home before he started school. He discovered he had a way with words at a young age. A poet in school, his early works were published, and he and his then girlfriend ⓞ **Heather Jones** discovered their singing voices. He formed a tongue-in-cheek vocal harmony group called Bara Menyn (Bread and Butter) with Heather and ⓞ **Meic Stevens**, and a poem of his appeared on ⓞ *Clywch-y-Bardd* (Hear-the-Poet), a seven-inch single of poems originally intended to be enjoyed over the telephone, released by the Welsh Arts Council.

In his mid twenties, Jarman was ready for action, beginning a prolific and remarkable journey.

The country guitar and its influence on *Gobaith Mawr y Ganrif* (The Century's Great Hope) is undeniable, particularly on 'I've Arrived' and 'Hyfryd Fore – Hyfryd Iawn' (Lovely Morning – Very Lovely), the latter almost a parody of a country song, which he pulls off beautifully. The spoken words added by Dewi Pws to 'Hyfryd Iawn' only add to its fun. That Jarman would dabble in acting throughout his career should come as no surprise: for all the seriousness and sober thoughts he raises, there is a playfulness and a knowing wink in his voice at times – almost as if Geraint himself is a character, as well as a very real young man trying to make sense of the world.

'*Merched Caerdydd*' (Cardiff Girls) is a stompy number celebrating the young women of Cardiff, with the beautiful love song to the city, '*Lawr yn y Ddinas*' (Down in the City) less crude. It tells of a sunny day by the River Taff, lovingly calling Cardiff the big bad city. He sings of a lover in Splott called Lott, and of a girl who's cute who lives down in Bute. Simple rhymes for simple, happy times. This was a city kid singing of his home, something which hadn't been done in Welsh before – a stark difference to the rural Wales of Edward H. Dafis or even Meic Stevens.

It's the sound of Jarman desperate to leave the middle classes behind and join the wild people he sings of in '*Lle Mae'r Bobl Wylltyn Byw*' (Where the Wild People Live), and the album closes with a duet: Jarman and Heather Jones singing '*Pethau Brau*' (Fragile Things), a beautifully tender, romantic number.

Geraint's lifelong friend Tich Gwilym plays guitar, a partnership that would last until Tich's untimely death in 2005. 15 albums would follow this debut – some of the most influential albums in Welsh-language music history. Each one shared more of Jarman and his close musician friends bringing their vision alive.

Hen Wlad fy Nhadau (Land of My Fathers), from 1978, is a heavier rock record, again focusing on Wales and its contradictions, which are keenly observed by Jarman. It was covered in its entirety by various artists for a 1990 compilation released by Ankst, who invited ⓞ **Llwybr Llaethog**, Jecsyn Ffeif and ⓞ **Tŷ Gwydr** along with ⓞ **Datblygu**, ⓞ **Maffia Mr. Huws**, Celt and Ffa Coffi Pawb to record their takes on the original.

Geraint Jarman has gone on to record several albums in the past decade alone, working with the Ankstmusik label. His love of reggae and dub harks back to the clubs of Cardiff, where he would hear these records, and a trip to Jamaica in the early 2000s, taking in Studio One in Kingston. He also worked on the influential *Fideo 9* series for S4C, directing videos for the next crop of young bands eager to stir things up – an urge he knew only too well.

Geraint Jarman
Gobaith Mawr y Ganrif

CASUALLY DRESSED & DEEP IN CONVERSATION
Funeral for a Friend
(INFECTIOUS RECORDS, 2003)

The influence of American music on the South Wales Valleys, as on so many communities around the world, has been substantial. With no American rock 'n' roll, there'd be no 🔘 Tom Jones, the exciting new genre finding its way to the Valleys and igniting a fire in young music fans that would be hard to put out. In the early Noughties, however, an equally big wave of American music would inspire another generation of young Welsh bands.

Formed in Bridgend and made up of members from various groups, Funeral for a Friend were originally only meant to play a few gigs, before realising they had something worth pursuing. Frontman Matthew Davies epitomised the band beautifully: apparently unassuming, his mellow vocals could erupt into a ferocious growl at any time, ready to burst forth when the song required it. Funeral for a Friend might not have reached as high in the charts as peers Lostprophets, or even had the sense of joie de vivre that Merthyr Tydfil's The Blackout would seem to display, but their thoughtful, intense playing made them stand out from the crowd, and they became pillars of the south Wales and UK-wide emo scene.

Mighty Atom – a Swansea-based independent label that was key in nurturing young bands – liked what they heard and released two EPs before this, their debut album, came out on Infectious Records in 2003. With the band riding high on a fervent fanbase and the patronage of *Kerrang!* magazine, it was a hit with fans and critics alike.

Different to their Cool Cymru predecessors, this wasn't indie music destined for the mainstream. This was post-hardcore, or emo music – so called since the 1980s, when Washington DC bands pioneered it – and like all genres, it had mutated and changed a little as the decades rolled through. Famed for being non-showy and wearing your heart on your sleeve, 'emo' really did stand for emotional. Given the backdrop of south Wales in the early 2000s, with its post-industrial landscape and promise of a brighter future, listening to music – and indeed making music – really was a lifeline for a lot of people: an escapism to immerse yourself in whilst talking openly about your feelings, hopes and fears. These were international themes, the band proving popular especially on the European touring circuit.

A re-recorded song from Funeral for a Friend's earlier EP, *She Drove Me to Daytime Television*, made it on to this debut album, as did a new version of 'Juneau', with its powerful riffs and heartfelt vocals. The crashing guitars throughout the album make for an enjoyably bumpy ride, visions of a throbbing moshpit and a thousand sweaty kids hard not to imagine.

Six studio albums followed this impressive debut. Funeral for a Friend have gigged sporadically since, and have managed to do justice to their albums by playing special shows concentrating on playing albums in full, much to the delight of their original, and new, fans.

In 2023, after these shows, singer Matt announced his departure from the band, declaring his love for his bandmates and the music, but wishing to move on with his life. The rest of Funeral For a Friend respected this, and declared their wish to continue with a new vocalist, promising updates on future plans.

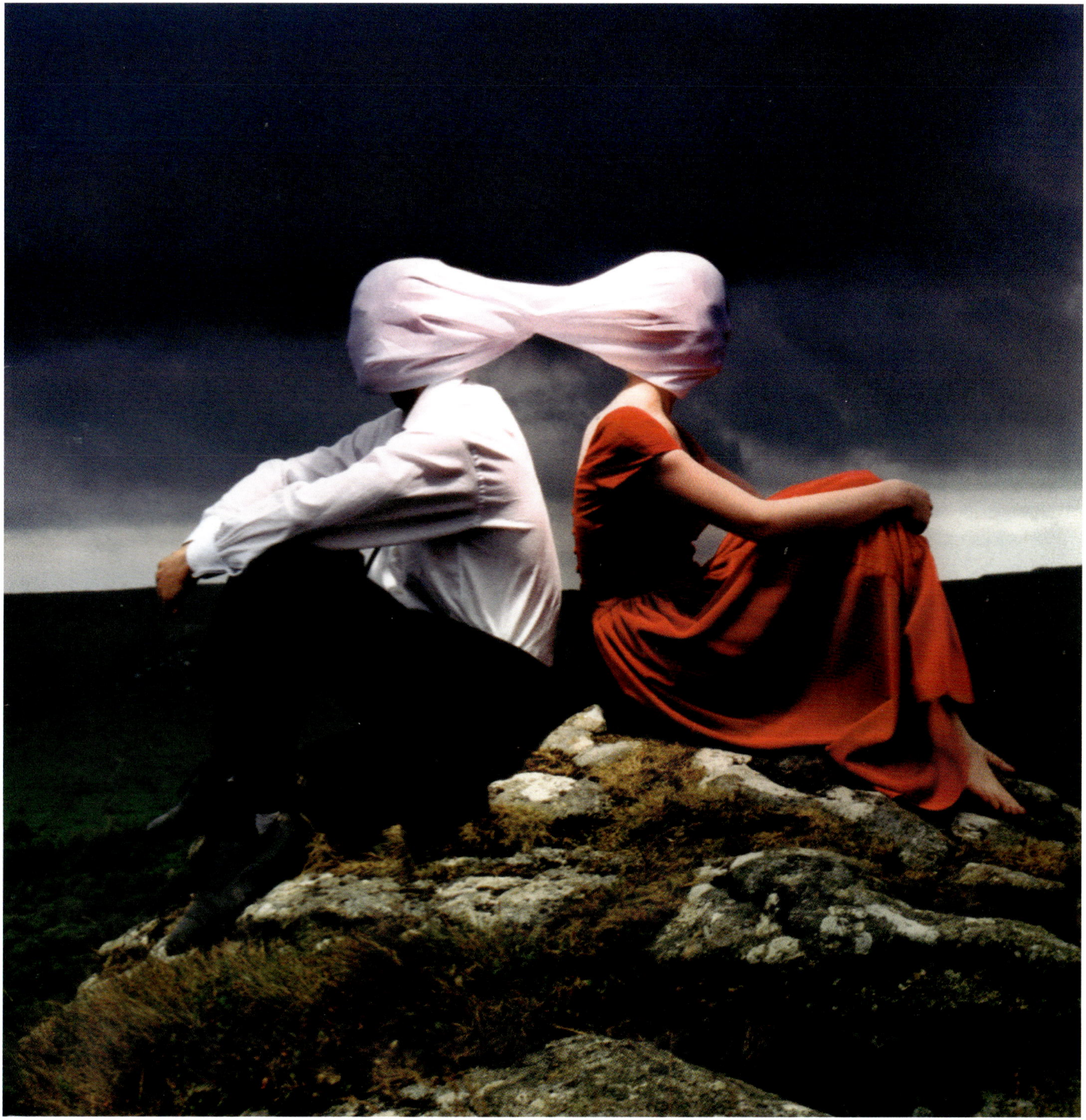

SHAMPŴ
Bando
(SAIN, 1982)

The Eighties were an exciting time for Welsh-language artists, keen to record songs in their own language that reflected the modern music they were hearing in the charts. Playful and with exceptional musicianship, the disco grooves of Bando caught young music fans' imaginations. Featuring Caryl Parry Jones – Caryl Ifans, as she was known at the time – her then husband Rhys Dyrfal Ifans, Gareth Thomas, Martin Sage and future husband Myfyr Isaac, the band was short-lived and this was their second album.

Caryl was an exceptional lyricist from a young age, and wrote the lyrics to all but one track on this raw, lovelorn and romantic album. In need of lyrics for a funky number the band had written, Caryl asked her friend Hywel Gwynfryn, lyric writer and media personality, if he had any words lying around. Hywel had been in a hairdresser's that day, watching the stylist massage a woman's head as she washed her hair, and the title track of this album was born. '*Tybed Wyt Ti'n Rhy Hen*' (I Wonder if You're Too Old) and "*Sgen ti Sws i Mi*' (Have You a Kiss for Me) are perfect disco numbers, accomplished and masterful, Caryl's voice and the band's musicianship gelling perfectly. Ballad '*Chwarae'n Troi'n Chwerw*', which means something like 'Playing with Fire', became an end-of-the-night dancefloor favourite in Welsh-language discos, along with Edward H. Dafis' '*Ysbryd y Nos*' (Spirit of the Night). Gruff Rhys covered it, closing his debut solo album *Yr Atal Genhedlaeth* with an epic version in 2004.

Caryl Parry Jones has remained one of the most popular singers in the Welsh music scene. Born in Ffynnongroyw, Flintshire, her father Rhys Jones was a highly respected musician. The bright lights of Cardiff soon called, and Caryl would go on to become a popular broadcaster on BBC Radio Cymru, a scriptwriter and Wales' most popular television comedian, with a host of memorable characters in sitcoms and films. She writes for her cousin Non Parry's band, the popular girl group Eden, and occasionally sings with her daughters to Myfyr's accompaniment as The Parry Isaacs, for charitable causes. Her daughter Greta Isaac is a professional musician who, as well as singing under her own name, is in the popular band FIZZ. Myfyr Isaac was a member of Budgie in the mid Seventies, playing live with the influential heavy rock band from Cardiff. He formed the supergroup Jîp with ○ **Endaf Emlyn**, John Gwyn, and two of ○ **Geraint Jarman**'s band, Richard Dunn and Arran Ahmun, and produced several albums, including Endaf Emlyn's *Dawnsionara* (Slowdancing) and this Bando record, which was to be their last.

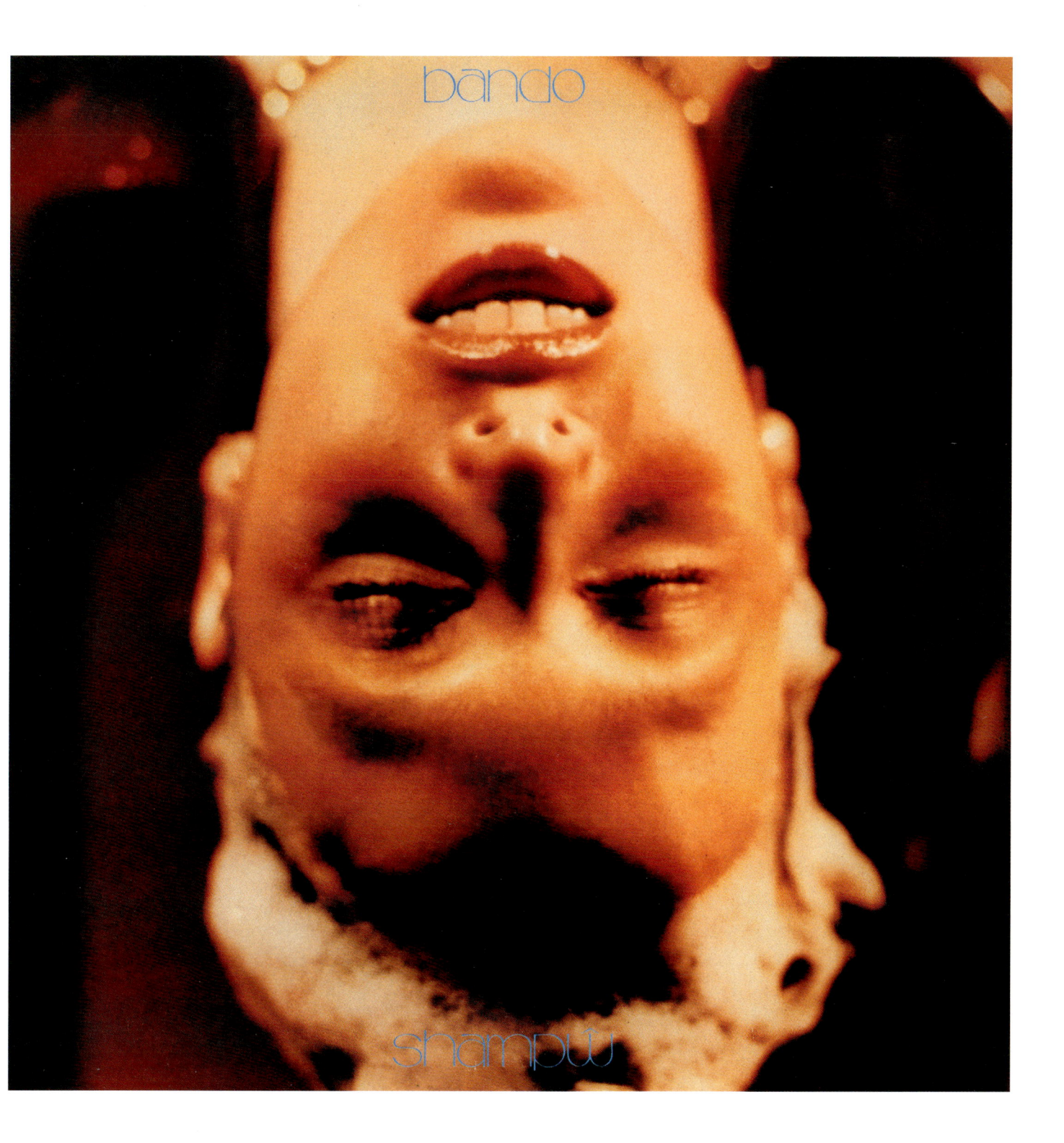

bando

shampoo

EYE OF THE HURRICANE
The Alarm
(I.R.S. RECORDS, 1987)

The Alarm have brought fans of anthemic, soaring rock together to hang on Mike Peters' every word and follow the band on a most remarkable journey since they formed in Rhyl in 1981. Originally called The Toilets, and then Alarm Alarm, they settled on The Alarm and never looked back. They found fame and broke through in a big way, touring with U2 and building a strong fanbase, which continually grew and have stuck with them through thick and thin.

Mike Peters has said 'The journey back into Wales began with this album,' and it's a big sounding record, with a melancholic feel to the lyrics, opulent production and a bold vision, captured triumphantly on the hit single 'Rain in the Summertime'.

Mike has always been very proud of his Welshness, learning the language and unafraid to sing about his home country. The 1989 album *Change* was translated into Welsh and re-released as *Newid* – produced by Tony Visconti – and takes Wales as its main inspiration. *Change* album-closer 'A New South Wales', featuring the Morriston Orpheus Male Voice Choir, is an emotional and bleak yet somehow optimistic song that remains an Alarm favourite. In the same way, their 1991 album *Raw* was also released in Welsh as *Tân* (Fire) – these were bold steps for such a commercially successful band to take. That was to be their last record, with Peters starting a solo career, before The Alarm MM++ regrouped in the early Noughties to tour and record for an audience delighted to have them back.

The Alarm's yearly Gatherings, often happening in Llandudno, when Mike and the band meet their fans, have allowed people to connect with the music in a unique, personal way which has been refreshing for both the group and their fans. In 2023 sold-out Gatherings took place in Cardiff and New York, with events happening around the gigs to spread Mike's message of love and community.

His passion for music, Wales and life have been an important factor in Mike's optimism as he faced enormous health issues: he was first diagnosed with cancer in 1995, and has been fighting it since. He and his wife Jules – a constant in Mike's life, on stage and off – have stayed connected with fans online to keep them updated on his health progress over the years, and they have remained living in north-east Wales.

Mike's other love, football, resulted in the fantastic 'The Red Wall of Cymru', Wales' official UEFA Euro 2020 song. Initially laid down by The Alarm at Rockfield, Peters then travelled to twelve locations across Wales to record the members of the *Wal Goch*/Red Wall. It's an upbeat, jubilant singalong of a single, like all good football songs, and is another milestone in the history of one of Wales' most successful rock bands. Much like Gareth Bale united football fans worldwide, Mike Peters has united music fans the world over, and always with Wales as the starting point.

THE ALARM
EYE OF THE HURRICANE

MAGI THATCHER
Dafydd Iwan
(SAIN, 1980)

'I have only one thing to say' is the first thing you hear on this track, with Margaret Thatcher's unmistakable voice letting us know what the theme for this 1980 single from Dafydd Iwan is. Tongue firmly in cheek, Dafydd urges us to sit by the fire and listen to him sing about Maggie Thatcher, but given its context, we know this isn't going to be a relaxing bedtime story.

This single was released a year before the government of the day reneged on their manifesto promise to establish a Welsh-language television channel: a controversial decision. Gwynfor Evans – Plaid Cymru's first elected Member of Parliament in Westminster – went on hunger strike, forcing Thatcher and then Home Secretary Willie Whitelaw to do a U-turn, as colourfully portrayed in 2023 film *Y Sŵn* (which would be translated as something like 'The Clamour' in this context), the story of the birth of S4C. Thatcher played such a large role in Welsh public life, whether she meant to or not, that her legacy is still felt in Wales all these decades on. Whilst some united behind her, many united in their hatred for her policies, her image an easy target for protest singers like Dafydd.

'*Mae'r fenyw â'r fwyell yn dod!*' (The lady with the axe is coming!) he sings, bringing the artwork by cartoonist and illustrator Elwyn Ioan alive. There is a punk ethos to the sleeve, something akin to a political flyer, her name all in lower case. The image of her striking an axe into the heart of Wales is a powerful one.

He mocks her policies, such as urging people without work to up their tents and move to Kent to find it. In the same way he derides Prince Charles on other singles, Dafydd's sarcastic tone suggests a very Welsh sense of friendliness: a reactionary song to capitalise on a feeling of unease and anger at the politics of the day. On the sleeve notes, *Magi a'r Ceidwadwyr* (Maggie and the Conservatives) are given a credit as backing vocalists, presumably without the artists' permission.

Dafydd's extensive back catalogue takes in so many issues, big and small, that have concerned Wales and those who live in Wales. Schools closing, the chapel closing, the Welsh leaving Wales, Tryweryn, taxes, road signs – Dafydd has really been the voice of Wales' concerns since he started singing. He is a respected preacher, and still travels Wales with his message. But more recently, he has found a new audience keen to welcome him to their schools and communities.

In 2022, Dafydd's 40-year-old song with Ar Log was put on a worldwide platform. '*Yma o Hyd*' (Still Here) became hugely important for the Football Association of Wales, under the guidance of their Head of Public Affairs Ian Gwyn Hughes. *Y Wal Goch*/The Red Wall had adopted it as their anthem, bursting into song spontaneously during games, and as a result Dafydd Iwan was invited to sing it before their World Cup qualifier matches. The song's message of defiance, of withstanding hardship and resisting just by continuing to exist, struck a chord with the football fans, true to their team. It was a perfect marriage, which captured the hearts of those both familiar and unfamiliar with the song. For many, it felt like Dafydd was finally getting the wider recognition he had long deserved.

"magi thatcher"

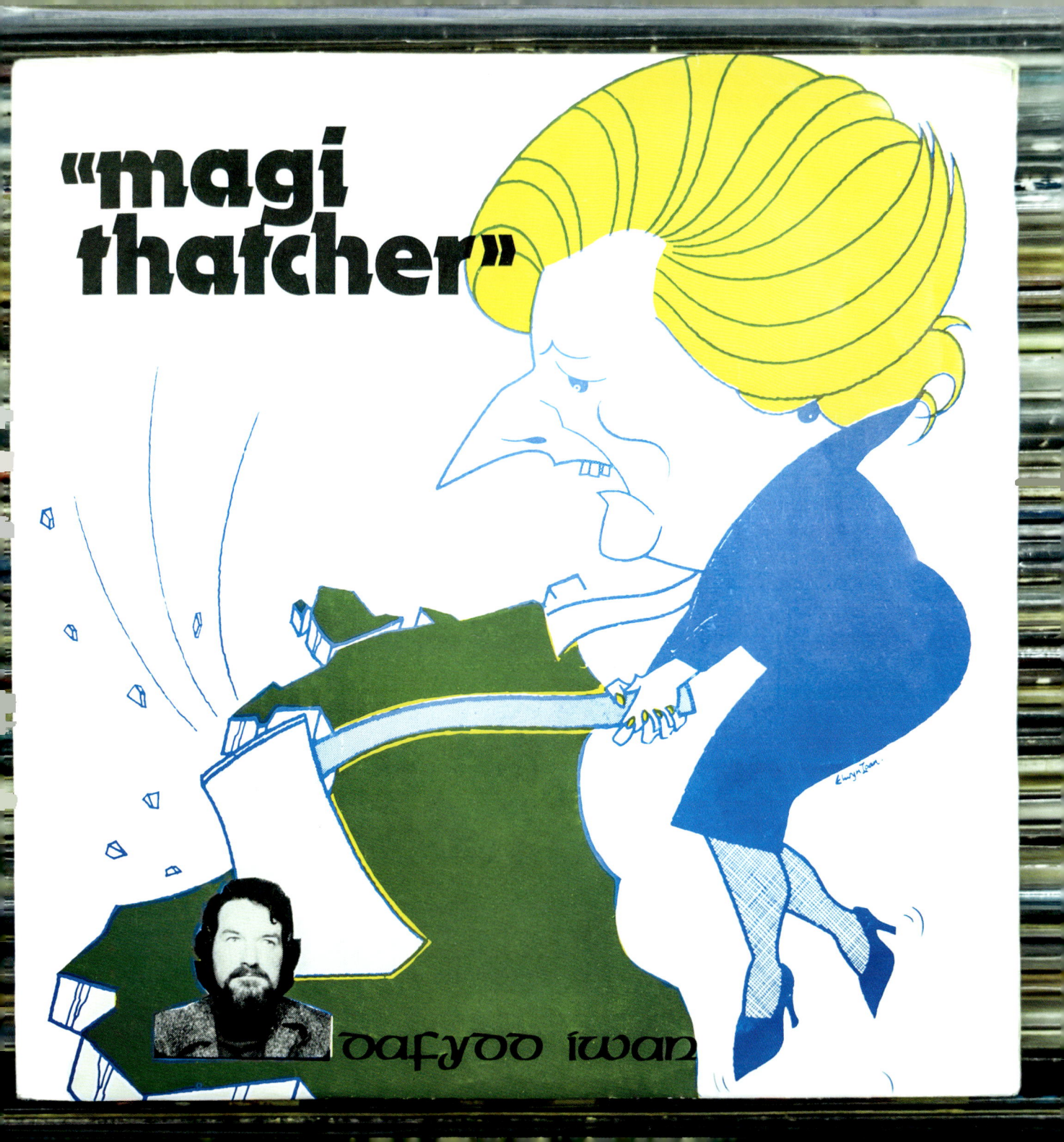

dafydd iwan

Ô SEASONS Ô CASTLES
Katell Keineg
(ELEKTRA, 1994)

Born to a Welsh teacher mother and Breton poet father, both political activists in Wales and Brittany, Katell moved from Breizh to Penpedairheol in the Rhymney Valley when she was 9 years old. Her upbringing and linguistic skills in Welsh, English, French and Breton have worked their way into her music, giving her a wide spectrum of bands, ideas, perspectives and influences to inspire her.

Moving to New York in the early 1990s, she was a regular at the respected Sin-é club, which showcased emerging singer-songwriters. She would become friends with like-minded musical nomads, including the late, celebrated singer Jeff Buckley, and was a regular on the live music scene of the bustling city. She sang on the Iggy Pop album *American Caesar* in 1993, and signed a deal with the iconic major label Elektra Records.

This is a heavyweight record, full of impressively composed songs. It showed the talent and great span of versatility Katell would bring to her musical career, and signalled the arrival of a true artist. *Ô Seasons Ô Castles* remains a breathtaking work of art of unrivalled depth and nuance, a hugely impressive debut album.

'Bop' is a hypnotic number, lilting and brooding before erupting into a frantic call to arms, deceptive in its breeziness, with no warning of the chaos to come. Katell's voice veers from vulnerability to an astute commandeering that oozes charisma.

The unaccompanied 'Conch Shell' demands you down tools to listen, and near the end of the album there is another a cappella rendition, this time of the hymn 'O Iesu Mawr', the only Welsh-language song on the record.

'The Gulf of Araby' is a devastating anti-war song, later recorded by renowned US songwriter Natalie Merchant, formerly of 10,000 Maniacs, who remains a huge fan and friend of Katell's. The song clocks in at almost seven minutes and is a compelling album closer.

Greater success would come for Katell with her second album *Jet* in 1997. Her song 'One Hell of a Life' was rediscovered by music manager Mark Woodward for his father **Tom Jones** to sing on the deluxe edition of his *Surrounded by Time* album in 2021.

Spending her time in Europe and the States, with Cardiff as her base since reconnecting with the city's creative spirit in the early Noughties, Katell continues to create and perform live. Her album *At the Mermaid Parade* was released via Honest Jon's Records in 2010, again getting hugely favourable reviews around the world. Katell is a special singer-songwriter with a small but dedicated fanbase who have fallen under the spell of her beautiful voice and intricate musical artistry, her creative journey continuing to take her on surprising and unexpected musical trips.

KATELL KEINEG

WINDRUSH BABY
Aleighcia Scott
(BLACK DUB, 2023)

The album cover for *Windrush Baby* shows a woman holding her baby. They are Aleighcia Scott's grandmother and uncle, at her uncle's christening, two years after moving to the UK. Aleighcia Scott was born in Cardiff, and this album is a tribute to her proud Jamaican and Welsh heritage. Its release coincided with the 75th anniversary of HMT *Empire Windrush* arriving in the UK, and for Aleighcia the album title was an obvious one.

Aleighcia's family roots are in Trelawny, Jamaica, where she spends time regularly, inspired by musician friends and the culture she holds so dear. The album was produced by Jamaican reggae legend Rorystonelove in Kingston, Jamaica, with ideas being sent back and forth between them, from Cardiff and Kingston, over five years.

The production here is outstanding: the drums crisp and rolling, the reggae rhythms soaked in sunshine. The echoing drumbeats and precise production bring out the best in Aleighcia, her honeyed vocals sounding stunning on both dub and lovers rock rhythms – the latter a uniquely Jamaican-British genre which lifts the spirits. Aleighcia's band on the record features backing vocalists Chevaughn and Roselyn Williams, and a superb horn section who play their mesmerising sound throughout the album. Single 'Do You' is a Brook Benton original, made famous by John Holt. 'Pretty Little Brown Thing' was brought to Aleighcia by Jamaican singer Racquel Jones. Aleighcia's voice and vision throughout the album proves a constant, with her love and understanding of the various rhythms running deep; it's an album that has taken time to make, and takes its time to play out.

Aleighcia is also a popular radio and television presenter. She has a regular show on BBC Radio Wales and has sat in on BBC Radio 1Xtra for David Rodigan, the reggae legend who has given his seal of approval to *Windrush Baby*. She fulfilled a childhood ambition of learning Welsh by teaching herself through the Say Something in Welsh app and appearing on the *Iaith ar Daith* programme on S4C, joining actress Mali Ann Rees on a tour of Wales to learn about the language she now speaks.

This led to her appearing at the National Eisteddfod in 2023, curating the first ever reggae night on the Maes – featuring herself, Eadyth and Morgan Elwy, amongst others. Aleighcia plays with a full band, has done sets at Glastonbury and Boomtown, and often performs at Notting Hill, Leeds, Bristol and Butetown's carnivals on August bank holiday. She's also a regular at the Green Man Festival, where the Chai Wallahs tent is packed every time she takes to the stage.

In a programme for S4C called *Curadur*, she looked into Wales' history with reggae, interviewing musician **Geraint Jarman** and founder of the Butetown Carnival Keith Murrell about Butetown's musical legacy, talking to Twmffat about why reggae resonates in north Wales communities like Blaenau Ffestiniog, and showcasing new artists Kiddus and Des1re.

RORYSTONELOVE / BLACK DUB PRESENTS

ALEIGHCIA SCOTT WINDRUSH BABY

RHAID I RYWBETH DDIGWYDD
Tystion
(FITAMIN UN, 1997)

A bold, uncompromising and riotous debut album, *Rhaid i Rywbeth Ddigwydd* (Something Has to Happen) had an urgency not heard previously in Welsh-language music. Although hip-hop itself was relatively young (roughly 20 years old), so many great and important records had made their mark globally, from Public Enemy's *It Takes a Nation of Millions to Hold Us Back* to *Enter the Wu-Tang (36 Chambers)* by Wu-Tang Clan. They'd certainly made their mark on a young Steffan Cravos, an early member of ◉ Gorky's Zygotic Mynci who fell in love with rap while at school in Carmarthen.

If a Tystion (Witnesses) live experience was chaotic and surprising, it wasn't for show but a lifestyle choice. Cravos and bandmate Gruff Meredith travelled all of Wales and occasionally further afield, with a wide circuit of contacts promoting and accommodating them and their band. They were joined onstage and on record by the late MC Chef (Gareth Williams), super scratch DJ and Cardiff hip-hop legend DJ Jaffa (Jason Farrell), and Dai Lloyd, who would later go on to form his own band, Skep. John Peel sessions for BBC Radio 1 followed, their audience consisting of those that thought this was a natural progression in the Welsh-language music scene, and those perhaps bemused that Welsh-language rap even existed. ◉ Llwybr Llaethog might have been the first to rap in Welsh, but Tystion were barely in their twenties, keen for a good time and politically minded. An early piece of marketing for the band was a matchbox with the words *MG yn y Tŷ* (MG in the House) written on it – a reference to the Meibion Glyndŵr movement, famed for burning down holiday homes in Wales, which their track of the same name is about.

Sitting alongside big political issues of the day on this album are some silly, softer songs. '*Fferins Nôl Mewn Ffasiwn*' (Sweets Are Back in Fashion) is about their love of sweets, extolling the virtues of Caramacs and Mars bars. '*Diwrnod Braf*' (Lovely Day) is a mellow jam that is simply about living a laid-back lifestyle, whilst its other Welsh-language BBC radio hit '*Gwyddbwyll*' (Chess), possibly the album's highlight, builds on a simple riff, claiming that they feel like pieces in a game of chess.

With Gruff Meredith calling himself MC Mabon, or occasionally G-Man, and rapper Curig Huws known as Lo-Cut, Cravos took the name Sleifar. Meaning a sly one, his was a quick, frustrated flow that didn't give a damn and wasn't about to leave the room quietly. Their rap style was loud, brash and heavy; there was no chance Tystion would burst into a love song. They wanted change in Wales, and on pre-referendum track 'Euro 96' they call for Welsh devolution, ask why young people have to leave Wales to find work and why Welsh beaches are polluted, and even manage to fit in a reference to Hong Kong gaining independence.

Listening to the album now, some 20 years on from the establishment of a Welsh Assembly – now a Parliament – some of the things they're demanding sound odd, in the same way that hearing artists in the Sixties' call for bilingual road signs in Wales does. A lot of us have grown up with these things and taken them for granted, maybe forgetting how much of a fight it was to get them, and how the singers of the day took to a studio to record their unhappiness with the situation.

Steffan Cravos went on to make one record with Lo-Cut and currently resides in Berlin, where he creates street art. Gruff Meredith made nine studio albums as MC Mabon, receiving a cult following thanks to their eccentric, madcap rap-and-rock fusions, with Gruff's unique take on modern life at the heart of the sometimes very catchy songs.

Rhaid I Rywbeth Ddigwydd...

tystion

FIT 004

CAM O'R TYWYLLWCH
Various Artists
(RECORDIAU ANHREFN, 1985)

The DIY spirit runs deep through this record, as it does through its label – Anhrefn Records – and the maverick spirit behind its release, Rhys Mwyn. The independent label's second release brought together some of the outsiders making music in Wales at that time – outsiders who would go on to become some of the most successful and important musicians Wales has produced.

Cardigan band ○ **Datblygu**, Llanrwst's Y Cyrff (The Bodies) and Smiths-inspired band Tynal Tywyll (Dark Tunnel) each contribute two songs to this hugely collectable record. Rhys hadn't heard Ian Morris of Tynal Tywyll sing before inviting them to record for this compilation: he asked them based on their image alone. Luckily they sounded as slick and as handsome as they looked, their breezy song *Paid â Synnu* (Don't Be Surprised) the poppiest contribution to this cult classic of a compilation. The most frantic song is a cut by Porthmadog's Elfyn Presli, described as 'farmer-psychopunk' and featuring the frazzled vocals of frontman Bernard Davey.

Datblygu were making a name for themselves as experimental underdogs with cassettes released on Malcolm Gwyon's Casetiau Neon, but this was their first release on vinyl. Singing about prostitution and heroin; David R Edwards' lyrics certainly didn't fit in with what was going on in the mainstream Welsh scene, something that struck a chord with Rhys Mwyn and Sion Sebon. '*Y Teimlad*' by Datblygu would later find a new audience thanks to ○ **Super Furry Animals**, who covered the song on their acclaimed 2000 album *Mwng*. SFA singer Gruff Rhys featured on *Cam o'r Tywyllwch* as the drummer in Machlud – a short-lived band from Bethesda, a small slate-mining community that has produced several bands and musicians over the years, including ○ **Maffia Mr. Huws**, Celt, Lisa Jên of ○ **9Bach** and Jackie Williams.

Y Cyrff possibly sound the most accomplished of the bands on this record,. They would release several short, sharp and impressive singles, plus some dazzling albums – including 1991's *Llawenydd Heb Ddiwedd* (Endless Joy) and 1992's *Mae Ddoe yn Ddoe* (Yesterday is Yesterday) – signalling a band in complete control of their art. Their track '*Cymru, Lloegr a Llanrwst*' (Wales, England and Llanrwst) became one of the most cherished and exciting songs in the Welsh language. Rhys Mwyn would later go on to release Y Cyrff singer Mark Roberts' next band ○ **Catatonia**'s first EP through Crai, a subsidiary of Sain.

○ **Anhrefn** (here credited as Yr Anhrefn) themselves have three tracks included on this important record, a sign of their confidence and popularity. 'Action Man', the anthemic '*Rhywle yn Moscow*' (Somewhere in Moscow) and '*Dagrau yn eu Llygaid*' (Tears in Their Eyes) fizz with excitement; accessible punk with an infectious energy. No wonder Anhrefn caught so many people's imaginations. Their singer, Rhys Mwyn himself, remains a hugely passionate advocate of the Welsh music scene and his shows on BBC Radio Cymru mix new artists with classic records from Wales and set them in a wider musical context. He has reflected in print on *Cam o'r Tywyllwch*, even naming his autobiography after the album and recognising its importance and influence on the music from Wales that followed. Peski Records would name a radio show and live event after this compilation, a collection that remains a brilliant document of the creativity on the scene in the mid Eighties. Another compilation, called *Gadael yr Ugeinfed Ganrif* (Leaving the Twentieth Century), would be released through Recordiau Anhrefn soon after this, building on the UK-wide interest in Welsh music.

CAM O'R TYWYLLWCH

GEDON
Bob Delyn a'r Ebillion
(CRAI, 1992)

It could be said that Wales has had a complicated relationship with its modern-day folk music. If things are more positive now – with bands like Calan, VRï, Trials of Cato and ◉ **9Bach** taking traditional Welsh music to a new audience, and organisations like Trac flying the flag for the scene – it wasn't always the case. In record shops you'd often find Irish and Scottish music sections, with trad music from those countries on display, and no Welsh sections. Even in the streaming age, our Celtic cousins still have more space dedicated to them, their music easier to digest, or maybe just easier to sell.

But in the 1990s, Bob Delyn a'r Ebillion were a constant on the live circuit. Their music is fun, moving and designed to be played live: you can almost envisage a smoke-filled back room of a pub, possibly at a stomping gig at Sesiwn Fawr Dolgellau, the audience having a proper jig to the trad tunes given a new lease of life by the young band. Twm's great friend Gorwel Roberts is on guitar and other stringed instruments throughout. Breton singer Nolwenn Korbell is a prominent vocalist on this album, a collaboration that would continue on the group's next album, *Gwbade Bach Cochlyd* (Little Red Flies). Her voice is used to comedic effect on the slightly ridiculous '*Trên Bach y Sgwarnogod*' (The Hares' Little Train). But next to the fun and lively numbers sit some breathtakingly beautiful songs – '*Y Sŵn*' (The Sound) and '*Mil Harddach Wyt*' (You Are a Thousand Times More Beautiful), a Welsh lullaby standard, especially.

Enigmatic frontman Twm Morys is a renowned poet, an expert in the strict meters of traditional Welsh poetry who has won accolades for his work, including the National Eisteddfod Chair in 2003. Over time he has gone from a young bohemian representing a new interest in Celtic music from a Welsh perspective to an elder statesman of Welsh poetry, still with a bohemian and mysterious image. He is the son of Jan Morris, the acclaimed writer who died in 2020, and more recently sings with his partner, Gwyneth Glyn (one quarter of ◉ **Pedair**). His voice is impeccably clear, and has an unmistakable depth captured on all the Bob Delyn records.

The name of the band is a play on Bob Dylan, *delyn* being the Welsh word for the harp, an instrument close to frontman Twm Morys' heart. His love for the Breton language is on display on the album cover, and the opening and closing tracks are in Breton, although the 47-second album closer is the 47-second album opener played in reverse. It's another surprising twist from a band that are keen to shake things up, to honour the past, and to look at it through a different lens. They play meticulously, and are rightfully respected as both progressive and professional experts in their chosen field. They still sporadically play live, their work occasionally gracing grateful ears.

gɛdõn

BOB DELYN A'R EBILLION

BROKE
Astroid Boys
(SONY MUSIC/MUSIC FOR NATIONS, 2017)

With a cover image of the band looking down at the lens through shards of shattered glass, *Broke* is the debut album from Cardiff grime collective Astroid Boys. The sound of the city's underground, this is an introduction to the world of two emcees: Phil Davies, aka Traxx, and Benjamin Kendell, aka Benji Wild, two rap artists who came together to create something very special.

After meeting at rap battles on the bustling Cardiff rap scene, the two rival emcees joined forces and worked for almost a decade before a couple of well-received EPs (with artwork by popular Cardiff artist Phil Morgan) were released, building the anticipation for something longer. The debut album from Astroid Boys landed through the Music for Nations label, funded by Sony, fusing heavy guitars and cold beats, the production values crisp and the two young vocalists' flows tight.

Mashing up genres between grime and rock, this album was a product of the band's live shows: sweaty and energetic experiences, where moshing and circle pits would erupt at the drop of a beat. There was no space to stand contemplating the music at these events – it was a case of getting involved or going home. This bringing together of two worlds and the genre crossover meant that Astroid Boys could play renowned rock festival Download and Reading and Leeds, on the traditionally heavier rock stages like the Lock-Up, as well as making waves in the grime world, earning the respect of DJ Target from BBC Radio 1Xtra and playing events predominantly showcasing rap.

Genre tags are meaning less and less to music lovers in the age of streaming: as long as it's good and speaks to you, it could be metal, grime, pop or R'n'B – what you call it doesn't matter. Newport's Skindred, another festival favourite, had found success merging metal and reggae, proving that finding your sound and running with it was the way forward. Astroid Boys blended their two loves to make something heavy and lyrical, and did it without alienating purists in either camp.

This is an album with a bite, which is clever in its use of language and isn't afraid to tell it as it is. Astroid Boys are in a unique position here, making music that is true to themselves but on a massive major-funded label, giving them a huge platform. They don't hold back, bringing what they do best to a new audience captivated by their style and their unique take on grime. Fellow Cardiff emcee Sonny Double 1 guests on the hypnotic, minimally produced beats of 'Foreigners', with a repetitive hook that is hard to shake, and other album highlights include 'Razz' and 'Soonish'.

Both rappers have gone on to release impressive solo albums, Traxx putting out *Sporting Peace* and Benji Wild releasing *Skull & Bones* and his latest album, simply titled *Welsh Grime*.

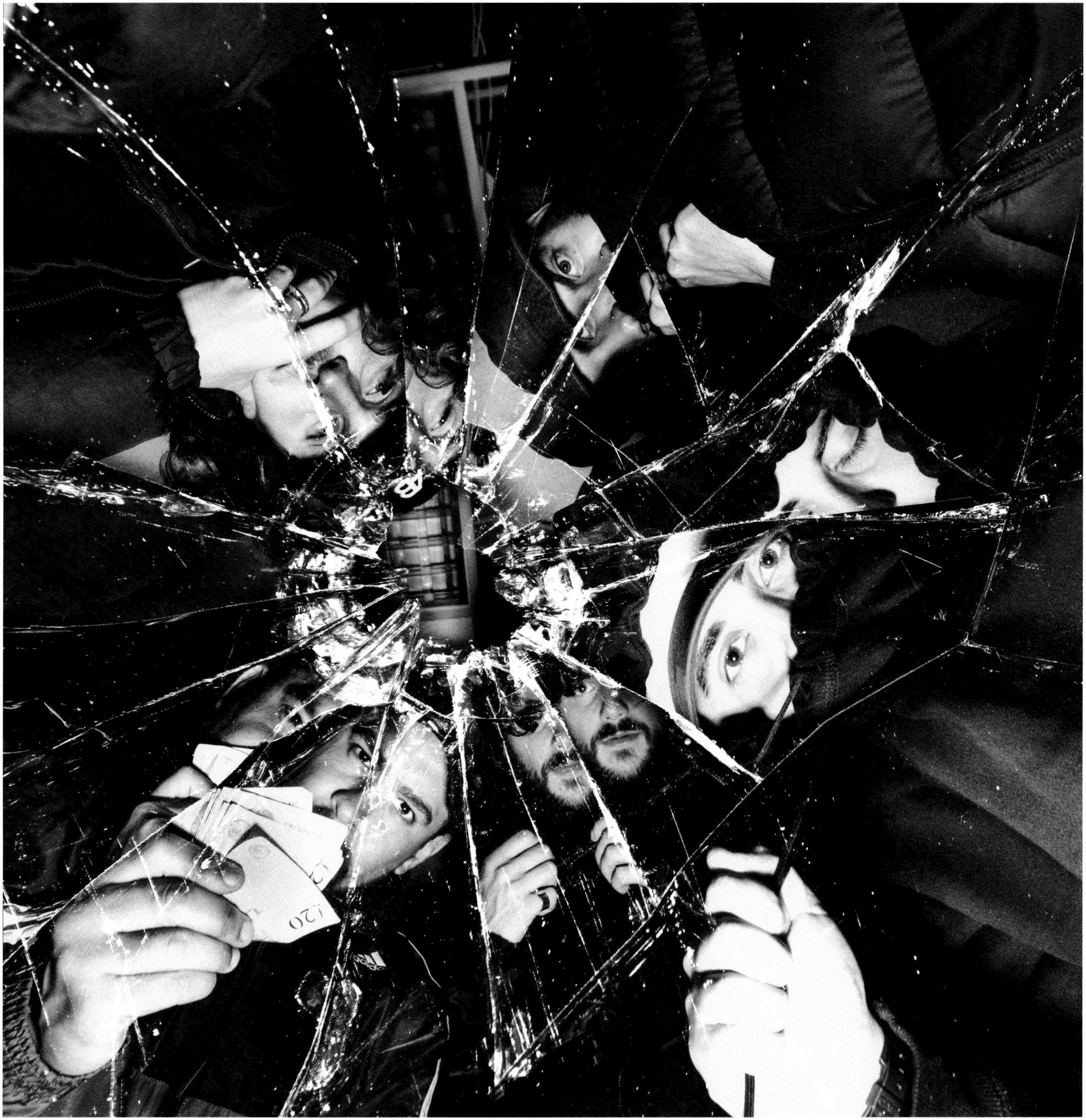

EDRYCH YN LLYGAID CEFFYL BENTHYG
Cate Le Bon

(PESKI, 2008)

Cate Le Bon hails from Pen-boyr, west Wales, and has released some of the most alluring and captivating music from Wales in recent times.

Peski Records, a small independent Cardiff label with a keen ear for new sounds from Wales, released the first official Cate Le Bon record. *Edrych Yn Llygaid Ceffyl Benthyg* (Looking a Gift Horse in the Mouth) was produced by Sir Doufus Styles, aka Kris Jenkins, a prolific musician who had worked with several bands, including ○ **Super Furry Animals**, and made his own music under the name Bench. Pressed on ten-inch vinyl and limited to a few hundred copies, Cate's debut record has become a much-sought-after release, more and more collectable as Cate's star has ascended.

An early friendship with Huw Evans, known as ○ **H. Hawkline**, started at the National Eisteddfod in 2002, held in Pembrokeshire, when Cate's first band Alcatraz shared a bill with Huw's first band Mwsog at Maes B. They would become lifelong friends and musical collaborators, with Cate producing his critically acclaimed 2023 album *Milk for Flowers*. He wrote the lyrics to the first two songs on this debut EP, '*Hwylio Mewn Cyfog*' (Sailing in Sick) and '*Mas Mas*' (Out Out), and also to '*O Am Gariad*' (Oh for Love), a rare number recorded for BBC Radio Cymru which made it on to extended versions of her debut album proper.

Euros Childs contributes backing vocals to '*Byw Heb Farw*' (Live Without Dying). His band ○ **Gorky's Zygotic Mynci** was a huge influence on Cate and her contemporaries, and Euros produced another Peski release, Radio Luxembourg's '*Byw Efo'r Anifeiliad*' (Living with the Animals). Cate herself would go on to produce her own and others' music, including John Grant's *Boy from Michigan*, Carmarthen's Alex Dingley's *Beat the Babble* album and more recently tracks for St. Vincent and Wilco, as her individual sound and taste for the esoteric struck a chord with like-minded musicians around the world. Gruff Rhys was an early fan, releasing her first album *Me Oh My* on his Irony Bored label in 2009, and Cate sang on Gruff and Boom Bip's Neon Neon project, contributing her vocals to *Stainless Style* banger 'I Lust U'.

Cate has gone on to release five albums since *Me Oh My* – *Cyrk*, *Mug Museum*, *Crab Day*, *Reward* and *Pompeii*. *Reward* was Mercury-nominated, and *Pompeii* marked a change in gear for Cate, her love of synths coming to the fore. Collaborating with US band White Fence vocalist Tim Presley, they formed the band Drinks, an outlet for Cate's noisier creative efforts.

An episode she curated for S4C's *Curadur* (Curator) music programme brought the band Pys Melyn to the same line-up as Australian singer Courtney Barnett and US-Venezuelean singer Devendra Banhart, a snapshot of Cate's wide ranging musical palate. She spoke as Devendra played, reminding us of the narrative nature of '*O Bont i Bont*' (From Bridge to Bridge), from this first release.

In 2021, Cate incorporated a ○ **John Cale** song, 'Big White Cloud', into her live set at Green Man. She had been a long-time fan of Cale, aware of his legacy but also in admiration of his constant creativity and looking forward. When she received an email informing her that 'John Cale is looking for you', she cried with happiness. He had reached out, hearing something special in her work.

There are similarities to Cale in Cate Le Bon. Proud of her Welsh roots, she too has found freedom in America, setting up home in the Joshua Tree in the Mojave Desert, ever eager to look forward whilst recognising and respecting her colourful musical past.

Cate Le Bon

EDRYCH YN LLYGAID CEFFYL BENTHYG

DEFAID, SKATEBOARDS A WELLIES
Anhrefn
(WORKERS PLAYTIME, 1987)

Inspired by Tony Wilson's Factory Records label in Manchester and Postcard Records in Glasgow, Rhys Mwyn and his brother Sion Sebon set up Recordiau Anhrefn in 1983, hoping to have a similar positive cultural impact on Wales and the Welsh-language scene. Their *'Cam O'r Tywyllwch'* compilation and subsequent releases certainly sparked a lot of interest in the right places.

Formed in Llanfair Caereinion, Mid Wales, and singing solely in Welsh, Anhrefn the band tried to live up to their name, which means 'Chaos'. They were a punk band from a small town in a small nation who sang in Welsh; they had a lot to be annoyed about. With nothing capturing their imagination in Wales, the band turned to mainland Europe for gigs. They found a keen network of DIY promoters who could recommend them to their contacts in nearby towns and cities, and Anhrefn found a home in these left-field, rebellious gigs, where smaller European languages were sung by bands whether the audience understood them or not. It was all about the music, the message, the ethos, and it was completely natural for this Welsh band to sing in their own minority language to a keen audience. In Wales, some audiences of Welsh speakers would tolerate them, while others were fans. But they would also play to audiences of non-Welsh speakers, who'd heard them on the John Peel show. Similarly to **Datblygu**, here was a band doing what they did while happening to sing in Welsh, not part of the safer, middle-of-the-road entertainment scene that the Welsh media was developing. They didn't fit in and they didn't want to.

Singer Rhys Mwyn has talked about how he wanted to take the punk ideas and ideals he consumed from artists worldwide and plant them in the Welsh garden. It could be said that he was justified in this endeavour, as he has seen the seeds he planted grow over several decades. The cultural impact of Anhrefn's music would be huge, their song *'Rhedeg i Paris'* (Running to Paris) covered by Candelas and becoming a hit in 2016 to mark Wales reaching the Euros that year. Anhrefn took Ffa Coffi Pawb on tour, with drummer Daf Ieuan a member of Anhrefn for a period. Daf also drummed for **Catatonia**, another support staple. Ffa Coffi members formed **Super Furry Animals**, and Catatonia went on to bigger things.

Defaid, Skateboards a Wellies (Sheep, Skateboards and Wellies) was released on Workers Playtime Records, a label set up by Bill Gilliam, who also managed the Dead Kennedys. The label would go on to release albums by renowned poet Benjamin Zephaniah, The Disposable Heroes of Hiphoprisy and Snuff, advocating young rebels with a lot to say. Intriguing TV's Andy Kershaw and the NME, this thrilling young punk band who sang in Welsh became favourites to write about and feature. Little did they know the amount of exciting Welsh-language music that was to follow in subsequent decades.

Anhrefn would finish making punk rock in 1995, but a new project, Hen Wlad fy Mamau – Land of my Mothers, was born, featuring Rhys and brother Sion Sebon. A multi-member production crew, they mixed traditional Welsh music with modern-day electronica, drum 'n' bass and techno to create a dancefloor-friendly breath of fresh air. Rhys hosts a popular weekly programme on BBC Radio Cymru, championing new sounds and ideas whilst connecting them to his musical past, and is also a keen archaeologist and tour guide, as captured in his excellent *Real Gwynedd* book.

ANHREFN

DEFAID, SKATEBOARDS A WELLIES

THE LONGEST DAY
Toby Hay
(THE STATE51 CONSPIRACY, 2018)

In 2024 Cambrian Records celebrated its 10th anniversary. The record label was founded by Toby Hay, the Rhayader-based musician responsible for this stunning album, a magical instrumental record that showcases Toby's intimate yet majestic guitar playing. His remarkable, otherworldly performance is transportative in its beauty, creating a sound that is enchanting and full of layers.

The music is directly inspired by the scenic, wild and impressive part of Wales where he lives. With the River Wye flowing through Rhayader and the stunning Elan Valley, it should come as no surprise that the music Toby Hay plays is so ravishing, so picturesque. On his debut album *The Gathering*, from 2017, Rhayader takes centre stage. Its name coming from the Welsh word *rhaeadr* (waterfall), the small market town is a busy one, with people travelling between north and south Wales, and has a proud history. That Hay named his label Cambrian after the mountains that surround his hometown shows their importance to him. He uses it to release his own music and albums by musicians of a similar ilk, occasionally transcendent, always moving, and always utterly beautiful.

Hay is inspired by many other individual artists, from ◉ **Llio Rhydderch** to Ali Farke Touré. Hay's distinctive style is captured on the album *New Music for the 12 String Guitar*, an album that came about when a one-off offer was made via his label. The State51 Conspiracy invited the Fylde guitar-makers to create a guitar especially for Hay, working together to create Hay's ideal instrument. The result is an album with no overdubs or edits, all performed by Hay at Real World Studios near Bath on this unique guitar, made by Fylde to suit his own specific playing style.

In 2020 he worked with two other songwriters very much inspired by nature, ◉ **The Gentle Good**, aka Gareth Bonello, and ◉ **Georgia Ruth**, on a song named 'Poacher River Song', commissioned by the National Library of Wales. It uses archive audio of a fisherman talking about seeing and catching fish in Tregaron, and field recordings along with the trio's musicianship to create a vivid, emotional piece.

On *The Longest Day*, Hay has one foot at home, one away, with his travels influencing the record. 'Leaving Chicago' was written after a train journey he took from there to Missouri, while 'Marvin the Mustang from Montana' is an ode to a horse Toby once rode. The US influence is heard as elements of jazz music, with some stunning saxophone and subtle violin making their way into Hay's arrangements here, conjuring up something very special. His dog Bear features on the album artwork on a particularly cold day, and has a track, 'Bear's Dance', named after him.

Playing on custom-made guitars, a 12- and a 6-string, his small band of musicians, including the double bass, lift this album, taking Hay's ideas and giving them wings. Indeed, on 'Curlew' (Parts I and II), sounds sweep and swoop immaculately, a joyous spring in the pieces' step. It is hard not to get lost and picture Mid Wales' nature at its very best whilst listening.

In 2023 Toby Hay released a collaboration album with Yorkshire's Jim Ghedi, and in 2024 a record with Aidan Thorne, who enjoyed the process of recording with Hay so much he moved from Cardiff to Mid Wales to live after the album was made.

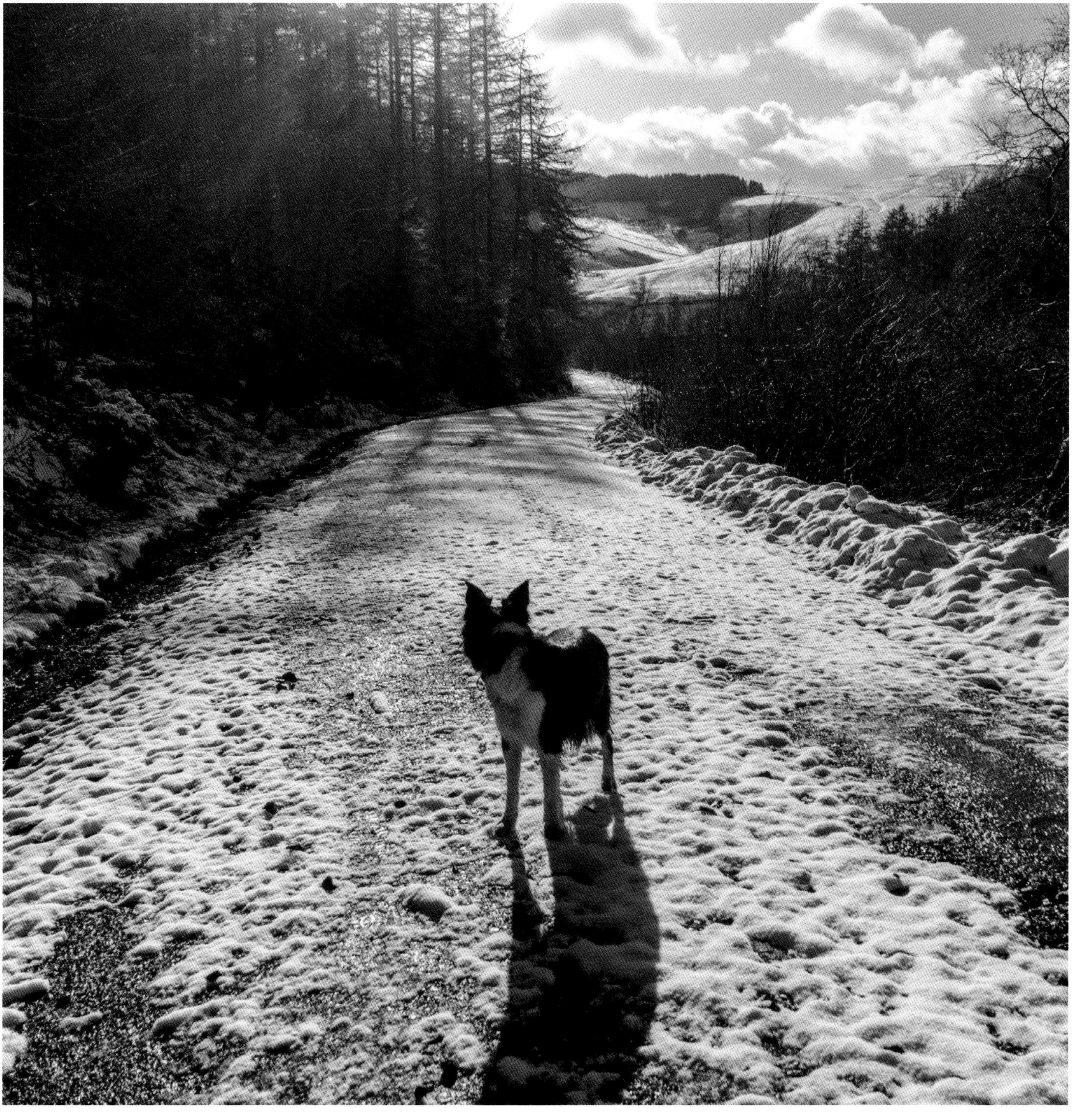

MAES B
Y Blew
(QUALITON, 1967)

Y Blew live on in Welsh music folklore as the first Welsh-language popular rock band, with 1967 the year that changed everything for the young members.

Frustrated by the lack of rock 'n' roll in the Welsh-language scene, Y Blew formed at Aberystwyth University, with Maldwyn Pate on vocals, Dafydd Prys Evans on bass, Richard Lloyd on guitar, Dave Williams on keyboards and Geraint Evans on drums. This was new for Wales – a clear breakaway from the choirs and pleasant duos who dominated Welsh-language culture. Politics in Wales in the 1960s was fraught, with Cymdeithas yr Iaith (the Welsh Language Society) and Plaid Cymru rallying young supporters to back the Welsh language campaign and the political party. Dafydd Evans' father was Gwynfor Evans, the first Plaid Cymru MP elected to Westminster, but Y Blew weren't a political band, aiming instead to create something exciting and relevant to the day's youth.

Influenced by flower power and the Summer of Love, 'Maes B' is a jaunty, free-flowing single with a pounding beat, charming from start to finish. Its crystal-clear vocals and melodic chorus swoop and circle, making it, to modern ears, a perfect pop single. B-side 'Beth Sy'n Dod Rhyngom Ni' (What's Coming Between Us) is a cover of 'You Must Believe Me' by Curtis Mayfield, a nod to the band's love of Motown and influences from further afield.

The sleeve was designed by Robat Gruffudd in the same year he established the publishing house Y Lolfa, who have published this book and thousands of others in both Welsh and English over the decades. Robat also designed many beautiful posters for the hip music acts of the day, and for large dances and get-togethers across Wales, enriching this vibrant scene with his colourful, psychedelic and surreal work.

Within a year of forming, Y Blew had split, having released only one single. That it remains to this day of huge cultural importance is testament to how brightly their star shone during those 12 short months. The group of friends, eager to push their culture forward, set the template for future rock bands, who would do it for longer and to larger audiences.

The title of the song, 'Maes B', remains significant in Wales to this day. It's the name of the youth field at the National Eisteddfod, and ⊙ **Datblygu** took the name and turned it into 'Maes E', David R Edwards' complex and witty lyrics full of drug references, mocking much of the Welsh establishment and criticising the competitive nature of the Eisteddfod. It displayed the anarchic spirit of a band that did much to move Welsh-language culture forward – a spirit that Y Blew would surely have approved of.

QUALITON

yblew

BE GOOD TO YOURSELF AT LEAST ONCE A DAY
Man

(UNITED ARTISTS RECORDS, 1972)

When it comes to prog (short for progressive) music, there's one name that fans of the genre mention in reverential terms: Man.

They were formed from the ashes of The Bystanders from Merthyr Tydfil, a popular rock 'n' roll band which briefly featured the now much-loved BBC Radio Wales presenter Owen Money as its vocalist. It was Deke Leonard's arrival in the band that changed the name of the group to Man, and the music from straight-up rock 'n' roll to something altogether more proggy – the genre that Man would make a real name for themselves in.

While signed to Pye Records, the influential label home to skiffle legend Lonnie Donegan and The Kinks, amongst others, they put out two albums and several singles. Popular in Europe, members came and went constantly, but the gigging and recording as Man continued despite – or maybe because of – the revolving door of musicians.

They recorded their 1971 album *Do You Like It Here Now, Are You Settling In?* in Rockfield Studios, near Monmouth, and released a live record, *Live at the Padget Rooms, Penarth* in 1972. In December '72, they held a Christmas party at the Patti Pavilion in Swansea, with by now former Man member Deke Leonard and revered pedal steel guitarist B J Cole guesting with the band Help Yourself, and Cardiff-born rock 'n' roll legend Dave Edmunds singing with Man. The gig was recorded and released as a beautiful ten-inch vinyl record, *Christmas at the Patti*. It became a hit, taking the name of the Italian opera singer who retired to Swansea, Adelina Patti, into the charts for the first time.

The positively titled *Be Good to Yourself at Least Once a Day* is Man's sixth album. With Dave Edmunds and the band themselves producing, it was recorded between August and October 1972, an incredibly busy year for the band.

An extraordinary vinyl edition of *Be Good to Yourself at Least Once a Day* features a gatefold sleeve that, when opened, reveals a fold-out map of Wales (see next page), designed by David Anstee. Towns and cities are noted, with a caption for each one:

Anglesey – joined to north Wales coast by two bridges
Aberystwyth – College of Wales, College of Beer
Penclawdd – cockles

Rockfield Studios is on the map; next to Cardiff is a list of bands from there, including **Amen Corner** and Budgie; Carmarthen has 'just a mad place' underneath it. On the right-hand side of the map, several men are reaching over the water with bargepoles, pushing England away: Man's map of Wales sees Wales as an island! It has to be seen to be believed.

The inner record sleeve itself is full of detailed notes, in-jokes and a family tree that is complex and exhaustive, taking in Man's numerous line-up changes, while acknowledgements include a mention for Deke Leonard's new band, Help Yourself. Underneath, in brackets, it continues: '(The most boring group in the world)'.

Prog might be a serious matter, but humour is clearly of equal importance in this unique album.

Many of the original members have died – including founding member Deke Leonard in 2017, having published four autobiographies and leaving a remarkable legacy – but Man continue to play live, and released their latest album in 2019.

MAN

Be good to yourself at least once a day

MANS MAP OF WALES
NORTH
SOUTH
EAST
WEST
TO IRELAND AND ALL POINTS WEST
HOLYHEAD
JOINED TO NORTH WALES COAST BY TWO BRIDGES
ANGLESEY
LLANDUDNO
BIGGEST RESORT IN WALES
POINT OF AIR
GIG AT AMERICAN AIR BASE
CAERNARVON
3560 FEET
SNOWDON
LLANYSTUMDWY
SNOWDONIA NATIONAL PARK
LLANGOLLEN
U.S.A.F.
IRISH SEA
WHALES
ABERYSTWYTH
DEVIL'S BRIDGE
TREGARON
NEW QUAY
THE BADLANDS
BADLANDS
FISHGUARD
CARMARTHEN
TENBY
LLANELLI
NEATH
SWANSEA
PORT TALBOT
MERTHYR TYDFIL
BRIDGEND
BARRY
CARDIFF
PENARTH
BRISTOL CHANNEL
SHARK FISHING

Map 1: Record stores

1. **Bangor:** Mudshark Records
2. **Abergele:** Noise Annoys
3. **Mold:** Vod Music
4. **Wrexham:** Moonlight Records; ReVibed Records
5. **Pwllheli:** The Definitely Maybe
6. **Porthmadog:** Cob Records
7. **Aberystwyth:** Andy's Records
8. **Hay on Wye:** Tangled Parrot; Tom's Records
9. **St Davids:** Dead Sea Records
10. **Haverfordwest:** Core of the Poodle; Terminal Records
11. **Tenby:** Dale's Music Store
12. **Carmarthen:** Tangled Parrot
13. **Llanelli:** The Second 45
14. **Swansea:** Derrick's Music; Tangled Parrot
15. **Ebbw Vale:** The Vault Collective
16. **Abergavenny:** Music One Vinyl
17. **Abertillery:** Kenny's Vinyl Vault
18. **Blackwood:** Heart of the Valleys Music Store
19. **Newport:** Diverse Vinyl; Kriminal Records
20. **Cardiff:** Cardiff Record Exchange; Diggers Club Records; D'Vinyl Records; Kelly's Records; Spillers Records

…and check Vinyl Daze for local record fairs!

Map II: 'All Wales is a Land of Song'

1. **Marian-glas:** Llio Rhydderch
2. **Benllech:** Carwyn Ellis & Rio 18
3. **Llangefni:** Tony ac Aloma
4. **Rhoscefnhir:** Super Furry Animals (Dafydd Ieuan & Cian Ciarán)
5. **Llangristiolus:** Pedair (Meinir Gwilym)
6. **Gaerwen:** Brân (Nest Howells)
7. **Llanfairpwllgwyngyllgogerychwyrndrobwllllantysiliogogogoch:** Rheinallt H. Rowlands
8. **Bangor:** Sasha
9. **Rachub:** Ffrancon
10. **Rhyl:** The Alarm
11. **Ffynnongroyw:** Bando (Caryl Parry Jones)
12. **Bagillt:** Kelly Lee Owens
13. **Dwyran:** Ren
14. **Rhiwlas:** Lleuwen
15. **Bethesda:** 9Bach, Maffia Mr. Huws, Super Furry Animals (Gruff Rhys)
16. **Trefriw:** Sweet Baboo
17. **Llanrwst:** Catatonia (Mark Roberts)
18. **Mold:** The Joy Formidable
19. **Waunfawr:** Big Leaves
20. **Llanberis:** Hogia'r Wyddfa
21. **Llanllyfni:** Sobin a'r Smaeliaid
22. **Snowdonia:** Daedelus
23. **Wrexham:** K-klass, Neck Deep
24. **Nefyn:** Duffy
25. **Llanarmon:** Pedair (Gwyneth Glyn)
26. **Blaenau Ffestiniog:** Llwybr Llaethog
27. **Pwllheli:** Endaf Emlyn, Pedair (Gwenan Gibbard)
28. **Llanystumdwy:** Bob Delyn a'r Ebillion
29. **Llanuwchlyn:** Dafydd Iwan ac Edward, Tystion (Gruff Meredith)
30. **Llanegryn:** Meredydd Evans
31. **Llanerfyl:** Pedair (Siân James)
32. **Llanfair Caereinion:** Anhrefn
33. **Aberystwyth:** Y Blew, Georgia Ruth, Murry the Hump
34. **Rhayader:** Toby Hay
35. **Llan-non:** Catrin Finch
36. **Cardigan:** Ail Symudiad, Datblygu
37. **Solva:** Meic Stevens
38. **Pen-boyr:** Cate Le Bon
39. **Freshwater East:** Gorky's Zygotic Mynci (Euros Childs)
40. **Carmarthen:** Adwaith, Gorky's Zygotic Mynci, Tystion (Steffan Cravos)
41. **Llandybie:** Datblygu (Patricia Morgan)
42. **Glanaman:** Ryan
43. **Brynaman:** Dafydd Iwan
44. **Ammanford:** Underworld (Rick Smith)
45. **Garnant:** John Cale
46. **Pontardawe:** Mary Hopkin
47. **Resolven:** Murry the Hump (Matthew Evans)
48. **Glynneath:** The Anchoress, Max Boyce
49. **Merthyr Tydfil:** Man
50. **Ebbw Vale:** The Flying Pickets (Brian Hibbard), Public Service Broadcasting
51. **Aberdare:** Don Leisure
52. **Rhymney:** The Byrds
53. **Llangennith:** Phil Tanner
54. **Swansea:** Badfinger, Bonnie Tyler, Helen Love, The Pooh Sticks
55. **Neath:** Bright Light Bright Light
56. **Cwmaman:** Stereophonics
57. **Treorchy:** Paul Robeson & Treorchy Male Voice Choir
58. **Penpedairheol:** Katell Keineg
59. **Blackwood:** Manic Street Preachers
60. **Ystrad Mynach:** Amen Corner (Andy Fairweather Low)
61. **Trefforest:** Tom Jones
62. **Taff's Well:** Gwenifer Raymond
63. **Caerphilly:** Tŷ Gwydr
64. **Newport:** 60ft Dolls, Dub War, Goldie Lookin Chain, Jon Langford & His Men of Gwent, Scritti Politti
65. **Bridgend:** Funeral for a Friend
66. **Cardiff:** Aleighcia Scott, Amen Corner, Astroid Boys, Bando, Catatonia, Deyah, The Gentle Good, Geraint Jarman, Gwenno, H. Hawkline, Heather Jones, Yr Hennessys, Huw Jones, Ivor Novello, Mace the Great, mclusky, Me One, Minas, Pino Palladino, Shakin' Stevens, Shirley Bassey, Super Furry Animals (Huw Bunford & Guto Pryce), Young Marble Giants
67. **Penarth:** High Contrast

Appendix I

Wales: 100 Records – A–Z by artist

artist/record	page
9Bach: *Tincian*	128
60ft Dolls: 'Happy Shopper'	100
Adwaith: *Melyn*	20
Ail Symudiad: *Sefyll ar y Sgwâr*	60
The Alarm: *Eye of the Hurricane*	170
Aleighcia Scott: *Windrush Baby*	176
Amen Corner: '(If Paradise Is) Half as Nice'	162
The Anchoress: *Versions*	148
Anhrefn: *Defaid, Skateboards a Wellies*	188
Astroid Boys: *Broke*	184
Badfinger: *No Dice*	142
Bando: *Shampŵ*	168
Big Leaves: *Pwy Sy'n Galw?*	150
Y Blew: 'Maes B'	192
Bob Delyn a'r Ebillion: *Gedon*	182
Bonnie Tyler: *Faster Than the Speed of Night*	98
Brân: *Brân*	106
Bright Light Bright Light: *Fun City*	56
The Byrds: 'The Bells of Rhymney'	144
Carwyn Ellis & Rio 18: *Joia!*	96
Catatonia: *Way Beyond Blue*	92
Cate Le Bon: *Edrych yn Llygaid Ceffyl Benthyg*	186
Catrin Finch & Seckou Keita: *Clychau Dibon*	158
Daedelus: *Of Snowdonia*	62
Dafydd Iwan: 'Magi Thatcher'	172
Dafydd Iwan ac Edward: *Yn ôl i Gwm Rhyd y Rhosyn*	32
Datblygu: *Wyau*	140
Deyah: *Care City*	64
Don Leisure: *Shaboo Strikes Back*	136
Dub War: *Westgate Under Fire*	110
Duffy: *Rockferry*	34
Endaf Emlyn: *Salem*	88
Ffrancon: *Gwalaxia: Belleville 1315/Machynlleth 1404*	36
The Flying Pickets: *Lost Boys*	120
Funeral for a Friend: *Casually Dressed & Deep in Conversation*	166

The Gentle Good: *Y Bardd Anfarwol*	160
Georgia Ruth: *Week of Pines*	112
Geraint Jarman: *Gobaith Mawr y Ganrif*	164
Goldie Lookin Chain: *Greatest Hits*	132
Gorky's Zygotic Mynci: *Tatay*	116
Gwenifer Raymond: 'Hell for Certain'	106
Gwenno: *Y Dydd Olaf*	54
H. Hawkline: *Milk for Flowers*	86
Heather Jones: *Colli Iaith*	26
Helen Love: 'Joey Ramoney'	130
Yr Hennessys: 'Ar Lan y Môr'	24
High Contrast: *True Colours*	30
Hogia'r Wyddfa: 'Safwn yn y Bwlch'	44
Huw Jones: 'Dŵr'	52
Ivor Novello: 'Keep the Home-Fires Burning'	50
John Cale: *Paris 1919*	28
Jon Langford & His Men of Gwent: *The Legend of LL*	84
The Joy Formidable: *The Big Roar*	154
K-klass: *Universal*	48
Katell Keineg: *Ô Seasons Ô Castles*	174
Kelly Lee Owens: *Inner Song*	14
Lleuwen: *Gwn Glân Beibl Budr*	108
Llio Rhydderch: *Sir Fôn Bach*	102
Llwybr Llaethog v. Tŷ Gwydr : David R. Edwards: *LL.LL. v. T.G : MC D.R.E.*	82
Mace the Great: *My Side of the Bridge*	80
Maffia Mr. Huws: *Hysbysebion*	114
Man: *Be Good to Yourself at Least Once a Day*	194
Manic Street Preachers: *The Holy Bible*	38
Mary Hopkin: *Llais Swynol*	66
Max Boyce: *We All Had Doctor's Papers*	78
mclusky: *Mclusky Do Dallas*	46
Me One: *As Far As I'm Concerned*	22
Meic Stevens: *Gwymon*	58
Meredydd Evans: *Welsh Folk Songs*	12
Minas: 'Chatty Patty'	26
Murry the Hump: *Songs of Ignorance*	146

Neck Deep: *Life's Not Out to Get You*	16
Paul Robeson & The Treorchy Male Voice Choir: *Transatlantic Exchange*	118
Pedair: *Mae 'Na Olau*	134
Phil Tanner: *The Gower Nightingale*	130
Pino Palladino & Blake Mills: *Notes With Attachments*	70
The Pooh Sticks: *'I Know Someone Who Knows Someone Who Knows Alan McGee Quite Well'*	50
Public Service Broadcasting: *Every Valley*	90
Ren: *Sick Boi*	162
Rheinallt H. Rowlands: *Bukowski*	68
Ryan: *Ryan*	148
Sasha: *Scene Delete*	76
Scritti Politti: *Cupid & Psyche 85*	18
Shakin' Stevens: *Take One!*	138
Shirley Bassey: *The Fabulous Shirley Bassey*	72
Sobin a'r Smaeliaid: *Sobin a'r Smaeliaid I*	156
Stereophonics: *Word Gets Around*	10
Super Furry Animals: *Mwng*	104
Sweet Baboo: *The Wreckage*	152
Toby Hay: *The Longest Day*	190
Tom Jones: *Surrounded by Time*	126
Tony ac Aloma: *Tony ac Aloma*	76
Tystion: *Rhaid i Rywbeth Ddigwydd*	178
Underworld: *Dubnobasswithmyheadman*	124
Various Artists: *Cam o'r Tywyllwch*	180
Various Artists: *The Collective*	94
Various Artists: *Dial-a-Poem* and *Clywch-y-Bardd*	122
Various Artists: *Dial M for Merthyr*	74
Various Artists: *Welsh Rare Beat*	42
Young Marble Giants: *Colossal Youth*	40

Appendix II

Wales: 100 Records – by year

1910s
1915   'Keep the Home-Fires Burning', Ivor Novello

1950s
1954   *Welsh Folk Songs*, Meredydd Evans
1957   *Transatlantic Exchange*, Paul Robeson & The Treorchy Male Voice Choir
1959   *The Fabulous Shirley Bassey*, Shirley Bassey

1960s
1965   'The Bells of Rhymney', The Byrds
1967   '*Maes B*', Y Blew
1968   *Llais Swynol*, Mary Hopkin
1969   '(If Paradise Is) Half as Nice', Amen Corner
1969   '*Safwn yn y Bwlch*', Hogia'r Wyddfa
1969   '*Dŵr*', Huw Jones

1970s
1970   *Ar Lan y Môr*, Yr Hennessys
1970   *No Dice*, Badfinger
1971   *Dial-a-Poem* and *Clywch-y-Bardd*, Various Artists
1971   *Colli Iaith*, Heather Jones
1971   *Ryan*, Ryan
1971   *Tony ac Aloma*, Tony ac Aloma
1972   *Gwymon*, Meic Stevens
1972   *Be Good to Yourself at Least Once a Day*, Man
1973   *Paris 1919*, John Cale
1974   *Brân*, Brân
1974   *Salem*, Endaf Emlyn
1975   *We All Had Doctor's Papers*, Max Boyce
1976   *Gobaith Mawr y Ganrif*, Geraint Jarman
1977   *Yn ôl i Gwm Rhyd y Rhosyn*, Dafydd Iwan ac Edward
1979   *Take One!*, Shakin' Stevens

1980s

1980	*Colossal Youth*, Young Marble Giants
1980	'Magi Thatcher', Dafydd Iwan
1982	*Sefyll ar y Sgwâr*, Ail Symudiad
1982	*Shampŵ*, Bando
1983	*Faster Than the Speed of Night*, Bonnie Tyler
1983	*Hysbysebion*, Maffia Mr. Huws
1984	*Lost Boys*, The Flying Pickets
1985	*Cam o'r Tywyllwch*, Various Artists
1985	*Cupid & Psyche 85*, Scritti Politti
1987	*Defaid, Skateboards a Wellies*, Anhrefn
1987	*Eye of the Hurricane*, The Alarm
1988	'I Know Someone Who Knows Someone Who Knows Alan McGee Quite Well', The Pooh Sticks
1988	*Wyau*, Datblygu
1989	*Sobin a'r Smaeliaid I*, Sobin a'r Smaeliaid

1990s

1991	*LL.LL. v. T.G : MC D.R.E.*, Llwybr Llaethog v. Tŷ Gwydr : David R. Edwards
1992	*Gedon*, Bob Delyn a'r Ebillion
1993	'Joey Ramoney', Helen Love
1993	*Universal*, K-klass
1994	*Dubnobasswithmyheadman*, Underworld
1994	*Tatay*, Gorky's Zygotic Mynci
1994	'Happy Shopper', 60ft Dolls
1994	*Ô Seasons Ô Castles*, Katell Keineg
1994	*The Holy Bible*, Manic Street Preachers
1996	*Bukowski*, Rheinallt H. Rowlands
1996	*Way Beyond Blue*, Catatonia
1997	*Dial M for Merthyr*, Various Artists
1997	*Word Gets Around*, Stereophonics
1997	*Rhaid i Rywbeth Ddigwydd*, Tystion
1999	*Pwy Sy'n Galw?*, Big Leaves

2000s

2000	*Mwng*, Super Furry Animals
2000	*As Far As I'm Concerned*, Me One
2000	*The Collective*, Various Artists
2001	*Songs of Ignorance*, Murry the Hump
2002	*Mclusky Do Dallas*, mclusky
2002	*True Colours*, High Contrast
2003	*The Gower Nightingale*, Phil Tanner
2003	*Casually Dressed & Deep in Conversation*, Funeral for a Friend

2004	*Of Snowdonia*, Daedelus
2004	*Greatest Hits*, Goldie Lookin Chain
2005	*Welsh Rare Beat*, Various Artists
2008	*Rockferry*, Duffy
2008	*Edrych yn Llygaid Ceffyl Benthyg*, Cate le Bon

2010s

2011	*The Big Roar*, The Joy Formidable
2013	*Week of Pines*, Georgia Ruth
2013	*Y Bardd Anfarwol*, The Gentle Good
2013	*Clychau Dibon*, Catrin Finch & Seckou Keita
2014	*Tincian*, 9Bach
2014	*Y Dydd Olaf*, Gwenno
2015	*Life's Not Out to Get You*, Neck Deep
2015	*The Legend of LL,* Jon Langford & His Men of Gwent
2016	*Scene Delete*, Sasha
2017	*Every Valley*, Public Service Broadcasting
2017	*Broke*, Astroid Boys
2018	*The Longest Day*, Toby Hay
2018	*Melyn*, Adwaith
2018	*Gwn Glân Beibl Budr*, Lleuwen
2019	*Joia!,* Carwyn Ellis & Rio 18
2019	*Sir Fôn Bach*, Llio Rhydderch

2020s

2020	*Care City*, Deyah
2020	*Inner Song*, Kelly Lee Owens
2020	*Fun City,* Bright Light Bright Light
2020	'Hell for Certain', Gwenifer Raymond
2021	*Notes with Attachments*, Pino Palladino & Blake Mills
2021	*My Side of the Bridge*, Mace the Great
2021	*Surrounded by Time*, Tom Jones
2021	*Gwalaxia: Belleville 1315/Machynlleth 1404*, Ffrancon
2022	*Shaboo Strikes Back*, Don Leisure
2022	*Westgate Under Fire*, Dub War
2022	*Mae 'Na Olau*, Pedair
2023	*The Wreckage*, Sweet Baboo
2023	*Milk for Flowers*, H. Hawkline
2023	*Windrush Baby*, Aleighcia Scott
2023	'Chatty Patty', Minas
2023	*Versions*, The Anchoress
2023	*Sick Boi*, Ren

Further reading

AP SIÔN, Pwyll & THOMAS, Wyn (gol.): *Cydymaith i Gerddoriaeth Cymru* (Y Lolfa, 2018)
BOYCE, Max: *Hymns & Arias: The selected poems, songs and stories* (Parthian, 2021)
CALE, John & BOCKRIS, Victor: *What's Welsh for Zen?* (Bloomsbury Publishing, 1999)
CHARNAS, Dan: *Dilla Time: The Life and Afterlife of J. Dilla* (Swift Press, 2022)
CHETTY, Darren; MUSE, Grug; ISSA, Hanan; TYNE, Iestyn (eds.): *Welsh (Plural): Essays on the Future of Wales* (Repeater Books, 2022)
COLLINS, Jeff: *Rock Legends at Rockfield* (Calon, 2022 [2nd edn.])
COLLINS, Neil: *International Velvet: How Wales Conquered the 90's Charts* (Calon, 2024)
DAFYDD, Elis & TUDUR, Marged (gol.): *Rhywbeth i'w Ddweud: 10 o Ganeuon Gwleidyddol 1979–2016* (Cyhoeddiadau Barddas, 2017)
DAY-WEBB, Robert: *On Track... Badfinger: Every album, every song* (Sonicbond Publishing, 2022)
EDWARDS, David R: *Atgofion Hen Wanc* (Y Lolfa, 2009)
EKPOUDOM, Aniefiok: *Where We Come From: Rap, Home & Hope in Modern Britain* (Faber, 2024)
EMLYN, Endaf: *Salem, a Fi* (Y Lolfa, 2024)
EVANS, Meredydd: *Hela'r Hen Ganeuon* (Y Lolfa, 2009)
FINCH, Peter : *The Roots of Rock from Cardiff to Mississippi and Back* (Seren, 2015)
GIBBARD, Gwenan: *Merched y Chwyldro: Merched Pop Cymru'r 60au a'r 70au* (Cyhoeddiadau Sain, 2019)
GLASPER, Ian: *Burning Britain: The History of UK Punk 1980–1984* (PM Press, 2014)
GLASPER, Ian: *Trapped in a Scene: UK Hardcore 1985–1989* (Cherry Red Books, 2009)
GWILYM, Arfon: *Cerddoriaeth y Cymry: Cyflwyniad i draddodiad cerddorol Cymru* (Y Lolfa, 2007)
GWYNFRYN, Hywel: *Ryan and Ronnie* (Y Lolfa, 2014)
HERBERT, Trevor; CLARKE, Martin V. & BARLOW, Helen (eds.): *A History of Welsh Music* (Cambridge University Press, 2022)
HILL, Sarah: *'Blerwytirhwng?' The Place of Welsh Pop Music* (Routledge, 2007)
IWAN, Dafydd: *Still Singing 'Yma o Hyd'* (Y Lolfa, 2023)
JARMAN, Geraint & WILLIAMS, Eurof: *Twrw Jarman* (Gwasg Gomer, 2011)
JONES, Huw: *Dwi isio bod yn...* (Y Lolfa, 2020)
JONES, Jack: *Swansea to Hornsey* (Strap Originals, 2023)
JONES, Richard & JONES, Wyn: *Fflach o Ail Symudiad* (Y Lolfa, 2014)
JONES, Tom: *Over the Top and Back: The Autobiography* (Penguin, 2016)
KING, Richard: *Brittle with Relics: A History of Wales, 1962–97* (Faber, 2022)
LORD, Peter & DAVIES, Rhian: *The Art of Music: Branding the Welsh Nation* (Parthian Book, 2022)
McNICHOLAS, Steph: *When Ponty Rocked!* (Graig Books, 2021)

MWYN, Rhys: *Cam o'r Tywyllwch: Hunangofiant* (Y Lolfa, 2006)
OWEN, Huw Dylan: *Sesiwn yng Nghymru: Cymry, Cwrw a Chân* (Y Lolfa, 2015)
PRICE, Simon: *Everything (A book about Manic Street Preachers)* (Virgin Books, 1999 [reprint])
RAWLINS, Ric: *Rise of the Super Furry Animals* (The Friday Project, 2015)
RHYS, Gruff: *Resist Phony Encores!* (Hat & Beard, LLC, 2020)
SANNEH, Kelefa: *Major Labels: A History of Popular Music in Seven Genres* (Canongate Books, 2021)
STEVENS, Meic: *Caniadau* (Dalen, 2022)
STEVENS, Meic: *Solva Blues; An autobiography* (Y Lolfa, 2004)
TREZISE, Rachel: *Dial M For Merthyr* (Parthian Books, 2007)
TYLER, Bonnie: *Straight from the Heart* (Coronet, 2023)
WALTON, Adam T: *On Making Music* (CreateSpace, 2014 [2nd edn.])
WYN, Hefin: *Ar drywydd Meic Stevens: Y Swynwr o Solfach* (Y Lolfa, 2015)
WYN, Hefin: *Be Bop a Lula'r Delyn Aur: Hanes canu poblogaidd Cymraeg* (Y Lolfa, 2002)
WYN, Hefin: *Ble Wyt Ti Rhwng?: Hanes canu poblogaidd Cymraeg 1980–2000* (Y Lolfa, 2006)

Diolch!

Thanks to all who gave permission and assisted us in bringing these records into the pages of *Wales: 100 Records*.

A massive *diolch yn fawr* to my editor Carolyn Hodges at Y Lolfa for her support, encouragement and patience in making this book happen: *diolch enfawr am dy waith caled! Diolch i Lefi am droi y syniad mewn i realiti, ac i bawb yn Y Lolfa am eich cymorth a'ch gwaith.* Thank you to Rich for the design. Thank you to Caio for the beautiful cover artwork. Thanks to Kasimiira for publicising. Thanks to Ren for the photos and Ed at Cardiff Record Exchange for the loan of the shop. Thanks to all who assisted in various ways – Meic Parry, Dyl Mei and all who kindly read various pieces. *Diolch i Tony Schiavone. Diolch Mam, Lowri, Heledd a Brengain. Diolch Sara.*

And finally, thank you for reading and sharing these records. And of course, I can't believe that record isn't in here either.

Huw Stephens
April 2024

Picture credits

Additional photography for the book by Ren Faulkner.

Thanks to the National Library of Wales for help with tracking down some of the rarer records.

Tincian by 9Bach: cover image reproduced by kind permission of 9Bach and Real World Records./'Happy Shopper' by 60ft Dolls: cover image reproduced by kind permission of Townhill Records./*Melyn* by Adwaith: cover image reproduced by kind permission of Adwaith and Libertino Records./*Sefyll ar y Sgwâr* by Ail Symudiad: cover image reproduced by kind permission of Sain./*Eye of the Hurricane* by The Alarm: cover image reproduced by kind permission of The Alarm./*Windrush Baby* by Aleighcia Scott: cover image reproduced by kind permission of Aleighcia Scott and Black Dub./*Versions* by The Anchoress: cover image reproduced by kind permission of The Anchoress and Drowned in Sound./*Defaid, Skateboards a Wellies* by Anhrefn: cover image reproduced by kind permission of Anhrefn./*Broke* by Astroid Boys: cover image used by permission of Music for Nations and Sony Music Entertainment UK Limited. All rights reserved./*No Dice* by Badfinger: cover artwork reproduced by kind permission of Apple Corps Ltd./*Shampŵ* by Bando: cover image reproduced by kind permission of Sain./*Pwy Sy'n Galw* by Big Leaves: cover image reproduced by kind permission of Sain./'Maes B' by Y Blew: cover image reproduced by kind permission of Y Blew and Robat Gruffudd./*Gedon* by Bob Delyn a'r Ebillion: cover image reproduced by kind permission of Sain./*Faster Than the Speed of Night* by Bonnie Tyler: cover image used by permission of Supermost Ents Ltd fso Bonnie Tyler, David Aspden Mgt. and Sony Music Entertainment UK Limited. All rights reserved./*Fun City* by Bright Light Bright Light: cover image reproduced by kind permission of Bright Light Bright Light./'The Bells of Rhymney' by The Byrds: cover image reproduced by kind permission of Sony Music Entertainment USA; with thanks to Sundazed Music./*Joia!* by Carwyn Ellis & Rio 18: cover image reproduced by kind permission of Carwyn Ellis and Banana & Louie./*Way Beyond Blue* by Catatonia: cover image reproduced by kind permission of Warner Music UK Ltd./*Edrych yn Llygaid Ceffyl Benthyg* by Cate Le Bon: cover image reproduced by kind permission of Peski./*Clychau Dibon* by Catrin Finch & Seckou Keita: cover image reproduced by kind permission of Catrin Finch & Seckou Keita./'Magi Thatcher' by Dafydd Iwan: cover image reproduced by kind permission of Sain./*Yn ôl i Gwm Rhyd y Rhosyn* by Dafydd Iwan ac Edward: cover image reproduced by kind permission of Sain./*Wyau* by Datblygu: cover image reproduced by kind permission of Recordiau Anhrefn./*Care City* by Deyah: cover image reproduced by kind permission of Deyah./*Shaboo Strikes Back* by Don Leisure: cover image reproduced by kind permission of Don Leisure./*Westgate Under Fire* by Dub War: cover image reproduced by kind permission of Earache./*Rockferry* by Duffy: cover image reproduced by kind permission of Universal Music Group./*Salem* by Endaf Emlyn: cover image reproduced by kind permission of Sain./*Lost Boys* by The Flying Pickets: cover image provided through the courtesy of Universal Music Operations Limited./*Gwalaxia: Belleville 1315/ Machynlleth 1404* by Ffrancon: cover image reproduced by kind permission of Ffrancon and Ankst/Ankstmusik./*Casually Dressed & Deep in Conversation* by Funeral for a Friend: cover image reproduced by kind permission of Warner Music UK Ltd./*Y Bardd Anfarwol*: cover image reproduced by kind permission of The Gentle Good and Bubblewrap Records./*Week of Pines* by Georgia Ruth: cover image reproduced by kind permission of Georgia Ruth and Sain./*Gobaith Mawr y Ganrif* by Geraint Jarman: cover image reproduced by kind permission of Sain./*Greatest Hits* by Goldie Lookin Chain: cover image reproduced by kind permission of Warner Music UK Ltd./*Tatay* by Gorky's Zygotic Mynci: cover image reproduced by kind permission of Ankst/Ankstmusik./'Hell for Certain' by Gwenifer Raymond: cover image reproduced by kind permission of Tompkins Square./*Y Dydd Olaf* by Gwenno: cover image reproduced by kind permission of Peski./*Milk for Flowers* by H. Hawkline: cover image reproduced by kind permission of H. Hawkline and Heavenly./*Colli Iaith* by Heather Jones: cover image reproduced by kind permission of Sain./'Joey Ramoney' by Helen Love: cover image reproduced by kind permission of Damaged Goods./*True Colours* by High Contrast: cover image reproduced by kind permission of Lincoln Barrett and Hospital Records./'Safwn yn y Bwlch' by Hogia'r Wyddfa: cover image reproduced by kind permission of Sain./'Dŵr' by Huw Jones: cover image reproduced by kind permission of Sain./Ivor Novello image: Bain News Service, restored by Adam Cuerden. Public domain, via Wikimedia Commons./*Paris 1919* by John Cale: cover image reproduced by kind permission of Domino Recording Co./*The Legend of LL* by Jon Langford & His Men of Gwent: cover image reproduced by kind permission of Country Mile Records./*The Big Roar* by The Joy Formidable: cover image reproduced by kind permission of Warner Music UK Ltd./*Ô Seasons Ô Castles* by Katell Keineg: cover image reproduced by kind permission of Katell Keineg./*Inner Song* by Kelly Lee Owens: cover image reproduced by kind permission of Kelly Lee Owens and Smalltown Supersound./*Universal* by K-klass: cover image reproduced by kind permission of Warner Music UK Ltd./*Gwn Glân Beibl Budr* by Lleuwen: cover image reproduced by kind permission of Sain./*Sir Fôn Bach* by Llio Rhydderch: cover image reproduced by kind permission of Llio Rhydderch and fflach:tradd./*LL.LL. v. T.G : MC D.R.E.* by Llwybr Llaethog v. Tŷ Gwydr : David R. Edwards: cover image reproduced by kind permission of Ankst/Ankstmusik./*My Side of the Bridge* by Mace the Great: cover image reproduced by kind permission of MacetheGreatMusic./*Hysbysebion* by Maffia Mr. Huws: cover image reproduced by kind permission of Maffia Mr. Huws and Pesda Roc./*Be Good to Yourself at Least Once a Day* by Man: cover and map images reproduced by kind permission of Warner Music UK. Map designed by David Anstee./*The Holy Bible* by Manic Street Preachers: cover image used by permission of Columbia Records and Sony Music Entertainment UK Limited. All rights reserved./*We All Had Doctor's Papers* by Max Boyce: cover image reproduced by kind permission of Warner Music UK./*Mclusky Do Dallas* by mclusky: cover image reproduced by kind permission of the Beggars Group./*As Far As I'm Concerned* by Me One: cover image provided through the courtesy of Universal Music Operations Limited./*Gwymon* by Meic Stevens: cover image reproduced by kind permission of Sain./*Welsh Folk Songs* by Meredydd Evans: cover image reproduced by kind permission of Folkways Records and the Smithsonian Institute./'Chatty Patty' by Minas: cover image reproduced by kind permission of Libertino Records./*Songs of Ignorance* by Murry the Hump: cover image reproduced by kind permission of the Beggars Group./*Life's Not Out to Get You* by Neck Deep: cover image reproduced by kind permission of Neck Deep and Hopeless Records./*Transatlantic Exchange* by Paul Robeson & The Treorchy Male Voice Choir: cover image reproduced by kind permission of the National Union of Mineworkers, South Wales Area./*Mae 'Na Olau* by Pedair: cover image reproduced by kind permission of Sain./*The Gower Nightingale* by Phil Tanner: cover image reproduced by kind permission of Veteran Tapes./*Notes with Attachments* by Pino Palladino & Blake Mills: cover image used with permission of Pino Palladino, Blake Mills and Impulse! Cover design by Sam Gendel./'I Know Someone Who Knows Someone Who Knows Alan McGee Quite Well' by The Pooh Sticks: cover image reproduced by kind permission of The Pooh Sticks./*Every Valley* by Public Service Broadcasting: cover image reproduced by kind permission of Public Service Broadcasting and Play It Again Sam./*Sick Boi* by Ren: cover image reproduced by kind permission of Ren and The Other Songs./*Bukowski* by Rheinallt H. Rowlands: cover image reproduced by kind permission of Ankst/Ankstmusik./*Ryan* by Ryan: cover image reproduced by kind permission of Sain./*Scene Delete* by Sasha: cover image reproduced by kind permission of LateNightTales./*Cupid & Psyche 85* by Scritti Politti: cover image reproduced by kind permission of the Beggars Group./*Take One!* by Shakin' Stevens: cover image used by permission of BMG Rights Management and Sony Music Entertainment UK Limited. All rights reserved./*The Fabulous Shirley Bassey* by Shirley Bassey: cover image reproduced by kind permission of Warner Music UK Ltd./*Sobin a'r Smaeliaid I* by Sobin a'r Smaeliaid: cover image reproduced by kind permission of Sain./*Word Gets Around* by Stereophonics: cover image provided through the courtesy of Universal Music Operations Limited./*Mwng* by Super Furry Animals: cover image reproduced by kind permission of Super Furry Animals, Placid Casual Recordings and Domino Recording Co. Cover art by Pete Fowler, cover design by Mark James./*The Wreckage* by Sweet Baboo: cover image reproduced by kind permission of Sweet Baboo and Amazing Tapes from Canton. Art Direction and Design by Emma Daman Thomas. Photography by Rhodri Brooks./*The Longest Day* by Toby Hay: cover image reproduced by kind permission of Toby Hay and The State51 Conspiracy. Cover photo by Toby Hay, cover design by Nic Finch./*Surrounded by Time* by Tom Jones: cover image reproduced by kind permission of EMI./*Rhaid i Rywbeth Ddigwydd* by Tystion: cover image reproduced by kind permission of Tystion and Fitamin Un./*Dubnobasswithmyheadman* by Underworld: cover image reproduced with thanks to Underworld. Art by Tomato./*Clywch-y-Bardd*: cover image reproduced by kind permission of Sain./*Dial-a-Poem*: cover image reproduced by kind permission of Sain./*Dial M for Merthyr*: cover image reproduced by kind permission of Fierce Panda and Townhill Records./*Welsh Rare Beat*: cover image reproduced by kind permission of Finders Keepers Records./*Cam o'r Tywllwch*: cover image reproduced by kind permission of Recordiau Anhrefn./*The Collective*: cover image reproduced by kind permission of Rounda Records./*Colossal Youth* by Young Marble Giants: cover image reproduced by kind permission of Domino Recording Co./ We have made best efforts to contact the copyright holders of all images. If we have failed to acknowledge any copyright holder, we should be glad to receive information to assist us.

Index

9Bach 90, 112, **128–129**, 160, 180, 182, 199, 200, 204
10 Records (label) 120
60ft Dolls 10, 34, 74, 84, **100–101**, 199, 200, 204

A&M Records (label) 34
Acid Casuals 150
Adam Walton 130, 150, 207
Adelina Patti 194
Adwaith 20–21, 150, 199, 200, 205
Aidan Thorne 190
Ail Symudiad 60–61, 140, 199, 200, 204, 206
Alan Holmes 68, 116
The Alarm 144, **170–171**, 199, 200, 204
Albwm Cymraeg y Flwyddyn/Welsh-Language Album of the Year 160
Alcatraz 186
Aleighcia Scott 176–177, 199, 200, 205
Alex Dingley 186
Amazing Tapes from Canton (label) 152
Amen Corner 56, **162–163**, 194, 199, 200, 203
The Anchoress 148–149, 199, 200, 205
Ani Glass 54
Andy Kershaw 188
Andy Votel 42, 136
Anhrefn 114, 134, 180, **188–189**, 199, 200, 204
Ankst (label) 68, 82, 104, 116, 140, 150, 164
Ankstmusik (label) 36, 82, 140, 164
Ann Matthews 68, 116
Apple Records (label) 66, 142
Ar Log 24, 106, 172
Ara Deg festival 114
Arran Ahmun 106, 168
Aruthrol singles club 154
Ascherberg, Hopwood and Crew Ltd. (music publishers) 50
Astar (label) 158
Astroid Boys 80, **184–185**, 199, 200, 205
Yr Atgyfodiad 106
Atlantic (label) 132
Atlantic Recording Corporation (label) 154
Audiobooks 54

Badfinger 130, **142–143**, 199, 200, 203, 206
Banana & Louie (label) 96
Band Pres Llareggub 150

Bandit (S4C programme) 86
Bando 88, 124, **168–169**, 199, 200, 204
Bangor University 102, 134
Bara Menyn 26, 52, 164
BBC National Orchestra of Wales 58, 96
BBC Radio 1 16, 74, 94, 130, 132, 150, 178
BBC Radio 1Xtra 176, 184
BBC Radio 6 Music 20, 64, 92, 136
BBC Radio Cymru 68, 82, 86, 92, 96, 112, 116, 122, 150, 168, 180, 186, 188
BBC Radio Wales 24, 130, 138, 150, 176, 194
The Beatles 74, 142, 162
Beaufort Male Choir 90
Beganifs 150
Bench 94, 186
Benji Webbe 84, 110
Big Leaves 28, 46, **150–151**, 199, 200, 204
Black Dub (label) 176
The Blackout 166
Blake Mills 70–71, 202, 205
Blanco Y Negro (label) 92
Y Blew 120, **192–193**, 199, 200, 203
Bob Delyn a'r Ebillion 122, **182–183**, 199, 200, 204
Bob Dylan 70, 120, 126, 144, 182
Boi 150
Bonnie Tyler 98–99, 199, 200, 204, 207
Boobytrap Records (label) 150
Boobytrap Singles Club (label) 46
Boomtown festival 176
Boy Azooga 54, 86, 136, 152, 160
Brân 42, **106–107**, 199, 200, 203
bravecaptain 46
Breichiau Hir 20
Brian Hibbard 120, 199
Bright Light Bright Light/Rod Thomas **56–57**, 199, 200, 205
Brit Awards 34
Brodyr y Ffin 48
Bronx River DJs 94
Bryn Derwen Studios 68, 112
Bryn Fôn 156
Bryn Terfel 8, 138
Bubblewrap Records (label) 112, 160
Budgie 168, 194

Burum 102
Buzzard Buzzard Buzzard 160
Bwchadanas 134
The Byrds 60, 90, **144–145**, 199, 200, 203
The Bystanders 194

Calan 182
Cam o'r Tywyllwch **180–181**, 188, 202, 204, 207
Cambrian (label) 24, 32, 66, 76, 78
Cambrian Records (label, est. 2014) 190
Camgymeriad Gwych/Beautiful Mistake (film) 8, 28, 102
Candelas 188
Canolfan Hamdden 140
Canvasback (label) 154
Caradog 7
carnival 176
Carwyn Ellis 96, 112
Carwyn Ellis & Rio 18 96–97, 199, 200, 205
Caryl Parry Jones 88, 124, 168, 199
Casetiau Neon (label) 140, 180
Casey Raymond (artist) 106
Casi Wyn 122
Cass Meurig 60
Catapult, Cardiff (record shop) 30
Catatonia 8, 10, 34, 50, 68, **92–93**, 100, 104, 114, 120, 150, 180, 188, 199, 200, 204
Cate Le Bon 86, 94, 106, 152, **186–187**, 199, 200, 205
Catfish and the Bottlemen 48
Catrin Finch 158–159, 199, 200, 205
CBS (label) 98
Celt 114, 164, 180
Cen Williams (artist) 32
Central Slate (label) 68
Central Station, Wrexham (venue) 16
Cerys Hafana 102, 128
Cerys Matthews 2, 12, 50, 92, 114, 126, 130
Chapter Arts Centre, Cardiff (venue) 124
Charles & Kingsley Ward 52
Charlotte Church 8, 102
Christian Fitness 46
Cian Ciarán 104, 199
Clwb Ifor Bach, Cardiff (venue) 30, 46, 54, 86, 92

Clywch-y-Bardd **122–123**, 164, 202, 203
Coal Exchange, Cardiff (venue) 28
Cob Records, Porthmadog (record shop) 34, 197
The Collective 8, **94–95**, 202, 204
Colorama 96, 154
Columbia (label) 72, 130, 144
Cool Cymru 10, 110, 166
Côr Cochion Caerdydd 54
Y Côr Mawr/The Big Choir 7
Côr y Penrhyn 128
Country Mile Records (label) 84
Cowbois Rhos Botwnnog 112
Crai (label) 54, 82, 92, 150, 180, 182
Creation Records (label) 50, 104
Crumblowers 34
Crysbas 156
Cubare 46
Curadur (S4C programme) 176, 186
Cwrw, Carmarthen (venue) 20
Cymdeithas yr Iaith 12, 32, 54, 156, 192
Y Cymylau 140
Y Cyrff 92, 180

Daedelus 62–63, 199, 200, 205
Daf/Dafydd Ieuan 102, 188, 199
Dafydd Iwan 8, 28, 32, 44, 52, 78, 106, 140, **172–173**, 199, 200, 203, 204, 206
Dafydd Iwan ac Edward 32–33, 199, 200, 203
Dafydd Rhys 68, 114
Damaged Goods (label) 130
Dan Charnas 70
Darkhouse Family 136
The Darling Buds 8, 50, 84
Das Koolies 104
Datblygu 20, 40, 60, 82, 104, **140–141**, 164, 180, 188, 192, 199, 200, 204
Dave Edmunds 138, 194
Davey Newington 86, 136, 152
David R Edwards 20, 60, **82–83**, 140, 180, 192, 201, 204, 206
David Rodigan 176
David Wrench 54, 68, 112
Decca Records (label) 126, 162
Deconstruction (label) 48
The Denims 138
Dennis Rees 44
Derrero 28, 74
Des1re 176
Dewi Pws 164

Deyah 64–65, 199, 200, 205
Dial M for Merthyr **74–75**, 202, 204
Dial-a-Poem **122–123**, 202, 203
Disc a Dawn (BBC TV programme) 24, 58, 78
Disco (band) 74
Diverse Vinyl, Newport (record shop) 100, 197
Y Diwygiad (band) 62
DJ Jaffa/Jason Farrell 8, 22, 94, 178
DJ Target 184
Dom a Lloyd 82
Dom Thomas 42
Don Leisure 136–137, 199, 200, 205
Download Festival 184
Drinks 186
Drowned in Sound (label) 148
Dub War 74, 100, **110–111**, 199, 200, 205
Duffy 34–35, 100, 199, 200, 205
Dylan Thomas 28, 122, 144, 148
Y Dyniadon Ynfyd Hirfelyn Tesog 42

Eadyth 176
Earache (label) 110
The Earth 104
Ectogram 116
Eden 168
Edward H. Dafis 52, 164, 168
El Goodo 46, 146
Elektra (label) 174
Eleri Llwyd 44
Elfyn Lewis (artist) 92
Elfyn Presli 180
Elin Fflur 106
Elinor Bennett 50, 158
Elwyn Ioan (artist) 172
EMI (label) 78, 126
Emma Daman Thomas 86, 152
Emyr Glyn Williams 82
Endaf Emlyn 70, **88–89**, 106, 168, 199, 200, 203, 206
Epic (label) 38, 138
Erban Poets 94
Ether 74
Euros Childs 116, 152, 186, 199
Eurovision Song Contest 98
Ewan Jones Morris (artist) 106
Exit International 100

Fabiana Palladino 70
Factory Records (label) 188
Far From Saints 10

Fernhill 102
Ffa Coffi Pawb 104, 106, 114, 164, 188
Fflach (label) 58, 60, 146
fflach:tradd (label) 60, 102
Fflaps 116
Ffrancon 8, **36–37**, 199, 200, 205
Y Ffyrc 92
Fideo 9 (S4C programme) 92, 164
Fierce Panda (label) 74
Fierce Recordings (label) 50
Finders Keepers Records (label) 42
Fiona Owen 104
First Word Records (label) 136
Fitamin Un (label) 178
Five Darrens 100
FIZZ 168
The Flying Pickets 120–121, 199, 200, 204
Flyscreen 100
Focus Wales 16
Folktracks Records (label) 130
Folkways Records (label) 12, 102
Frank Hennessy 24
Freur 124
Frug! Records (label) 100
Funeral for a Friend 8, **166–167**, 199, 200, 204
Future of the Left 46
Fuzzbox (label) 46

Gareth Bonello 160, 190
Gareth Edwards 78
Genod Droog 62
The Gentle Good 128, **160–161**, 199, 201, 205
Georgia Ruth 112–113, 152, 160, 190, 199, 201, 205
Geraint Jarman 26, 52, 82, 88, 94, 114, 122, **164–165**, 168, 176, 199, 201, 203, 206
Geraint Watkins 138
Gilles Peterson 136
Glastonbury Festival 20, 72, 148, 176
Goldie Lookin Chain 80, **132–133**, 199, 201, 205
Gordon Mills 126
Gorky's Zygotic Mynci 8, 10, 28, 68, 100, **116–117**, 178, 186, 199, 201, 204
Gorwel Owen 102, 104, 116, 140
Grassroots Studio 94
Green Man Festival 94, 96, 146, 176, 186
Greta Isaac 168
Group Listening 86, 152
Gruff Owen 20

Gruff Rhys 42, 68, 88, 104, 114, 128, 136, 152, 168, 180, 186, 199, 207
Gulp 104
Guto Pryce 104, 199
Gwawr (label) 76, 106
Gwdihŵ, Cardiff (venue) 86
Gwenan Gibbard 134, 199
Gwenifer Raymond 106–107, 199, 201, 205
Gwenno 54–55, 82, 86, 140, 150, 199, 201, 205
Gwion Llŷr Llewelyn 106
Gwymon (label) 112
Gwyneth Glyn 134, 182, 199
Gwynfor Evans (politician) 172, 192

H. Hawkline/Huw Evans **86–87**, 106, 152, 186, 199, 201, 205
Hanner Pei 86, 94
Harri Webb (poet) 26
Heather Jones 8, **26–27**, 42, 52, 164, 199, 201, 203
Heavenly (label) 54, 86
Hefin Wyn (author) 58
Helen Love 50, 74, **130–131**, 199, 201, 204
Help Yourself 194
Hen Ogledd 102
Hen Wlad Fy Nhadau (Welsh anthem) 42, 118, 164
Yr Hennessys 24–25, 76, 78, 199, 201, 203
Heno Bydd yr Adar yn Canu (Radio Cymru programme) 68, 92, 116
High Contrast/Lincoln Barrett **30–31**, 138, 199, 201, 204
High Mileage, Low Life (label) 64
HMS Morris 86, 160
Hogia'r Wyddfa 44–45, 199, 201, 203
Honest Jon's Records (label) 174
Hopeless Records (label) 16
Hospital Records (label) 30
HTV Wales 24, 58, 60, 88, 124
Huw Bunford 104, 199
Huw Jones 8, 42, **52–53**, 199, 201, 203, 206
Huw/Hue Williams 50, 100
Hywel Gwynfryn 24, 86, 168

I.R.S. Records (label) 170
Idris Davies (poet) 90, 122, 144
Immediate (label) 162
Impulse! (label) 70
Infectious Records (label) 166
Infinity Chimps 116

Injaroc 88
Iris Williams 8, 78
Irony Bored (label) 186
Island Records (label) 22
Islet 86, 152
The Iveys 142
Ivor Novello 50–51, 199, 201, 203

Jack Jones 122, 206
Jackie Williams 108, 180
Jakokoyak/Rhys Edwards 54, 140
James Dean Bradfield 20, 28, 38, 52, 72, 90, 112, 126, 142, 148
Jecsyn Ffeif 164
Jessica Lee Morgan 66
Jig Cal (studio/label) 150
Jîp 88, 106, 168
John Cale 8, 14, **28–29**, 88, 102, 186, 199, 201, 203, 206
John Grant 106, 186
John Gwyn 106, 168
John Hughes (hymnwriter) 108
John Lawrence 68, 116
John Lennon 148
John Peel 40, 74, 82, 94, 116, 130, 140, 146, 150, 178, 188
John Sicolo 74
Jon Langford 84, 100
Jon Langford & His Men of Gwent 84–85, 199, 201, 205
The Jonah Hex 100
Jools Holland 8, 70
The Joy Formidable 154–155, 199, 201, 205
JT Mouse 46
Julie Murphy 28, 60, 102
Junior Boy's Own (label) 124
Just the Duce 94

K-klass 8, **48–49**, 199, 201, 204
Kari 94
Karl Hyde 30, 124
Karl Jenkins 88
Katell Keineg 126, **174–175**, 199, 201, 204
Keith Cameron (journalist) 38
Keith Murrell 176
Kelefa Sanneh (author) 158
Kelly Lee Owens 14–15, 199, 201, 205
Kenneth Budd (artist) 110
Kerrang! 16, 166
Kevs Ford 82, 94

Keys 146
The Khasi-Cymru Collective 128, 160
Kiddus 176
Kizzy Crawford 150
Kliph Scurlock 88

LateNightTales (label) 76
Lauren Laverne 136
Le Pub, Newport (venue) 20, 74, 100
The Legendary TJ's, Newport (venue) 74, 100, 110
Les Morrison 50, 114
Lews Tunes & Nobsta Nuts 80
Libertino Records (label) 20, 26
Lisa Jên (Brown) 90, 128, 160, 180
Little Miss/Sophie Barras 94
Lleuwen (Steffan) 82, **108–109**, 112, 199, 201, 205
Llio Rhydderch 8, 28, 60, **102–103**, 190, 199, 201, 205
Llion Robertson 160
Llwybr Cyhoeddus 114
Llwybr Llaethog 82–83, 94, 164, 178, 199, 201, 204
Llwyd Owen (author) 82
Los Blancos 20
Lostprophets 166

Mace the Great 80–81, 199, 201, 205
MaceTheGreatMusic (label) 80
Machlud 114, 180
Madlib 40, 62
Maes B (Eisteddfod stage) 20, 150, 186, 192
Maffia Mr. Huws 114–115, 164, 180, 199, 201, 204
Malcolm Neon/Malcolm Gwyon 8, 60, 140, 152, 180
Man 194–195, 199, 201, 203
Manchild 94
Manic Street Preachers 8, 10, 20, 28, **38–39**, 52, 54, 72, 74, 90, 112, 118, 120, 122, 130, 142, 148, 154, 162, 199, 201, 204, 207
Manon Steffan Ros 108
Marc Evans (director) 28, 34
Mark Radcliffe 150
Mark Roberts/MR 92, 104, 180, 199
The Martini Henry Rifles 46
Mary ac Edward 32
Mary Hopkin 32, **66–67**, 199, 201, 203
Matthew Evans 146, 199

212

The Mavron Quartet 160
Max Boyce 24, 50, **78–79**, 84, 102, 199, 201, 203, 206
MC Chef 178
MC Mabon/Gruff Meredith 46, 178, 199
mclusky 46–47, 199, 201, 204
Me One/Eric Martin 8, **22–23**, 94, 199, 201, 204
Mei Gwynedd 150
Meibion Glyndŵr 156, 178
Meic Stephens 122
Meic Stevens 8, 12, 24, 26, 42, 52, **58–59**, 78, 88, 112, 160, 164, 199, 201, 203, 207
Meinir Gwilym 134, 199
Melody Maker 40
Melys 74
Mercury Prize 54, 64, 186
Meredydd Evans 8, **12–13**, 26, 134, 160, 199, 201, 203, 206
Michael Sheen 14
Mighty Atom (label) 166
Mike Peters 144, 170
Mim Twm Llai 114
Minas 20, **26–27**, 80, 199, 201, 205
miners 78, 90, 118, 120
Miri Madog festival 150
MOBO Awards 80, 110
Mo-Ho-Bish-O-Pi 46
Monnow Valley Studio 16, 126
Morgan Elwy 176
Morriston Orpheus Male Voice Choir 170
Moshi Moshi (label) 152
Mr Phormula/Ed Holden 62, 82
Murry the Hump 146–147, 199, 201, 204
Music for Nations (label) 184
Mwldan Records (label) 158
Mwsog 86, 186
Myfyr Isaac 106, 168

N.U.M. (label) 118
Nansi Richards 102
National Eisteddfod 20, 44, 66, 82, 102, 118, 134, 140, 150, 156, 160, 176, 182, 186, 192
National Library of Wales 102, 160, 190, 208
National Youth Orchestra of Wales 28, 88
Neck Deep 16–17, 48, 199, 202, 205
Neon Neon 186
Nest Howells 106, 199
Neuadd Ogwen, Bethesda (venue) 114
Neud Nid Deud (label) 82
New Deal Records (label) 70

The New York Times 12
Newport Rising 84, 110
N'Famady Kouyaté 20
Nia Melville 68, 116
Nicky Wire 2, 38, 72, 122
Nid Madagascar 112
NME 74, 146, 188
Noson Lawen 26, 32, 44, 76
Novocaine 74, 100

Ochre (label) 68
Ofn (label) 140
Ofn Studios 102, 104, 116
The Other Songs (label) 162
Owen Money 194
Owen Powell 34, 92

Pale Blue Dots 104
Pappy 36
Papur Wal 20
Parc Troli 74
Parlophone (label) 48, 88
Patricia Morgan 82, 140, 199
Patrick Jones (poet) 28, 122
Patti Pavilion, Swansea (venue) 194
Paul Jones (Catatonia) 92
Paul Jones (Group Listening) 86, 152
Paul McCartney 66, 138, 142, 148, 152
Paul Robeson 8, **118–119**, 199, 202, 203
Pedair 134–135, 182, 199, 202, 205
Pep le Pew 82
Pererin 106
Pesda Roc (label) 114
Pesda Roc festival 114
Peski (label) 54, 154, 180, 186
Pete Fowler (artist) 104
Pete Seeger 66, 144
The Peth 104
The Pharmacy/The Bunker/ROC2 (studio) 48
Phil Tanner 130–131, 199, 202, 204
Phyllis Kinney 12, 134, 160
Pino Palladino 70–71, 88, 162, 199, 202, 205
The Pipettes 54
Placid Casual Recordings (label) 104
Plaid Cymru 32, 140, 172, 192
Plant Bach Ofnus 104
Play It Again Sam (label) 90
Plu 96
Plug Research (label) 62
Plyci 36

The Point, Cardiff (venue) 28
The Pooh Sticks 50–51, 199, 202, 204
Pop Negatif Wastad 82
Postcard Records (label) 188
Pretenders 96, 126
Public Service Broadcasting 8, **90–91**, 199, 202, 204
Pye Records (label) 194
Pys Melyn 186

Qualiton (label) 118, 192
Questlove 34, 70

R. Seiliog/Robin Edwards 54, 86
Race Horses 106
Radio Luxembourg 186
Ralph Rip Shit 80
Rasal (label) 82
RCA Records (label) 98
Reading & Leeds festivals 132, 150, 154, 184
Real World Records (label) 128
Real World Studios 126, 190
Rebecca Riots 84
Recordiau Anhrefn (label) 82, 140, 180, 188
Ren 162–163, 199, 202, 205
René Griffiths 156
Reprise Records (label) 28
Rheinallt H. Rowlands 8, **68–69**, 199, 202, 204
Rhodri Davies 102, 140
Rhys Mwyn 92, 134, 180, 188, 207
Rich Chitty 160
Richard Dunn 106, 168
Richard Jackson 74, 110
Richard Parfitt 34, 84, 100
Rick Smith 30, 124, 199
Robert Wyatt 18, 116, 152
Rocco Palladino 70
Rockfield Studios 16, 52, 126, 170, 194, 206
The Rockin' Chair, Wrexham (venue) 16
Rogue Jones 20
Ronnie Williams 12, 148, 206
The Roots 22, 34, 70
Rorystonelove 176
Rough Trade (label) 18, 34, 40
Rounda Records (label) 8, 94
Roy Saer 130
Royal Welsh College of Music & Drama 72
Rufus Mufasa 176
Ryan & Ronnie 12, 148, 206
Ryan (Davies) 12, **148–149**, 199, 202, 203, 206

S4C 14, 24, 34, 52, 60, 86, 88, 92, 120, 146, 148, 156, 164, 172, 176, 186
Sage Todz 82
Sain (label) 8, 26, 32, 44, 52, 58, 60, 76, 82, 88, 92, 108, 112, 134, 136, 156, 164, 168, 172, 180
Sam Dabb 74
Sammo Hung 46
Sasha 76–77, 199, 202, 205
Sassie Rees 32
The Screen Gemz 124
Scritti Politti 18–19, 34, 84, 199, 202, 204
Seb Goldfinch 160
Seckou Keita 158–159, 200, 205
Sêr (HTV programme) 60
The Serpents 8, 68
Sesiwn Fawr Dolgellau 182
Sgrech Awards 114
Sgrech (magazine) 60, 114
Shakin' Stevens 30, 138–139, 199, 202, 203
Shape Records (label) 86, 152
Shirley Bassey 72–73, 138, 199, 202, 203
Siân James 134, 199
Sibrydion 150
Sidecar Kisses 154
Silent Kid Records (label) 26
Simon Williams (journalist) 74
Sion Sebon 180, 188
Sir Doufus Styles/Kris Jenkins 94, 186
Skep 178
Skindred 84, 110, 184
Sleifar/Steffan Cravos 8, 178, 199
Smalltown Supersound (label) 14
Sobin a'r Smaeliaid 156–157, 199, 202, 204
Sonny Double 1 184
Sony Music (label) 184
Sosban (BBC radio programme) 60
Sothach (magazine) 114
Sound Space Studios 38
Spillers, Cardiff (record shop) 8, 197
St David's Hall, Cardiff (venue) 64
St Fagans National Museum of History 108, 130
The State51 Conspiracy (label) 190
Stereophonics 8, 10–11, 74, 100, 126, 162, 199, 202, 204

Steve Eaves 108
Steve Lamacq 130
Stitches 154
StudiOws 152
Super Furry Animals 8, 10, 50, 68, 94, 100, **104–105**, 114, 120, 140, 150, 180, 186, 188, 199, 202, 204, 207
Swansea Sound 50
Swansea University 98
Sweet Baboo/Stephen Black 86, 106, **152–153**, 199, 202, 205
Sŵn Festival 40
Y Sŵn (film) 172
SYBS 20

Talking Heads 40, 120
The Tangled Parrot, Carmarthen (venue) 20
Y Tebot Piws 42, 52
Technotronic 8, 22, 94
Teen Anthems 74
Texas Radio Band 46
Tich Gwilym 42, 164
Tips Wyn Gruffydd 146
Toby Hay 190–191, 199, 202, 205
The Toilets 170
Tom Jones 2, 8, 10, **126–127**, 138, 146, 166, 174, 199, 202, 205, 206
Tommy Scott 126
Tompkins Square (label) 106
Tony ac Aloma 76–77, 199, 202, 203
Tony Visconti 66, 170
Too Pure (label) 46, 146
Top Rank nightclub, Swansea (venue) 148
Townhill Records (label) 74, 100
Traddodiad Ofnus 82
Trampolene 122
The Treorchy Male Voice Choir 8, **118–119**, 199, 202, 203
Trials of Cato 182
Triawd y Coleg 12
Tricky Nixon 154
Y Trwynau Coch 60
Tryweryn 26, 52, 172
Twin Town (film) 120
Twm Morys 122, 182

Twmffat 176
Tŷ Gwydr 82–83, 164, 199, 201, 204
Tynal Tywyll 180
Tystion 8, 28, 46, 82, 94, **178–179**, 199, 202, 204

U Thant 104
The UK Chinese Ensemble 160
Underworld 30, **124–125**, 199, 202, 204
United Artists Records (label) 194
Universal Music Group (label) 94
University of South Wales 146

V2 (label) 10
The Velvet Underground 28
Veteran Tapes (label) 130
Virgin (label) 18
Visage 138
VRi 182

We Are Animal 154
Welsh Arts Council 122, 164
Welsh Music Foundation 22, 50
Welsh Music Prize 12, 14, 20, 54, 64, 80, 112, 160
Welsh Rare Beat 42–43, 202, 205
Welsh Teldisc (label) 26, 32
Whipcord Records (label) 150
Will Barras (artist) 94
Will Paynter, NUM 118
Words of Warning (label) 110
Workers Playtime (label) 188
Wren Records/Recordiau'r Dryw (label) 44, 58, 122, 148
Wwwzz 104

Xenith 94

Ynys 20
Young Marble Giants 40–41, 199, 202, 204
Yskwn! (label) 56
Yws Gwynedd 150

Zabrinski 8, 46
Zefur Wolves 104

Wales 100: Records is just one of a whole range of publications from Y Lolfa.

For a full list of books currently in print, check out our website

www.ylolfa.com

for secure online ordering.